PATRONAGE AND PIETY

Patronage and Piety

The Politics of English Roman Catholicism, 1850–1900

Dermot Quinn

Stanford University Press
Stanford, California
1993

Stanford University Press
Stanford, California
© 1993 Dermot A. Quinn
Originating publisher: The Macmillan Press Ltd,
    Hampshire
First published in the U. S. A. by
    Stanford University Press, 1993
Printed in Hong Kong
ISBN 0-8047-1996-9
LC 91-75051
This book is printed on acid free paper.

To
T. J. Q. and K. P. Q.

Contents

Preface

Historical fashions come and go. The novelty of one generation is the orthodoxy of the next and the archaism of the next after that, because academic historians are intellectually curious, and properly suspicious of ideas too casually accepted, too readily assumed. They may also have access to sources denied to their predecessors and find merit in different theories of causality. Again, some will conceive an interest in grand design, and others a distaste for it.

Even so, it is one of the wearier paradoxes of the historian's art that the only thing which is constant is change. Sometimes it appears that nothing changes at all. Consider, for instance, two accounts of the history of English Catholicism in the second half of the nineteenth century. Both take as their text the death of a cardinal, the first Manning, who died in 1892, the second Vaughan, who died eleven years later. Both men are made to reflect the era through which they lived. Thus Manning:

> The chain of old associations, linking the beginning of the century with its end, the early beginnings of the Catholic Revival in England with the glorious results witnessed today all over the land, was broken by the death of Cardinal Manning.[1]

Thus also Vaughan:

> So the last of the great Catholic prelates of Victorian England brought a triumphant era to an end. On 19 June 1903, with a lucid mind and great fortitude, impressed by the frailty of human faith, tired in spirit and yet attaining an ultimate serenity, Vaughan was delivered into eternity. It was the Feast of the Sacred Heart.[2]

What is striking about these obituary notices is not the similarity but the fact that nearly a hundred years separates the writing of the second from the first: the Manning piece comes from Purcell's famous *Life*, published in 1896, the Vaughan from Edward Norman's

English Catholic Church in the Nineteenth Century, published in 1984. It is as if a century of scholarship had never happened.[3]

Other authors leave much the same impression. 'There were giants in those days,' writes E. E. Reynolds of the heroic leadership of Wiseman and Newman.

Norman, Reynolds and Purcell form part of a tradition of Catholic historiography which holds, as its unshakable orthodoxy, that the years from 1850 to the end of the century were triumphant times. Nor are they capricious. Contemporaries thought similarly, and pointed to material evidence: churches built, parishes formed, missions preached. Perhaps this explains the unvarying style: they are heirs to an idiom of formal ecclesiastical history which conforms to literary conventions entirely its own and is a way not merely of writing but of thinking. But History as Revelation is seldom very revealing and histories of holiness are often full of holes.

This book has different credentials. Its aims are, on the contrary, entirely sublunary. The temptation to deal in grand themes must be resisted, less because it leads to overblown rhetoric, more because it enshrines a faulty and misleading generalisation. That generalisation is this: the idea that Catholic life in England is simply the history of a spiritual confraternity, a unitary body which may be adjudged to be in decline or ascent as circumstances change. The Catholic world was more complicated than that. Even as an institution, as a man-made collection of dioceses and parishes, convents and schools, the English Church resists easy description. In some places religious observance flourished, in others it withered. And geography alone is a poor index: among different groups in the same area a similar pattern of devotion and indifference may be discerned. Besides, there is a further complication: time. If generalisation is hazardous about one place at one point, how much more so about many areas over a period of fifty years?

This is to say nothing of Catholic politics, the burden of the present work. Here the situation was even more confused, the patterns of experience yet more varied. Catholicism was not merely a spiritual condition; it was a tag of social and political identity as well. At one level, this is scarcely controversial: *of course* Catholics have an existence outside their churches and their convents; *of course* they are residents of this world as well as travellers to the next. Therein lies the problem. Free agency in politics was not granted to Catholics any more than to their contemporaries: like it or not, they all had to co-operate with other parties and other groups. English Catholics, being a highly self-conscious collection, found this at once fascinating and melancholy. One of the themes of this book is the way in which this self-consciousness had political consequences: Catholics took themselves very seriously and expected the parties to reciprocate. In this they were deluded. The parties had other constituencies to please and Catholics on the whole did not rank high with them. This caused formidable tensions and highly intricate schemes of political behaviour on both sides.

It is important, then, to understand something of the Catholic mind before attempting to plumb Catholic politics. Chapter One, entitled *Liberal Catholics and Catholic Liberals 1850–1874*, attempts this. It uses the so-called Liberal Catholic movement as a way of introducing some of the wider themes of English Catholic life – the enthusiasm for the restored hierarchy; the social, political and intellectual challenges of the modern era; the tensions between old Catholics and converts; the continuing importance of anti-Catholic feeling; the impact of the *Syllabus of Errors* and (even more dramatic) the Vatican Council, Ultramontanism's finest hour. It also explores the tangled relationship between Catholics and the Liberal Party until the fall of Gladstone's first ministry. From the story of the Vatican Council valuable conclusions may be drawn about English Liberal responses to Catholicism, and about Catholic responses to Liberalism. This is important because it touches the very nature of their political disposition. How was Gladstone's party received in the light of its hostility to Infallibility? Were Catholics reliable or even predictable political allies? It is here argued that the only thing that could be relied on was their touchiness, their political self-absorption and their tactical ignorance. And, in ways less obvious but no less demonstrable, Gladstone's ministers – to say nothing of Gladstone himself – were similarly self-absorbed. Unaware that Catholics did not think in the same way as they did themselves, the Liberal ministers expected the former to follow their own patterns of political behaviour.

Much of Chapter One is concerned with the politics of personal relationships – the Manning-Gladstone connection, for instance, and the friendship between Gladstone and Acton. The same is true of Chapter Two, *Catholics and Tories 1850–1868*. Though 'Glorious Era' historians like Purcell and Reynolds are slow to acknowledge *any* divisions in English Catholic life, there was in fact a thriving Catholic Tory world as well as a Catholic Liberal one. More than that, there was often cordial loathing between the two. This chapter examines the belief – a crucial one for Catholic Tories for several years in the late 1850s and 1860s – that Catholics and the Tory party were 'natural allies'. The idea is found seriously wanting, partly because of the palpable unevenness of the alliance, and partly because of the tactical unsubtlety of Catholic Tories (they shared that at least with their Liberal counterparts). As with Chapter One, it is suggested that patronage, not just piety, was the dynamic of Catholic politics. Catholics were eager for political reward and were prepared to use their Catholicism as an instrument to achieve it. This had the consequence (for example) that Catholic Tories spent much of their time explaining to their leaders how awful Catholic Liberals were. In a sense, political preferment demanded of them Catholicism and anti-Catholicism in roughly equal measure. The careers of some Catholic Tory figures – notably Edward Ryley and John Pope Hennessy – are closely investigated. They are both important figures, in that they form links between Tory high politics and the altogether lesser world of Catholic jobbery and jealousy.

Chapter Two ends in 1868, an *annus mirabilis* in Catholic-Tory relations, when Disraeli felt himself abandoned on the Irish Church question. He found it nearly impossible to forgive English as well as Irish Catholics this 'stab in the back'. But the politics of that year are by no means straightfoward. For Catholic Tories, too, the abandonment lived long in the memory; but with them, ironically, it served rather to reinforce their attachment to the Conservative Party.

Chapter Three, *Catholics and Tories 1868–1874*, continues the investigation of the Catholic-Tory nexus until the fall of Gladstone. For Disraeli, opposition brought respite from Catholic claims, not release. Patronage still bulked large in their world; Protestants still bulked large in his. This chapter also begins to develop the full parallel and paradox of Catholic politics: just as it was Gladstone's Liberal Catholics who unwittingly persuaded him that Catholics were not to be relied on, so it was Disraeli's Catholic Tories who convinced *him* of the same thing. Both sets of supporters, seeking to establish their especial claims on their respective parties, merely proved their querulousness and redundancy.

Chapter Three also investigates the networks of patronage so crucial to the political pressures on Disraeli; pressures which his Catholic followers failed to appreciate. Tory interest in Catholicism in the early 1870s consisted mainly of the belief that it was a handy smear with which to besmirch Gladstone and his party. Thus the chapter ends with the sharpest irony of all: Catholics embraced the

Tories in 1874 (as enthusiastically as they had rejected them in 1868) but failed to realised that the Tories had hardened in their antipathy towards them.

Chapter Four introduces a central figure in this work: Lord Ripon. Converted to Rome in 1874, Ripon was for thirty years a key connection between Liberal high politics and the Catholic world. Much hope reposed in him: Catholics believed they had found a sectional spokesman of real weight, a statesman of the first rank. In this they were mistaken, but in ways they scarcely understood. Ripon was indeed an important Catholic in Liberal circles, but his value to the party – and in a real sense to his co-religionists – lay in lowering Catholic hopes, not raising them. Here, then, are three variables – how Catholics viewed Ripon's role, how the party viewed it, and how he viewed it himself. The interaction of the three tells much of Catholic attitudes towards Liberals, Liberal attitudes towards Catholics (who formed only one of several contending sectional interest-groups), and Ripon's skill – perhaps duplicity – as a statesman.

Investigation of Ripon properly falls into two parts: the first, *Ripon: A Catholic in Politics*, takes the story to 1880, with a few references to 1886 and 1892; the second, *Ripon: a Catholic in Government*, concerns itself exclusively with the post-1880 period. Chapter Five deals with *Catholic Toryism During Disraeli's Second Ministry*. A contrast is proposed: between the jealous eagerness with which Catholics sought preferment (the main technique being to black-guard their own bishops and Gladstone-supporting co-religionaries) and the calculating knowingness with which Party leaders either withheld or dispensed it. There were several reasons why ministers should have been cool towards Catholics: one was simple distrust; another was pressure from the Queen; a third, the pugnacious Protestantism of their 'rank-and-file' support. The way these tensions resolved themselves is examined, and it is suggested that they often had surprising implications – in publicising foreign policy initiatives, for example, when the party leadership occasionally had the choice of cultivating its Protestant or its Catholic following at home by its actions abroad.

Foreign policy, particularly Tory responses to the Eastern question, was an important reason for Catholic support in the late 1870s. The relationship between Disraeli and Manning was partly instrumental here, and it yields another contrast, between their hostility of the late 1860s and their warmth ten years later. But the chapter ends where it began, showing the one-sidedness of Catholic Toryism, and how closely the Party relied on Protestantism for its successes.

Chapter Six resumes the Ripon story. Its central theme is the conflicting claims which the Liberal Party and the Catholic Church made on him, and how Ripon manipulated the latter in the interests of the former. Ripon's view of his co-religionists is explored, as are the methods which he used to reach the very heart of Catholic politics.

The final chapter – *The Duke of Norfolk, Catholics and Tories 1880–1900* – examines the career of another key figure in the politics of Party and of pressure. As with Ripon, Catholics invested much hope in Norfolk, the ultimately respectable spokesman. They were not to realise the extent of his partisanship: in every respect which mattered, Norfolk put the Tory Party first. Yet, as with Ripon, Norfolk's relationship with political colleagues was intricate: there is much to be learned both from the way he treated them and the way they treated him. With Norfolk at their head, English Catholics seem by the end of the century to be firmly Tory in their loyalty. But was *he* much of a leader and were *they* much better off for following him?

The appendix closely examines Catholic voting strength in key English and Welsh constituencies. Only by such systematic analysis may Catholic claims to political potency be adjudged.

It will be clear that the method of this book is at once chronological and topical. Its purpose is also two-fold. To discover how Catholic politics actually worked has a value in itself. But there is an extra benefit to be derived, like tackling those jigsaw puzzles which have two pictures, one on the front, one on the back. Do the first and you have done the second. So too with English Catholicism in this period. On the back of the picture marked 'Catholic Politics' is another, taken as it were from a distance, its variety of detail perhaps not so clearly marked, but its salient features still plainly visible. It is called 'English Politics'.

Notes

1. E. S. Purcell, *The Life of Cardinal Manning* (1896), II, p. 817.
2. E. R. Norman, *The English Catholic Church in the Nineteenth Century* (London, 1984), pp. 372–3.
3. *Qua* political historian, Norman is, of course, outstanding.

Introduction

This book examines Catholic politics, High and Low, in the years between 1850 and 1900. There is no mystery, though there are many difficulties, about High Politics. Most readers will be familiar, at least in part, with the lives of Gladstone and Disraeli, Manning and Newman, Churchill and Chamberlain; perhaps also with some of the lesser personages who together constitute the public face of 'Victorianism'. Beneath them, however, lies a world which is more opaque. Thanks to some splendid historical writing – the efforts of Joyce, Clarke and Pelling come to mind – we know a good deal more about the social geography of Victorian politics than we previously did. Likewise, Swift and Gilley have added much to our knowledge of the Irish in the Victorian city. Still, they are all engaged in uncovering subterranean existences – and such work, in truth, is never completed. The view from Westminster is all very well, but it is a partial one. It must be supplemented by some account of politics at constituency level.

What was the strength of Catholicism in the constituencies? Was there, indeed, a Catholic 'vote'? If so, was it easily managed? These questions – vital to the present survey – can only be answered by close examination of individual constituencies: not every parliamentary seat, of course, but a representative sample where the Catholic presence may have been expected to make a difference. To this end, the appendix provides a systematic analysis of some forty seats in England and Wales. All politics is local, it has been said. The appendix makes this clear. It is a complex story, better told at the end of this volume than the beginning. It would be well, however, to summarise its findings at the outset.

In 1851, there were 679,067 Catholics in England and Wales. That number had risen to about a million and a half by the turn of the century. This was a substantial advance, but it would be wrong to infer that Catholics enjoyed commensurate political progress. The reasons are several. Many Catholics did not have a vote, either because they were ineligible or because, though eligible, they failed to register. Most were Irish working class, and many fell outside the terms of the Reform Act of 1867, whose purpose, as Disraeli boasted to his followers shortly after its passage, was not to bring democracy to England but to prevent it. Many Irish people did not receive the vote until the Reform and Redistribution Acts of 1884 and 1885. It would be nearer the mark to say that no more than 150,000 Irish born or second-generation Irish Catholics were enfranchised in 1885.

These are technical considerations; there are also considerations of political culture which lessened the electoral significance of the Catholic vote. In some places (most of Wales, for example, and all of East Anglia), Catholics were too thinly scattered to have had any impact. In other places, they were densely clustered – parts of Lancashire and London most notably – but, again, care is needed in interpreting that fact. The more formidable the Catholic presence in a constituency, the more likely that it would call forth a counter-vailing Protestant response. Consider the history of the Irish National League, founded in 1882 to marshall the Irish vote in England for the Home Rule cause. For all its undoubted vigour, only one English constituency ever voted for a candidate on Home Rule grounds alone – Liverpool Scotland, seat of the larger than life T. P. O'Connor. Catholics might dominate a constituency, but that was not always – or even usually – translatable into electoral gain.

Lancashire illustrates the point. As the heartland of Catholicism in England, it should have been fertile territory for votes. Its native recusant population was prodigiously supplemented by Irish immi-gration, with the result that by 1880 there were over half a million Catholics in the county. That they transformed the politics of, say, Liverpool, is not to be denied. Sheer weight of numbers ensured that. Yet consider a town like Preston. Catholics formed a solid *bloc* there, too (over 20 per cent of the population), but they were never able to dominate the politics of the town, except in a negative sense. In 1868, their support for Gladstone called forth even greater Protestant support for Disraeli. In 1885, following instructions from Manning and Parnell, they backed the Tory, thus adding to a majority which was safe anyway. The Liberals could not win with them; the Tories could win without them: altogether a melancholy fate for such an apparently powerful group.

It would, moreover, be dangerous to assume that the Catholic vote was unitary. In some places it was far from that. Denomination was not the primary identifier for every voter, certainly not for every Catholic. Class mattered too, especially towards the end of the century. Local party managers knew better than to imagine the

Catholic vote to be obediently firm. Consider Middlesborough, where Catholics never formed a reliable *bloc*. In the first place, there was always some tension between English and Irish Catholics, the former tending towards Toryism, the latter Liberalism. Even then there were subdivisions. In 1880, a few Irish Catholics eccentrically canvassed for the Tories. In 1885, the local bishop urged support of the Tory, who nonetheless flopped. In 1892, the Irish vote split, not between Tory and Liberal, but between Liberal and Labour. In 1895, the Tories tried (as they had in 1880) to appeal specifically for Catholic support: they lost handily. In that election, the local clergy declined to give any political advice to their flock, leaving them free to vote as they wished. The point is plain: over the years, Middlesborough Catholics declined to be classified in any simple or predictable way. Those who wish to understand Victorian Catholic politics would do well to treat other constituencies with similar caution.

To suggest that the Catholic vote may have been exaggerated is not to imply that it was unimportant. Catholics made a difference in some constituencies. Their numbers were never negligible. More to the point, the propensity among Catholics to overstate their electoral significance was itself significant. It encourged in them a political peremptoriness which occasionally damaged their cause. Such is the besetting, though forgivable, sin of most minority lobbies. In extenuation, it might be said that the major parties sometimes erred in similar ways. In the 1890s, Herbert Gladstone believed that over forty seats could be won for Liberalism by appealing to the Irish Catholic voter in England and Wales. He was mistaken: but it suited the Home Rule party (especially after Parnell's fall) to have him act on the belief. Political actors are adept at cloaking irrational behaviour in the language of rationality. Viewing the electoral landscape, both English Catholics and their party sponsors found it convenient to see greater strength than actually existed.

1

Liberal Catholics and Catholic Liberals 1850–74

THE POLITICS OF *THE RAMBLER*

The 1850s and 1860s have been characterised by historians of ideas as the years of the Liberal Catholic movement in England. Quite when it began and quite when it ended are hazy questions: ideas do not admit of the same exactitude of chronology as a political revolution or the fall of a ministry. Even so, the movement has handy signposts. The first is the appearance in 1848 of *The Rambler*. This was one of the most notable of Victorian periodicals and is an invaluable source of articulate, mid-century lay Catholic debate. Another is the Syllabus of Errors of 1864, when Pius IX pronounced himself irreconcilably opposed to 'progress, liberalism and modern civilisation'; less a signpost for Liberal Catholics than the end of the road. Some grant the movement a fitful existence into the 1870s, but by 1875 an infallible Pope had plainly triumphed over his fallible, indeed impotent, critics. Liberal Catholicism was dead and its surviving spokesmen – men like John Acton, Richard Simpson, and Thomas Wetherell – were anachronisms in the body of English Catholicism. This was recognised by non-Catholics, too. Gladstone once wished that he might have the same control over his party as the Pope had over his church; an unappetising notion, but one which acknowledged the finality of the Papal victory.[1]

Though its boundaries are uncertain, the Liberal Catholic movement does pass Voltaire's tripartite test: it was liberal, it was Catholic and it was a movement. It was also distinctively English. Although Liberal Catholics in England shared many of the assumptions of their continental counterparts – such as Döllinger's idea of historical theology and Montalembert's of 'liberalised' nationalism – they naturally addressed themselves to the unique features of English Catholicism. What were those features? The mid-century Catholic Church in England underwent a dramatic change of life, symbolised by the restoration of the diocesan hierarchy in 1850. This recreation of long-unused ecclesiastical machinery was both cause and effect. It was a response to the administrative problems of a significantly enlarged Church;[2] to the challenges to social cohesion, inside the Catholic community and outside, of the arrival in the 1840s of the famine-stricken Irish;[3] it was a reflection, apparently, of a new political tolerance towards Catholics whose origins lay in the Emancipation Act of 1829. It was a manifestation of the new confidence which the Oxford Movement had given the English Catholic Church. It spoke of the re-awakening of Old Catholics, whose stewardship of the Faith had hitherto been intellectually moribund. All these things made diocesan restoration sensible. A new set of bishops indicated how the English Church had grown. It was the first fruit of the second spring.

However, the restoration created problems as much as it responded to them. English Protestantism had watched the Catholic revival with anxious interest. It raised fundamental questions. Catholicism, even in its home-grown variety, seemed essentially a foreign bloom. Protestantism, not Popery, was the seed of English greatness. English liberties were Protestant liberties; English oppressions had been Catholic oppressions. This was a pleasingly simple dichotomy, versatile too. It explained the past in a way which made the present understandable. Thus when Cardinal Wiseman formally announced the Restoration (7 October 1850), he misread his audience. To Catholics, the exuberance of his pastoral letter 'From the Flaminian Gate' may have been inspiring, but to Protestants it provoked another response: Rome was once again expanding its empire.

Protestant anxiety was compounded by self-doubt. Consider the impact of the Oxford Movement on the English mind. Its leaders had tried the Church of England and had found it lacking. Many of 'Rome's Recruits' were men of the highest calibre whose rejection of Anglicanism could not be dismissed as fashionable whim. The social isolation (and often financial embarrassment) of conversion, was evidence of that.[4] Besides, the sheer number of conversions allowed Catholics to talk – with a massive *naiveté* which ought to have lessened, not heightened, a Protestant sense of threat – of the 'conversion of England'. This was a dream designed to make bearable the pains of proselytism, but it had serious consequences. The most obvious of them was Lord John Russell's 'No Popery' campaign of 1851. Catholic triumphalism was an expensive and dangerous commodity, liable to produce an emphatic Protestant response, however disporportionate to the real threat. Political insiders felt uneasy with Russell's anti-Papal opportunism,[5] but there was always a ready market for it.

These were the circumstances out of which liberal Catholicism grew and to which it responded: a revitalised but by no means untroubled English church. Liberal Catholicism was also a response to the *ideas* of the modern world as to its particular challenges. The new orthodoxies of science and democracy, liberalism and nationalism, industrialism and socialism, all demanded attention. Liberal Catholics attempted to reconcile the Church to progress, liberalism and modern civilisation, thus rendering her less vulnerable to their threats. Men like John Acton and Richard Simpson considered it their duty to inject small doses of liberalism into a church unaware of how to tackle its effects. There was excitement about this task: urgency too. John Moore Capes, a convert and an astringent critic of his new co-religionists, found in the English Catholic body a 'grievously deficient' level of cultural attainment, a 'cautious conservative spirit', a need for 'fresh vigour and a deeper philosophy'.[6]

In this spirit he founded and, for a while, edited *The Rambler*, for thirteen years the focus of Liberal Catholicism in England. It was the organ of many troubled souls: Henry N. Oxenham, a convert parson, devoted to Newman, but highly critical of his inconsistency; James Spencer Northcote, who believed that the Church had nothing to fear from scholarship which might falsify some of her historical claims – perhaps the most generally held Liberal Catholic belief; Thomas F. Wetherell, whose liberalism in ecclesiastical matters extended to hero-worship of Gladstone in political; Rowland Blennerhasset, a Döllingerite and Gladstonian Liberal, later an Irish Home Ruler; William Monsell, an Irish Liberal MP, who, critical of those who were 'first Whigs and then Catholics',[7] nonetheless seemed to imply that the conjunction was as natural as the contradistinction; and John Acton, of whom more later. The list is by no means exhaustive, but it indicates the variety of liberal Catholics; perhaps also their potential fissiparousness. Both characteristics are well exemplified in the history of *The Rambler*, which is worth examining as an introduction to the themes and controversies of English Catholic life in the 1850s and 1860s.

Variety was clear from its first year of existence, with articles on Communism, Liberal Catholics in France, the rise of democracy, Church and State, the dangers of the Gothic Revival, the state of the Catholic poor, the social *insouciance* of the Catholic rich, the inadequacy of Catholic education, the paucity of Catholic churches, and so on. For many old Catholics, this smacked of impertinence. They took the criticisms of converts as a personal affront. Gothic, in particular, was a touchy subject: converts preferred Italianate styles in vestments, devotions and architecture, old Catholics preferred Pugin's rood-screens; converts recognised a social need for cheaper and less fanciful churches, old Catholics saw this as a dilution of the Faith. It was not a straightforward division (Pugin was himself a convert, though an eccentric one) but recusants resented that a 'body of mutineers' had excited an 'insane ... almost impious movement against ... Old Catholic Solemnity'.[8]

The Gothic row blew itself out, but it adumbrated future divisions. For a while, however, Liberal Catholics remained confident of their creed.

By the middle of the 1850s the euphoria of the restoration of the hierarchy began to dissipate. English Catholics lost their sense of being *fratres in unum*, an evanescent quality at the best of times. Catholic social inequalities, for example, were enormous. With lurid relish, one *Rambler* contributor contrasted two worlds. On the one hand, there were those who thought that the poor liked nothing better than high masses and penny pamphlets. On the other were the poor themselves, more accustomed to 'the gin shop, the penny gaff, the police court, the gaol and the gallows'.[9] This was excessive. There was a less dramatic reason for abandoning triumphalism:

> We have had a great many converts but as a mass the English nation remains untouched.... Worldliness, heresy, infidelity, delusion, prejudice and pride are still absolutely dominant in [England].[10]

So far from converting England (the argument went), Catholics were still regarded as unfit citizens of it. The belief remained that 'a man in becoming a Catholic ceases to belong to the British or Irish nation'.[11] Having noticed this 'falsehood' however, Catholics themselves perpetuated it. They held themselves to be not as other men. They were not, for instance, an interest-group amenable to political bribery. They could not be bought off like Nonconformists[12] or neutered like 'sleek and well-fed' Anglican divines who prayed for the all-providing Tory party. On the contrary, 'a designing Government cannot [easily] ... divide us in order to govern us'.[13]

By the mid-1850s, therefore, English Catholicism had become more self-critical. There was a greater preparedness to engage in debate. Self-congratulation, tolerable in 1850, when there was some-thing to celebrate, was tiresome in 1855, when there was nothing. It became obvious that the task of the Church in England was to secure its modest gains, not gloat over imagined ones. However, those who took this lead from the *Rambler* differed sharply in analysis from their more conservative co-religionists. They underestimated the traditionalists' resistance to change, and traditionalists underesti-mated their liberalism, which in some instances was theologically suspect.[14] As well as this, the Old Catholic/convert division began to be superseded by one between different types of convert: Manning and W. G. Ward, for example, were Ultramontanes, Newman and Richard Simpson plainly not.

The case of Richard Simpson bears examination. He was a brilliant polemicist who enjoyed controversy for its own sake. Thus in 1856 he denounced 'the little remnant of Catholic England' who wanted no more than to read 'nice stories in illustration of the pleasantness ... of the Catholic religion'.[15] This was an undisguised reference to Cardinal Wiseman and the *Dublin Review,* both of them devoted to a '*couleur de rose*'[16] view of English Catholic unity. A protracted row between the *Rambler* and the *Review* followed. From Wiseman's point of view, it was singularly self-defeating. His was an odd notion of denominational unity if he thought it best preserved by denuncia-tion of his flock. Even so, it was ironic that liberal Catholics, having denied Catholic unity, found themselves more isolated than ever, opposed, obviously, by the 'little remnant' of old Catholic England, but also by many Ultramontane converts who resented their un-bridled intellectualism. In that sense, the liberal wing of the English Church *had* created an improbable unity where none had existed before.

In the years which followed, liberal Catholics became more isolated, more divided, and more querulous. The *Rambler*'s attacks on the hierarchy began to appear egregious. One article on the politics of Catholic education, for example, condemned ecclesiastical authorities 'whose infirm and baby minds are gratified by mischief'.[17] This enabled the bishops to condemn from the pulpit 'the enemy' who had used the pretext of education 'to sow the tares of division among Catholics'.[18] As a result Richard Simpson had to resign as editor to make way for Newman, the only candidate acceptable to Bishops and liberals alike. Even this was an unhappy decision. Newman, as he often did, made matters worse. Quite uninten-tionally he isolated the liberals further, by producing a classic expression of their position – 'On Consulting the Faithful in Matters of Doctrine' – for which he was reported to Rome for heresy. Such treatment might have frightened real heretics as much as imagined ones. It certainly kept him quiet for the rest of the 1860s.[19]

Newman's retreat had an important but unforeseen consequence: it meant that there was now little check on livelier spirits on the liberal wing of the Church – Simpson, Wetherall and, especially, Acton.[20] In the 1860s they became more active politically (theology being out of bounds), and the politics were explicitly Gladstonian.

ACTION AND GLADSTONE

Acton's place in the liberal Catholic movement is well known, his political career less so. As far as he was concerned, the two were not separable. There was a 'wavy line'[21] between religion and politics which he intended to straddle:

> I would have a complete body of principles for the conduct of English Catholics in political affairs, and ... I will gradually unfold them. The Catholics want political education.[22]

Acton was prepared to give it to them, good and proper, either through *The Rambler* or, after 1859, in the House of Commons. His stepfather was Lord Granville (the source of much of his Whiggism), who undertook to find the young man a seat. This was not easy, Acton being Catholic, but Granville was pleased to note that 'although he is only a moderate Whig, he is also a very moderate Catholic'.[23] Zealotry in religion did not lend itself to Whiggery in politics. Cardinal Wiseman also hoped that he could get a seat, but his reasoning was less secure than Granville's. The Archbishop anticipated that Acton would speak 'with independence and in a thoroughly Catholic spirit',[24] a meaningless endorsement, making little sense in logic, and none in politics where a thoroughly Catholic spirit, as Wiseman ought to have remembered, was generally answered by a thoroughly Protestant one. As for Acton himself, he had no need to be encouraged to be independent, nor any desire to become an archiepiscopal mouthpiece.

In 1859 he was elected as Liberal member for Carlow, a boisterous affair which had all the elements the popular historical imagination requires of an Irish election – drunken mobs, inflammatory speeches, extensive bribery, priestly influence.[25] In the General Election itself, clerical pressure was explicit.[26] Wiseman urged the Catholics of England and Ireland to re-elect the government in order to keep out Palmerston and Russell, who were sympathetic to the Italian Revolution and opposed to the temporal power of the Pope. This was a risky strategy. Not all Catholics wanted to vote for 'those who [had] always been their bitterest enemies',[27] the Tories, simply to keep the Whigs out. Clerical dictation was foolish because it revealed the poverty of choice open to Catholics. It widened the gap between clergy and hierarchy in some Irish dioceses,[28] it failed of its immediate purpose to re-elect the government, and it encouraged a belief that the Catholic laity were not allowed to think for themselves.

It was hard to know in 1859 which side Catholics would take, because they did not know themselves. Acton is a case in point. He was too subtle a thinker for party politics. In 1857 'reasons of religion' made him declare 'most positively' that he could not always vote for Palmerston's government 'or for any other';[29] in 1859 he did not deny authorship of an article which argued that it was a 'precarious experiment' for Catholic MPs to act 'as mere Catholics instead of English or Irish statesmen and gentlemen'.[30] This kept both bishops and chief whips at bay. It could justify political neutrality on Catholic grounds[31] and justify precisely the opposite – support of Palmerston, Italian policies notwithstanding, because it was nonsense to say that 'the interests of religion must over-ride the precepts of politics'.[32] This was sophisticated thinking. Most Catholics were less capable than Acton. He was able, as they were not, of arriving at exquisite distinctions which showed that, from a purely Catholic perspective, neither party was especially attractive.

For all its confusions, the General Election of 1859 made one thing clear: the threat to the Papal States was the central consideration of Catholic politics. Unfortunately Catholics did not agree among themselves about the Temporal Sovereignty of the Pope. It was therefore unreasonable of them to expect greater consistency in the political parties. Wiseman's policy, articulated in the Commons by Sir George Bowyer, MP for Dundalk, was to oppose Palmerston at every turn because of his government's Roman policy. Acton thought this self-defeating. He preferred to support Palmerston in order to soften the administration's antipathy towards the Vatican. In so doing, he fell between several stools. Indeed, he annoyed almost everyone: constituents who believed he preferred 'the in-

terests of his step-father to those of the Holy Father';[33] Whig
Catholics who wanted a united Parliamentary front; Ultramontanes
like Manning (who prompted the Vatican to request that Acton
change the pro-Government policy of *The Rambler*); even Liberal
colleagues who were never sure when such a finely-tuned conscience might change its course again.

It is highly significant that Manning, exasperated by Acton's
continued support for Palmerston, attempted (unsuccessfully) to
silence *The Rambler*. It revealed a number of things. The first was that
the Vatican was prepared to interfere in domestic politics by adopt-
ing, then trying to enforce, a certain political line. It also showed that
Ultramontanism was politically unsubtle, indeed avowedly so,
being intent on one aim, Temporal Power, and one method, opposition to those who disagreed. This was self-defeating if it stirred up
another 'no popery' cry. More immediately, however, Manning's
belligerence showed that liberal Catholics had no real stomach for a
fight. Newman, for example, was not prepared to stand with his
former allies. He thought that the isolation of *The Rambler* and its
contributors was deserved. He had no sympathy for those who
believed that they could invite ecclesiastical sanction for political views, then oppose that authority when it found against them.

The Rambler last appeared in May 1861 and re-emerged in 1862 as
The Home and Foreign Review. Its history was no quieter than its
predecessor, but it was considerably shorter. After appearing to libel
Wiseman,[34] it was publicly condemned by every bishop, Acton's
excepted, for its unCatholic insolence. A familiar dialectic ensued:
Acton repeated liberal principles, Bishop Ullathorne condemned
them; Newman moved closer to the bishops, Acton began to fear for
Newman's liberalism; Newman, as ever, pronounced himself much
misunderstood; Simpson claimed in a pamphlet that Ullathorne had
misunderstood the purpose of free inquiry, Ullathorne claimed in
another that he had understood it all too well. The row eventually
petered out, but, as with all dialogues of the deaf, it raised tempers
and made them coarser for their next discussion.

The *Home and Foreign* was never a Catholic organ or even a purely
religious one. Its politics were largely Gladstonian, in keeping with
the enthusiasms of Acton and Wetherall. Gladstone's links with it
were informal and, though Acton invited articles from him, he
acknowledged privately,[35] and Simpson publicly,[36] that the review
could not be directly linked to one party or another. The Glad-
stonianism, however, was never in doubt: as Acton wrote to

Gladstone, 'the objects and principles of the *Review* fit it to be your organ on many important matters, perhaps more than any other journal'.[37] Acton's enthusiasm for Gladstone displeased his constituents, who were annoyed that they heard so little from him on Catholic matters in the Commons. (If they had known what he was likely to say they would have counted themselves lucky.)[38] His speaking record as a denominational spokesman was patchy, and this weakened him in the eyes of both constituency and hierarchy. The best reason the formerly favourable *Carlow Post* could propose for his re-election was that the constituency had been served so often in the past by ultra Protestants that the electors, having for so long 'swallowed a Protestant camel,... should [not] now strain at a Catholic gnat'.[39]

Catholic gnat: the phrase says much for the way both the politics and the religion of Acton's set were derided. They were too liberal for the Catholics and too Catholic for the Liberals. In 1864 this became abundantly obvious. In March of that year, the Papal Brief to the Archbishop of Munich decisively rejected Döllinger's historical theology (in which theological error was seen as an unavoidable and therefore tolerable element in doctrinal development).[40] Acton recognised that this undermined the liberal Catholic position, philosophically, by making inquiry impossible; tactically, by making loyal opposition to Rome impossible; politically, by seeming to prove that Catholics were uncivically obscurantist. He therefore closed the *Home and Foreign* in April 1864. Worse was to follow. The *Quanta Cura* and the *Syllabus of Errors* devasted the liberals. They had long claimed that unbridled Ultramontanism made bad politics. The *Syllabus* and the reaction to it proved their point.

THE SYLLABUS OF ERRORS OF 1864 AND THE GENERAL ELECTION OF 1865

The reaction to the *Syllabus* in England was, according to its historian, theologically unsubtle.[41] What the public failed to realise, the argument goes, was that Pio Nono's apparent condemnation of the modern world and all its works was addressed to fellow theologians in the shared language of theology, and as such was easily misunderstood. It was obscure, but not in its contents obscurantist. This is disingenuous. Would clarity have won the *Syllabus* any more friends? It is unlikely. Nevertheless, it is important not to exaggerate

Protestant outrage. Derision more than anger seemed the natural response.[42] Even so, the surprise was real enough and it made Catholic politics awkward. 'What are we to do in Parliament,' William Monsell MP asked Newman, 'when the Encyclical is thrown in our faces?'[43] There was not a great deal they could do. Gestures such as Acton's refusal (along with Lord Vaux, a prominent Oxford convert) to sign an Address of English Catholics thanking the Pope for his documents, were too puny. They could never convince Liberals that Catholics were to be trusted or that their votes were worth cultivating. Witness the *Morning Advertiser*. The Liberal Party, it averred, could not 'lower itself to the point of seeking Popish votes when its principles stood in opposition to all that the Encyclical spoke for'.[44]

In the election of 1865, the *Syllabus* provided Liberal politics with many of its images, not all of them predictable. The 'intemperate missive'[45] was, of course, condemned. When Wiseman died, obituaries hoped 'that Ultramontanism has [now] passed its highest flood tide,... [to be] replaced by more sound and sober opinions among our Roman Catholic fellow citizens'.[46] These were standard responses. More subtly, the encyclical offered politicians a metaphor. Any policy which was unenlightened and despotic, any opponent who was overmighty and insensitive, was best condemned by being likened to the Pope.[47] Liberals, it should be noted, were keen to condemn Ultramontanism but not Catholicism itself. The former was a corruption of the latter. They wanted Catholics to realise that they had much in common with other supporters of the Liberal Party – Dissenters, for instance, who were in the same position with regard to the Established Church. Liberal candidates, in short, attempted to appeal to so many groups that they ran the danger of appealing to none.[48] But were the Tories in any better position to court Catholic support? Clearly not. Lord Derby had recently spoken of the danger of 'unmuzzling the Catholics', a reference to the Parliamentary Oaths Bill (1865) which would have removed elements of the Oath supposedly offensive to Catholic MPs. This was a poor basis for any appeal for Catholic votes.

If in the election of 1865 the parties were uncertain of how to treat Catholics, so too were Catholics of how to treat the parties. Ultramontanism turned out to be an political *point de départ*, as the curious election of Sir John Simeon for the Isle of Wight indicated. On that occasion W. G. Ward, the Ultramontane, supported Sir Charles Locock, the 'no popery' Conservative, rather than Sir John Simeon, the liberal Catholic, arguing that it was better to have a Protestant MP, even one who wanted to investigate the convents, than a Catholic who was motivated by principles that had been 'authoritatively condemned by the Church's infallible voice'.[49] And the irony of an Ultramontane supporting a 'no popery' candidate was paralleled by Liberal claims that Simeon's election was proof of their religious toleration. This was doubtful. Without ever denying his religion, Simeon formulated its politics in a wholly anodyne way. As he told his electors, 'he would never give a vote that was at all calculated to injure or endanger the Protestant Church of England'.[50]

Other Catholic candidates were equally eirenic. Lord Eustace Cecil, a Tory, complaining that he had been the victim of 'no popery', was able to assure the voters that 'he was a staunch supporter of the Protestant Church'. Pressed to deny that he opposed the Oaths Bill and every other measure of Catholic relief, he could only manage the feeble retort that he did not give pledges as to how he would act 'with regard to any particular political question'. Acton's election as a Catholic for the Protestant borough of Bridgnorth presents a similar picture (he had parted from Carlow, with mutual pleasure). Bridgnorth was near the family seat of Aldenham, and Acton had told his constituents that he belonged 'rather to the soul than the body of the Catholic Church':[52] hardly a clarion call of the Church Militant.

The isolation of Catholics like Acton derived in part from the fact that they were Liberals by conviction, not *faute de mieux*. They were *for* Gladstone, not merely against his foes. The contrast with the former idol, Newman, was stark:

> I have no great love of the Conservatives, as being Erastians of a type which I do not think you can admire – but I speak of them as a party – as to individuals, I know what excellent, estimable men there are among them – and I shall rejoice at their coming into power, if, without upsetting the state-coach, they can keep it from running off the highroad, the king's highway.[53]

This was too timid for Acton's taste. By 1868, with Gladstone's coming to power and the increasing extravagance of Ultramontane claims, he and his allies committed themselves more fully than ever to Liberal party politics.

THE VATICAN COUNCIL: 'FRANKENSTEIN'S MONSTER'

By 1868 Gladstone was Prime Minister, Manning was Archbishop of Westminster, and Pius IX was contemplating, though the agency of the First Vatican Council, his *coup de théâtre*: the declaration of Papal Infallibility in matters of faith and morals. The first two had their thoughts on the third. Gladstone's Roman preoccupation[55] is well known. Ultramontanism threatened his dream of a reunited apostolic Christendom, it endangered his vision of the pluralist state, it insulted his intelligence.[56] These were personal considerations. Politically viewed, Romanism was equally complex. Gladstone wished to pacify Ireland, whose hierarchy had to be appeased and whose Liberalism revitalised. But it was no easy task to reform the Irish Church, Irish land law, and the Irish educational system in a way that would satisfy his conscience, the grievances of his complainants, the social presumptions of his Whig cabinet colleagues, and the religious sensibilities of his Anglican and Nonconformist support. Ultramontanism made it even harder. Gladstone led a cabinet which rarely shared his urgency about Rome and a party which, in its nonconformist wing, shared it too much. His cabinet-making and his party management indicated a desire for 'balance' – between Whigs, Peelites and Radicals, and between Anglicans, Nonconformists and Catholics – and the ministry's reforms (of the land, the army, the civil service, the Church and the schools) openly expressed this balance, indeed ultimately undermined it.[57] Gladstone's personal religiosity, and events in Rome from 1868 to 1871, complicated already delicate politics.

The Vatican Council did for all Liberals what the *Syllabus* had done only for liberal Catholics: it traumatised them. As it unfolded, as Papal pretensions became clearer, Gladstone and his party were staggered by the implications, diplomatic, domestic, and theological. The Prime Minister derived his information from a notably Whiggish, diplomatic chain of family connections. Odo Russell (Clarendon's son-in-law, Earl Russell's nephew, the son of a Catholic mother and Britain's unofficial representative at the Vatican) wrote to Clarendon, now Foreign Secretary, and sometimes directly to Gladstone. Acton, in Rome as the correspondent of the *Chronicle*,[59] wrote to Gladstone (on terms, now, of intimacy) and to Clarendon's successor at the Foreign Office in 1870, his own stepfather, Earl Granville. These relationships might have confirmed Protestant fears that Catholics were to be found at the very heart of the establishment, but that

would have been a *canard*. There was never any danger of Gladstone's being deprived of an overwhelmingly liberal view of the
Council. None of his Roman correspondents, except Manning, held
any brief for the Pope. Russell's letters were shrewd though change-
ably optimistic or pessimistic, Clarendon's more intemperate, Granville's more world-weary, Acton's the impassioned products of one
who felt himself so threatened by Jesuits that he went around Rome
in disguise.

Apart from diplomatic information, these correspondences reveal
several things. The first is the imaginative inadequacy of the Liberal
response to Infallibility. An event so inexpressible in the language of
progress and perfectibility reduced Whiggish optimism to bathos,
the hope that some 'good may come out of ... such ... a monster glove
thrown down not alone to the spirit of the age but to the common
sense of mankind'.[60] This was at once desperate and Panglossian. It
was also politically naive, reflecting a desire to impute Liberal
rationality to Ultramontane opponents who in no wise shared it.
Whatever Pio Nono was, he was not a landed Whig. His priorities
were not Gladstone's. It mattered little to him how affairs in Rome
were interpreted in terms of their domestic consequences – on
Ireland, on Catholic civil rights, on Scottish Protestant feeling, on the
Nonconformist vote. Those who thought that these considerations
could be made to weigh with him misunderstood their man.

Bemused and ironic disbelief is the *leitmotiv* of Odo Russell's early
dispatches from Rome. One of them captured all the themes that
would dominate the next two years: a mischievous Manning, a
freebooting Pope, an illusory Council, a deceived clergy, a naive
laity, and a Russell confident that his voice was listened to:

> The Pope himself, who is a wonderful force, thinks of nothing but
> his Oecumenical Council and the Divine glory he is to enjoy from
> its miraculous effects. Cardinal Antonelli had some misgivings on
> the subject, but his prudent objections have been overruled by the
> Pope and the Jesuits and he now submits in silence to the religious
> caprices of his Pontifical Master.... This Council is certainly a very
> popular measure in the clergy who flatter themselves generally
> that they are to have an Ecclesiastical Parliament.... No one seems
> yet to realise that the Pope merely intends the Council to be a grand
> Ceremony in St. Peter's for his own glorification.... When Dr.
> Manning comes to Rome next year he may possibly upset all the

good you did last year – for he is said to have set his heart on mischief.[61]

The reference to Manning concerned his desire to see a restoration of the Catholic hierarchy in Scotland. Clarendon was spared this. 'Whatever Manning may [have said],' he claimed, 'it would have had a disastrous effect in Scotland.'[62] But in 1869 that was the least of his worries. Ireland was much more pressing, and Manning, a mischief-maker in December 1868, had become a potential miracle-worker in January 1869. This was because Archbishop Cullen's attitude to the distribution of Irish Church property had complicated Disestablishment negotiations, requiring Gladstone to enlist Vatican support for government policy, and the Tories to secure Vatican opposition to it.[63] Momentarily, Pio Nono's outrageous pretensions were forgotten. As Clarendon confided to Russell,

> I wish, tho' of course in vain, that some check could be put on Cullen. I told the Pope that he was the bitter and pertinacious enemy of the English govt ... and it really is too bad that this viper Cullen should be permitted to create difficulties in addition to those which already exist....[64]

Clarendon felt that Cullen, by embarrassing Gladstone, played into Tory hands, and that Manning therefore was the prelate whom the Liberals ought to trust. This he expressed with unwitting irony. Having begun his letter to Russell with thanks that the disastrous Scottish hierarchy had been averted, he ended it with the observation that Cullen's conduct was 'a bitter pill to Gladstone whose object is to satisfy the Catholics'.[65] He deplored the fact that Cullen had given 'an enormous triumph to the Tories', and fresh vigour 'to the ultra Protestants in England'.[66] If Manning could deaden this, then it mattered little that Manning himself had been the embarrassment only a month before. There could be no clearer demonstration of the complexities of religious politics than that Manning the Ultramontane could be regarded, however much in a fit of bad temper, as the best means of soothing Gladstone's ultra-Protestant support, or his ultra-Protestant enemies.

Manning continued to be crucial for the first months of 1869. Russell reported that the Archbishop's 'strongly expressed Gladstonian convictions' had caused no alarm at the Vatican because the Pope had 'implicit faith and confidence in him'.[67] Confident that

Manning and Cullen were the men to win over, he thought that the Tories had missed out:

> I took a walk ... with Dr. Manning and found him personally and politically devoted to Mr. Gladstone of whom he spoke with the *warmest affection*. He also said twice that he was 'sincerely glad' you [Clarendon] had replaced Lord Stanley at the F.O.[68]

He even held out the prospect of 'using'[69] Manning's influence in Rome to make the *English* Catholics more manageable. For a while, there was optimism about Catholic politics, based on Cullen's apparent moderation, Manning's emollient approach to Temporal Power, and the enthusiasm for Gladstone among Irish priests in Rome. In April 1869 Russell thought that 'our present relations with the Court of Rome are better than ever'.[70]

This was the bliss of ignorance. Three weeks later, in May 1869, the good mood had vanished, sunk beneath the weight of Irish violence and the renewed disloyalty of Cullen. Faced with this, Vatican support seemed hardly worth the trouble. Clarendon failed to see 'the slightest sign of Vatican influence in Ireland' and began to question the wisdom of relying upon the well-meaning but ineffectual Manning who 'desires to check evil-doers but has no authority in Ireland'.[71] Whether Cullen had any more authority was moot: Clarendon was inclined to blame the violence on priests who had fed their flocks on disloyalty to England and then found it impossible to wean them off it.

Why did Russell in Rome and Clarendon in England differ so markedly in their reading of Irish affairs? One reason is obvious: distance from the problem. Even after the despairing letter quoted above, Russell still held that Gladstone's Irish policy 'appears to be giving the Vatican and the Irish Priesthood in Rome and the most perfect and unmingled satisfaction'[72] – an over-optimistic view of things as far as Clarendon was concerned, who was more interested in the behaviour of the Irish priesthood in Ireland. Notice, too, that Clarendon's attempt to see Ireland as a problem of diplomacy helped make the government feel less remorseful about being unable to solve it. Diplomacy was an elaborate form of self-exculpation because it made a complex problem appear susceptible to relatively straightforward solution. Consider the changing images of Manning and Cullen and the rapidity of the changes. Manning was up to mischief in December; was 'most agreeable ... thoroughly straightforward ... and all Powerful at the Vatican' in February; and had no authority in Ireland in May.[73] Cullen, more dramatically, was a viper in December, 'most friendly' in February, and 'thoro'ly disaffected'[74] in May. These modulations reflected the state of Ireland, or what was taken to be the state of Ireland. Russell and Clarendon seemed not to realise that they amounted to little more than an attempt to make others personify the failure of their own policy, both diplomatic *and* domestic.

The rapidity, it is true, worked both ways. A better mood prevailed in June 1869, possibly because, as papal claims became clearer, Liberals gave themselves up to the pleasures of self-righteousness. Gladstone imagined that it might be possible, by intelligent diplomacy, 'to do what the Reformation did – to save the Pope and the Roman Church from themselves'.[75] Russell thought this confidence misplaced, believing that

> the policy of Rome is clearly tending to the establishment through the Council of a 'free Church in free States,' only the free Clergy will become a Politico-Ecclesiastical reactionary party that will give the State a vast amount of trouble.[76]

Clarendon's thinking was more wishful. He held that 'the influence of the clergy has been exercised beneficially in Ireland' (a clear change from his earlier view that Rome had little influence over Ireland)[77] – for which he hoped Russell would thank Cardinal Antonelli:

> There have been none of these outrages for the past month that the opposition gloated over as proofs that disestablishing the Irish Church would do nothing for the pacification of Ireland.[78]

What do these observations mean? Simply this: the government needed the Vatican's support because it kept alive the hope that disestablishment was not a waste of time. The government thought it possible to win that support by hinting at Catholic 'measures' while at the same time keeping the support of its majority by hinting at no such thing[79] – a duplicitous course. Russell summarised the government's position nicely, arguing that one reason for disestablishment and disendowment was that 'when the Catholic clergy have no real grievance left wherewith to excite the Irish people against England, the Pope and his priests will lose half their influence in Ireland and become uninteresting and tiresome as in Italy'.[80] This was, for three reasons, a delusion – it assumed that the Church question *was* the grievance, that clerical influence would be weakened by its solution, and it forgot what Russell himself once noticed, the ingratitude of Romanists in general, the Irish in particular. It was not apparent how a world was to be brought about in which the political embarrassment of Catholic 'measures' would be unheard of because unnecessary, unnecessary because unasked for, unasked for because the Pope and his clergy were no longer a force, and no longer a force because Catholic grievances had already been relieved, quite *apart* from the possibility that this hypothetical relief might whet, not satisfy, an appetite for reform. Russell's observation was typical of a Catholic policy which merely hoped that all, eventually, would come right.

What the Vatican Council exposed therefore was the ambivalence of a policy which relied on clerical influence in Ireland as a means of social control and excoriated it elsewhere as a cause of social decay. Clarendon predicted to Gladstone that in about three or four years the Council would 'cause trouble to States in which there are R. Catholics'[81] on the grounds that clergy of all ranks were 'sure to adopt the dogma eagerly as it will enable them to speak with greater authority, and the "faithful" ... will be more ready ... to obey orders';[82] precisely the reason why Gladstone hoped to *strengthen* moderate clerical influence in Ireland. (The Queen, it might be added, experienced the same changing moods as her government: four months after Russell reported that 'the Queen's message to the Pope on his Jubilee ... produced a marvellously good effect',[83] Gladstone wrote to Clarendon that 'the Queen will be pleased if you can find any legitimate opportunity of throwing dirt on the Council'.)[84]

Gloom, then, defined the government's attitude to events in Rome and, by extension, violence in Ireland. One source of comfort was the thought that the Pope would soon be dead. Alternatively, there was a conspiracy theory (Jesuits featuring prominently) which made things seem better by the sombre recognition of how bad they were. The images of a senile Pope or a wily one both had their comforts: Infallibility could be reduced to Jesuit worldliness or geriatric whim, the Council made to seem a ridiculous 'medieval prank', as Clarendon put it, the tawdry fantasy of a 'poor old man'.[85] Either way, the hope was kept alive that Vatican diplomacy might pacify Ireland. The hope foundered. Clarendon concluded that it would prove unavailing, for the 'splendid ingratitude of Cullen and Co.'[86] always stymied measures of moderate reform. The last chance to check Rome's socially menacing advances was 'the common sense of our R.C. countrymen ... and a very vain hope it will be', for even English Catholics were liable to reject 'progress and civilisation'. Political 'boobyism', as he implied, was their abiding characteristic.[87]

GLADSTONE, ACTON, MANNING AND THE POLITICS OF PATRONAGE

There was an exception, in Gladstone's eyes, to Catholic political eccentricity: men like Acton and Wetherell who were still devoted to the cause of common-sense. In 1868 Acton again stood for Bridgnorth (having been unseated in 1866 by a corruption petition). This time he was beaten, perhaps the least mourned of the Catholic casualties in that election.[88] His correspondence with Simpson makes plain the political disadvantages of a Catholicism even as rarefied and unRoman as his. He was defeated by a No Popery cry got up by local Tories; an odd fate for one who had spent much time making similar noises himself.[89] His defeat removed the sheen of the general Liberal triumph.[90] Catholics, especially in Ireland, liked to think that they had given Gladstone his victory and were entitled to special treatment, but Richard Simpson knew better: 'I fear me for the prospects of Catholics in the English or Scottish side of the Dom. Com. [House of Commons]',[91] he wrote to Acton. A Liberal victory did not mean a Catholic one.

Liberal Catholics were thus disowned by both the English electorate and the Pope. This was no mean feat. Gladstone, however, rewarded their loyalty. Acton was elevated to the peerage in November 1869, a promotion which has caused needless puzzlement,[92] misplaced Catholic self-congratulation (then and since), and faulty exuberance in certain historians.[93] Professor Chadwick claims that Acton's peerage 'smashed centuries of prejudice against Roman Catholics'.[94] This tabloid view does not withstand much examination. Acton's peerage did not smash anti-Catholic prejudice; in a curious way, it re-affirmed it. The peerage was one of Gladstone's balancing acts, an attempt to weigh the claims of two important areas of support, the Catholic and the Nonconformist.

This is clear from simple chronology. On 3 August 1869 Gladstone wrote orotundly to C.S.P. Fortescue that 'the time has come for giving some honours ... I am inclined to recommend ... two English

R.C.s, Edw. Howard, & J. Acton for the peerage'.[95] The next day he wrote to John Bright asking if he knew anyone who might go to the Lords 'on behalf partly of trade & manufactures, but especially of Nonconformity'.[96] Catholic claims were thus intrinsically no stronger or weaker than those of Nonconformists, even of Jews: for political purposes, they were merely comparable. Catholics only understood this when it suited them. They complained, for instance, if they thought they were getting less patronage than Jews, but believed that when they *were* favoured, their merits had been recognised on an absolute and not a relative scale.

Another consideration was the likely attitude of the Queen; and it was the inclusion of the Jew, Baron Lionel de Rothschild, and the two Catholics, in Gladstone's list, which angered her. 'To make a *Jew a peer*,' she told Granville, 'is a step she *could not* consent to.' As for the Catholics, even if one of them was his stepson,

> At *this* moment when there is *not* a doubt that the measure just passed respecting the Irish Church is looked upon as a triumph to the R. Catholics, she would not wish to create two R. Catholic Peers, though personally they are most unexceptionable, & at some other time the Queen might not be indisposed to make them.[97]

This was a general view. Catholic claims were measured against a double balance: their relation to other minorities, and to their own state of historical advance. There was an unspoken timetable of Catholic progress which could not be tampered with – the RCs should not get too much too soon.

Granville played on the Queen s prejudices without yielding to them. The government's Catholic policy was based on equity. It recognised social realities – he could not 'remember the creation of a Catholic peer, notwithstanding their wealth and bulk'. Above all, it was politic. What better way to strike a blow against the worst elements in English Catholicism?

> The old Catholic peers cannot speak. They cannot think for themselves and are under the direction of their bishops.

And Granville had a clinching argument:

Sir John Acton would be excluded if Dr. Manning had the power to do so.[98]

Paying off a debt, building up credit, liberating the Catholic voice, undercutting Manning and his bishops: all these things lay behind Acton's honour. It would be wrong to think that it implied favouritism. As Granville wrote to Gladstone, wondering how to raise an obviously delicate subject with the Queen,

> I shall leave it to you to discuss in conversation whether it will be wise as a general principle for the future to treat R. Catholics with disfavor [*sic*] in order to rescue the Protestant religion.[99]

So much for the view that the prejudice of centuries had been smashed.

Meanwhile, in Rome the Ultramontanes appeared unstoppable. They were immune to the argument, either as plea or threat, that Infallibility would put English Catholics in 'social and political danger'.[100] Diplomacy was unavailing; on the contrary its weapons were being used to good effect by Ultramontanes themselves. For example, Acton warned that Manning had been trading on his relationship with Gladstone to convince the doubtful that no political harm would come to English or Irish Catholics by the pronouncement of Infallibility[101] – a drastic change from the view that Gladstone could trade on Manning's name to win approval for his Irish policy. Another problem: Acton was no diplomat. His reputation in Rome was dubious. Granville wondered whether he was not, perhaps, 'too black a sheep'[102] to be of much use to the government. One of the advantages of Acton as would-be peer (he was recognisably not a bishop's man) was a positive disadvantage for Acton the would-be diplomat.

Gladstone had another adviser on Catholic matters, domestic and foreign: Manning. The Archbishop thought of himself as a political worthy in his own right, one who could write as 'a politician and good subject only' or could assure Gladstone that some of his flock were 'strangely confused in political opinions', as if his own were unimpeachably sensible.[103] His support for Gladstone took several forms: he acted as occasional go-between with the Irish MPs; he encouraged Irish Disestablishment;[104] he urged support for the Irish bishops (without ever reconciling that with his observation that the more bishops were praised the more their authority in Ireland declined, because 'it renders us suspect of the English policy of contempt and coercion');[105] he warned of the political consequences of legislation which would jeopardise his ability 'to view all public questions from [Gladstone's] position'; he praised Gladstone's 'patience and command of [his] supporters'[106] and suggested a few Catholics for preferment; he argued that concurrent endowment was not worth 'the political danger to the Government, and to the unity of its supporters';[107] he warned against 'stirring up the prejudices of the English Dissenters and the Scotch Presbyterians',[108] a somewhat obtuse admonition from an Ultramontanist.

These intimacies were valuable but suffocating. By seeming always to take Gladstone's part, he made things harder, not easier for the Prime Minister. For example, writing from Rome he claimed that he 'fully recognised that the excitement raised by the newspapers in England respecting what passes here, makes it less easy for the Government to do as it would to us'.[109] This had the paradoxical effect of exculpating the government for any anti-popery activity and yet increasing the pressure on it to be pro-Catholic. Nor did he further his own cause by blackguarding Acton, then whom, he told the Prime Minister, 'a more dangerous adviser you could not have'.[110] This only increased Gladstone's disillusion with the whole body of English Catholics. Manning had only to warn him that the 'shadow of Lord Acton between you and the Catholics of Great Britain' was a grave obstacle, for Gladstone to reply that he had 'never supposed him to be ... representative of the general body of English Roman Catholics.... You will not be surprised by my adding that ... I wish he were'.[111]

Manning, in short, was occasionally the author of self-defeating advice. It was easier, for example, for Gladstone to warn that any anti-social dogmas of the Council would 'certainly have an influence on legislation in this country which ... will be hostile to R.C. interests and feelings',[112] when the Archbishop half expected the threat and its execution. Not that he needed much reminder of the nuisance value of Catholics. 'The R.C.s are bothering me again about the Pope,'[113] he could write, annoyed and amazed by their single-mindedness. And there was another point. Bother from the RCs often meant bother from Nonconformists as well. Each group jealously watched the other's political progress. Gladstone exploited this. He used Protestant criticism to keep Catholics quiet. As he wrote on one occasion to Granville, when the *Daily News* had condemned him for seeming to favour the Pope's territorial independence, 'this is well as it might help to keep the RCs in order'.[114]

As the beneficiary of both Acton's advice and Manning's, Gladstone could discern which of the two was in the ascendant. It was, of course, the latter. As a declaration of Infallibility became inevitable, Acton and his ilk began to be seen in a new light. Their failure to influence the Council changed their political value. Having been useful to the government for once holding out the prospect of success, they now became useful for proving the certainty of defeat. Notice how Clarendon distanced himself from them after May 1870:

> Acton and co. have made a great torrent but they have known for a long time that it was carrying them away and that the straws they caught at could not prevent their being drowned.[115]

Other members of the government also seemed less concerned by events in Rome. Consider the irony that as Gladstone was attempting to prevent Infallibility, his ministry was simultaneously and successfully sponsoring the Repeal of the Ecclesiastical Titles Act of 1851. Earl Kimberley was responsible for guiding the legislation through the Lords, and his view of Papal pretensions was much more urbane than the Prime Minister's:

> It is amusing to see how an Act which made such a noise when it was passed is now snuffed out with the consent of all parties. It must be admitted that its original enactment was a mistake. The popular outburst against Popery might have been appeased by a short Declaratory Act or by Resolution, if it was absolutely necessary to do something; but [the] Act was a mere display of impotent anger.[116]

Here was common sense. The original Act was a dead letter which prevented the government from harnessing the 'great influence'[117] of the Irish bishops to the Liberal cause in Ireland. Protestant fears, he admitted, had not been entirely unfounded in 1851. He implied that they were equally exaggerated in 1870.

The passage of the repeal proved more troubled than Kimberley had anticipated, but his refusal to take anti-Popery much more seriously than Popery itself is worth noting. Gladstone was different: he took both very seriously, and it was he who defined the public face of the ministry. As far as Catholics were concerned, it was a

ministry increasingly secular in its tenor. In domestic legislation, this
was particularly so. What the *Tablet* called the 'monstrous'[118] Education Bill is a case in point. It posed a threat to denominational
schools, and galvanised Catholics into defence of them. Manning
urged 'redoubled' efforts on their behalf, and lobbied extensively
among ministers to that end. The usual mechanisms of popular
protest were deployed – a mass meeting at St James's Hall in
London, a St Patrick's Day demonstration in Liverpool, letters to the
editor, petitions – but to no avail. Events in Rome made it impossible
for Gladstone to yield. Pressure from his Nonconformist following
(who equally disliked the Bill, but for quite different reasons) also
helped ensure that Catholic objections would be discounted.[119]
Catholics noticed that 'Conservative and Religious Protestant'[120]
Members of Parliament had the same interest as themselves in
opposing the measure, and they accordingly moved in the direction
of the Tories, as they had a year before on the Scottish Education Bill.
Manning believed that an alliance of Catholics, Anglicans and well-
disposed Nonconformists would halt the Bill. All it did, in the end,
was to make Gladstone even more disillusioned with all of them. The
prospects for a Liberal-Catholic alliance for the rest of the ministry
therefore seemed poor, ameliorative legislation in Ireland notwithstanding.

LIBERALS AND CATHOLICS TO 1874

Infallibility was duly proclaimed, the Education Bill duly passed.
The *Tablet* became more stridently Ultramontane. The politics of
liberal Catholicism languished: Acton's political career, like his
literary career, began its long journey to the realm of 'promise
unfulfilled'. Relations between Gladstone and Manning, once intimate, became self-consciously strained.[121] Catholics continued to
prove that political self-importance often led to poor judgment.

Gladstone was still distrusted. Herbert Vaughan's letters to Lady
Herbert of Lea (important documents which indicate how an
Ultramontane Liberal became a Tory, and anti-Irish)[122] show some-
thing of this. In one, he wrote that

A petition is being got up throughout the Dioceses to Parliament
on behalf of the Pope. Of course, it will bring out a disagreeable

speech from Gladstone: but it will be a record of Catholic feeling.[123]

This was naive and realistic, but in precisely the wrong proportions: it was right to recognise anti-Catholic feeling, and right to see that concerted Catholic action could bring it forth; but it was wrong to underestimate the strength of it and also to imagine, without actually giving voice to the thought, that concerted Catholic action would also win a good deal of Protestant respect.[124]

Suspicion of Gladstone extended to his party. Newman, admittedly 'much perplexed between Mr. Disraeli and Gladstone',[125] regretted that the latter was 'the leader of a mixed multitude, who profess a Babel of religions or none at all'. This was a good description, but one which seemed unaware that Catholics, too, formed part of the Babel of Gladstone's support, and could not be treated with any special favour.[126]

The suspicion was mutual, in small matters as in large. From a party perspective it, Catholicism made patronage problematic. Thus in diplomacy:

Lytton (foolishly) has refused Munich – West does not wish for it. Petre has the next claim. But I doubt its being a good thing to send another Catholic to Munich.[127]

Thus also in peer-making:

I am for Rothschild being made a Peer – and in one sense his Peerage would be a complement to that of the Catholic. But for this especial purpose I should prefer some one to whom the Queen nor anyone else could object.[128]

Ultramontanism, or even the suspicion of it, was a handicap. Granville knew of no objections to Sir Augustus Paget 'except ... that Manning does not speak ill of him'.[129]

The Irish Education Bill widened divisions between Catholics and Liberals.[130] Irish Catholics could not conscientiously attend either Trinity College, Dublin, an Anglican establishment, or the Queen's Colleges of Belfast, Cork and Galway, which were 'Godless', that is to say undenominational. Their flock thus effectively denied third-level education, the Irish hierarchy hoped for a state-funded university under their own control: a touchingly naive wish which would have been out of the question even without events in Rome. Gladstone attempted compromise, proposing a new Dublin University, undenominational in its governing body, secular in its curriculum, unendowed by the state, to which Catholic and Presbyterian colleges could attach themselves if they so chose. Manning saw some merit in the scheme (it excluded 'mixed' or undenominational religious teaching) but the Irish bishops saw none. Theirs was the decisive voice. When the Bill came to Second Reading, all but five Catholic MPs opposed it. With its defeat, by a majority of three (287–284), Gladstone's first ministry was, for all practical purposes, broken. He resigned, but Disraeli refused office. Forced to continue in power for another eleven months, the administration was without moral or political authority.

Gladstone, a hero to Catholics in 1868, was thus condemned for a position on Irish education which was 'politically unwise, philosophically indefensible and in every respect unjust'.[131] Catholics much resented that the Liberals, of all people, should prove unworthy of the trust once invested in them. To Newman, the Education Act was 'a great tyranny – and is brought about by the exigencies of a Liberal Government'.[132] For others, Gladstone's treachery went deeper still. Consider the views of William Monsell. In September 1873, he wrote to Newman that

> my belief is that Gladstone is determined to break off his Catholic alliance. He told me in the spring that the action taken on the Irish University Question must separate the Catholics from the Liberal Party. He is almost fanatically anti-Catholic himself. He was furious with Lady Mary Herbert when she became Catholic. He said to me once 'I do not believe that we could do now what we did in 1868 [Disestablishment of the Irish Church].' He is not a Protestant. It is his Catholicism that resents those developments which separate still more Catholicism from high Anglicanism.[133]

There were elements of truth in this, but its analysis was one-sided – Gladstone the fanatic, Gladstone the furious, Gladstone the irrationally confused. Monsell never considered *why* the enactments of 1868 could not have been achieved in 1873. Gladstone had broken the alliance, not the Catholics.

There were other indications, it appeared, of the ministry's dangerous radicalism. The *Tablet* believed that the resignation of Lord Ripon, a denominationalist rather than a secularist in education policy, was a sop to the Nonconformists; the journal was 'scarcely disposed' to believe the official line that he had resigned for personal reasons.[134] This argument was ill-judged: in its zeal to prove that Ripon's removal was the act of an anti-Catholic government, the *Tablet* refused to be duped by the 'personal reasons' argument. It happened to be true. Ripon himself was about to become a Catholic and was suffering a crisis of conscience as a result. As for other members of the government, Lyon Playfair was a pure secularist, and Vernon Harcourt was a prominent opponent of 'a policy supposed to be too favourable to Catholics'.[135]

The defeat of the ministry in 1873 and its slow, lingering decline into 1874 put such strain on the Liberal-Catholic alliance that the General Election proved of decisive importance in their floundering marriage. Gladstone, once praiseworthy for having been amenable to their special interests, was now condemned for a programme which was little more than an opportunist attempt to please 'the jarring sections of the Liberal Party'.[136] For conceding the desires of Catholics, he had been a statesman: for yielding to the vested interests of others, he was 'to a large extent ... squeezable'.[137] The key issue was education. Bishop Vaughan of Salford, in a letter which was read at all churches in his diocese, reminded his flock of moral theology:

> There is one general moral principle to be insisted upon in the coming Elections, viz., that we cannot do evil that good may come of it. The application of this principle in the present crisis is very plain, and it comes to this: that no Catholic can vote for any candidate who proposes to saddle the country with a secular and godless system of education.[138]

Officially, this was an argument, not for voting against Liberal candidates but for discovering their views on the denominationalist-secularist controversy. Privately, though, Vaughan made plain the practical application of the principle:

> The Radical creed was precisely the three condemned proposi-tions in the Syllabus on popular Education. How could Catholics vote for that?... Better suffer a little tyranny from the Tories than vote for the Radical programme in Education.[139]

This was not a sanguine view of Catholic political prospects. A choice between Liberal godlessness and Tory tyranny was no choice at all. Catholics were nonetheless forced into the choice, and for the most part they chose the Conservatives. Both parties, however, were palpably anti-Ultramontane in their rhetoric. 'The emphatic repudiation of Ultramontane pretensions' was the platform of Sir Thomas Chambers, Liberal candidate for Marylebone. Resistance to the Pope's attempt 'to enforce slavery on mankind' was the unsurprising boast of Charles Newdegate, perennially successful Conservative candidate for North Warwickshire. There were three threats, an Orange flier claimed, which made it imperative for Protestants to vote Conservative in Glasgow: 'secularism, mammon, and Popery'. 'Faithfulness to the principles of the Reformation' secured a seat for Lord Sandon in Liverpool.[140]

Education was one reason for Catholics turning Tory; Home Rule was another. Liberals set their face against Home Rule in 1874, and duly suffered the consequences in Ireland. Some Catholic voters in England and Wales also punished them for it, thinking that support for the Conservatives would constitute a suitable rebuke. Here was double irony: on Catholic educational grounds, they supported a Protestant party; on Home Rule grounds, they supported a Unionist one. Gladstone, his ministry destroyed by attempts to assuage them on both, justifiably felt very ill-used.

Given the eccentricity of their position, it was rash of Catholics to claim the election as demonstration of their political potency. The *Tablet*, however, was sure of it, while simultaneously and contradictorily holding that Gladstone should not blame Catholics for his defeat:

> The lesson which we hope Mr. Gladstone will draw from the elections is this: that he must not trust the Radicals unless he is prepared to become one of them himself. It is they who have thrown him out; it is they who have forced the mass of Catholic voters into an attitude of opposition.[141]

What of Gladstone himself? The Catholic performance convinced him more than ever of the dangers of clericalism. He did not dissent from John Bright's observation that Catholic electors 'vote as the Priests tell them, and the Priests are for public money for Catholic schools, and they have no politics apart from the Church'.[142] Gladstone embellished the point. If the first principle of Catholic politics was loyalty to the Church, it followed that loyalty to any particular party was out of the question. Writing at the end of the year, in circumstances more heated than the election itself, he appeared for that reason to write off the Catholic vote, even to loathe it:

No R.C. vote is to be had except for a price. Those who can pay the price will have the vote whether they be L. or C. But the price must lie in the future, not in the recollections of the past. And it is probable that for each R.C. gained we lose several Protestants. Even in the fervour of 1868 we could not carry Liverpool; perhaps because we had there a large and enthusiastic R.C. support.

And now you must be tolerably weary of the subject.[143]

Such were the acerbities prompted by six years in the company of Catholics and their problems.

2

Catholics and Tories 1850–68: A Natural Alliance?

THE ROOTS OF CATHOLIC TORYISM

By the early 1870s Liberals and Catholics were beginning to part company, and by 1874 Gladstone was saying farewell – to the Catholic mind as much as to the Catholic vote – with such undisguised relief as to make reconciliation unlikely. In every facet – philosophical, political, personal – the Liberal-Catholic marriage had broken down. Gladstone recognised this and sued for divorce on grounds of mental cruelty: Catholics could be forgiven those faults which grated on the nerves – failure ever to be satisfied in Ireland, their self-absorption and sense of historic persecution, social pretensions which made them rejoice over a Marquis who converted,[1] even occasional flirtations with the Tories – but the claim to Infallibility was an assault which even the most indulgent partner could not support.

Catholics did not contest the case, but put a different construction on the facts. Where Gladstone had seen political infidelity, they saw impartiality; where Clarendon had discovered unreliability, they saw pragmatism; where others had felt a presumptuous intimacy – suffocating advice in public and in private – they saw the honest intercourse of political partners. And if the intimacy of the advice was unhelpful, much more so was its quality. Did they not realise, as they revealed to the Prime Minister the secret of political longevity (a formula easily remembered: the Catholic vote), that he had other parties to please? It seemed to Bright,[2] to Granville, still more to Gladstone, that they did not.

To speak of a Catholic-Liberal alliance, however, is to tell only half the story. What about the links between Catholicism and Conservatism? As with Catholic Liberalism, these existed at different levels – from a vague assumption that Catholicism was, in the broadest sense, a conservative creed, to subtle expressions of the same view; from political dalliance to passionate belief, at least on one side, that Catholics and Tories were, as Lord Derby once put it,

32

'natural allies'. This was a portentous notion. Natural allies in what way? For what reason? According to whom? Since when? The phrase was meaningless, by virtue of having too many meanings. Was it the case, for instance, as W. G. Ward claimed, that Tories ought to have seen in Popery not a threat to social peace but its guarantor?[3] Ward was an Oxford movement convert who, it was said, would have like nothing better than a Papal Bull with his *Times* at breakfast every morning: evidently a Tory by temperament. His argument led in an obvious direction: Catholicism not only preached but also produced social quietude. Cruder expressions of the same view abounded. Even Ward would have been embarrassed by a typical *Tablet* letter:[4]

In Lancashire among the working classes we have:

Brutality
Vulgarity   } and Bibles in Abundance
Cruelty and Drunkenness

In Belgium among a similar class, it is:

Humility
Civility   } and priests and nuns
Charity and Sobriety   everywhere

This need not have been an argument for a 'natural alliance' between Catholics and Conservatives. If it was, it was stupid: pointless to curry favour with Tories by condemning some of their best friends – the Protestant drinking classes of Lancashire. But Catholics, like the ideal Victorian child, wished to be good and to be seen to be good. Some, it is true, went too far in this respect. They won social acceptance only at the price of vapidity:

Our Catholic newspapers have never made an effort ... to introduce a single Catholic interest into what has been called 'practical politics ...'. This is shunned as being ungenteel and out of fashion.[5]

Too much can be made of this putative Catholic conformism. A desire to please did not make Catholics into Tories; but it may have helped.

The natural alliance of Catholic and Conservative may have been

less exalted than Ward thought and less self-denying than the
Tablet's correspondent implied. Some Catholics were Tories by social
calling, and denomination had little to do with it. Think of the world
revealed in his letters by Herbert Vaughan, future Cardinal Archbishop of Westminster. It was peopled by Howards, Denbighs,
Norfolks and Stonors – conventional grandees who expected deference and paid for it by philanthropy. Vaughan himself was an old-
fashioned paternalist:

> The Catholic aristocracy and gentry have not learned what the
> Protestant have, viz., that if they do not wish to be left behind they
> must *work*, and that if they wish to act upon society they must love
> *public duty*. If we had but men capable of leading and moulding
> this "little flock" what a grand work it might achieve upon the
> country....[6]

Here was sharp social perception vitiated by soapy idealism, but the
Toryism was clear. English Catholicism was a doll's-house world, a
self-sufficient society in miniature; no surprise, then, that its leaders
wished to educate their masters.

Vaughan's anxiety was misplaced. His class was safe enough.
Catholics could drop names as easily as Nonconformists could quote
Scripture. They were deferential to a fault. That said, one of the
illusions of English Catholicism was its classlessness. The *Tablet*, for
example, could report a pilgrimage to Pontigny in 1874 with
novelettish romanticism:

> By eight o'clock this morning the Victoria Station was alive and
> astir, and all the cabs and carriages which arrived brought fresh
> accessions of pilgrims bound for Pontigny.... There were old men
> as well as young; clergy as well as laymen; country squires and
> men with handles to their names; lawyers and merchants, clerks
> and tradesmen; old Catholics and converts; there were ladies,
> too....

In every way, a Catholic outing. But heterogeniety did not imply
equality. By the time they got to France, rank reasserted itself:

> The following, we understand, was the order of the procession –
> Lord E. Howard, the banner on the pilgrimage, and fifty pilgrims.
> The Earl of Gainsborough and the banner of St. Edward ...

The honourable and Right Reverend Monsignor Stonor ...
The Reverend Lord Archibald Douglas and the banner of St. Thomas of Canterbury.[7]

Catholics could be notable snobs. It would be no surprise to find some of them voting Tory as a supposed mark of social distinction.

The 'alliance' was more precise than this, however. Catholics were Tories by political conviction as well as by social desire. They had been made so by the Italian revolution. In 1859 Wiseman advised the Catholic electorate that Derby was a better friend to the Pope than Gladstone. Palmerston entered Catholic demonology as the friend of the revolution and it proved hard to dislodge him. Catholics found it easy to associate Liberalism with Italian revolution, and (what did not follow) Toryism with papal freedom. (Liberals could not complain: they did the same in reverse, by considering Ultramontanism a synonym for political ineducability.) More to the point, Tories, while not sharing Catholic enthusiasm for the Pope, seemed well disposed towards him. It was, after all, Derby who coined the phrase 'natural allies' to describe Toryism and Catholicism, a piece of inexpensive flattery which did no real harm.

Disraeli provides even more impressive evidence of a rapprochement with Catholicism. The political journals of Edward Henry, Lord Stanley, are full of it. Witness this entry in February, 1861:

Dined H. of C. with Disraeli: who was full of the expected victory at Cork: he says that the union of the R. Catholics with the Conservative Party has been his object for twenty years.[8]

Four years later, almost to the day, the theme recurs:

Long debate on Irish Administration of Justice ... Disraeli's disgust at the whole proceeding was amusing to watch: he looked at it as possibly endangering the Catholic alliance, his favourite idea since 1852....[9]

Disraeli was thinking of Ireland, but there was more to it than that:

Much talk last night with D. as to the representation of Lancashire: he is anxious to bring forward Sir R. Gerard ... who is a Catholic.[10]

And if there were personal considerations, there were general ones, too:

> The Catholics could be no worse off in our hands than in those of the Whigs. He wanted, he said, to break off the connection between Toryism and Orangeism, it was merely accidental, of late growth: the first Orangemen were Whigs. The real struggle of the present day was between country and town: Ireland was wholly agricultural, and therefore ought to side with us against Manchester.[11]

This was the long view, but there were short term calculations, too:

> The Italian policy of ministers has alienated the Catholic support they might otherwise have reckoned on: and something may be gained, for Disraeli, by coquetting with the Pope's party, has aroused a good deal of suspicion among their opponents.[12]

Sceptics about the 'naturalness' of a Catholic-Tory alliance have a weapon here: 'the ... support they might otherwise have reckoned on', and Stanley's 'coquetting' metaphor both suggest that the relationship was, from a Tory perspective, a contrivance. Even so, it needs to be investigated.

THE PARLIAMENTARY CONTEXT OF THE CATHOLIC-TORY 'ALLIANCE'

Before investigating the Catholic-Tory alliance, it needs to be given parliamentary context. In particular, the importance of denomination as a political weapon must be established. Mid-Victorian Parliaments were well supplied with men whose stock-in-trade was the representation of confessional interests. In the late 1850s and early 1860s, they did not lack custom. The Parliament of 1859–65 was dominated by religions controversy. During that period, Lords and Commons considered a variety of matters touching denominational interest: the provision of Roman Catholic chaplains in prisons, the Maynooth grant, the abolition of church rates, the threat to the papal states posed by the Italian revolution, the national education system in Ireland, the reform of the parliamentary oath required of Catholic MPs, the investigation of convents, the provision of burial grounds for dissenters. This formidable list constituted what Gladstone called 'a multitude of questions, each of which represents a separate knot as yet untied'.[13]

Party leaders distrusted 'enthusiasm'. Yet they could not do without it. Parties needed votes: the churches could provide them. As we have seen, statesmen deplored sectarianism while unblushingly accepting its fruits. Aberdeen in 1853 was greatly exasperated by 'confounded Church matters'.[14] Sir Charles Wood in 1854 held that 'you cannot reason about [religion] and control men's feelings on such subjects'.[15] Sir James Graham concurred: confessional issues provided 'sources of difference which it is always most difficult to reconcile'.[16]

Aberdeen, Wood, Graham, Stanley provide a view from the top. Even more telling is a view from below. Consider Sir John Salusbury-Trelawny. Trelawny was Liberal MP for Tavistock in the Parliament of 1859–65. For fourteen years, from 1859 to 1873, he kept a diary, an impressionistic and instructive record of days spent at the House. Its theme was the frequency and frivolity of religious dispute. 'What a Convocation Parliament has become! Enter it when you will, the chances are members are discussing Theology.'[17] Religion, he noticed, seemed always to be 'the topic least wisely and religiously treated',[18] calling forth 'unusual frivolity and unseemly jesting – mingled with no little bitterness and fanaticism'.[19]

Trelawny assumed (sometimes unfairly) that denominational debates in the Commons were as much a contrivance of politics as a product of reasonable *a priori* religious disagreement. In identifying this, he also identified culprits. The most conspicuous were the Irish. To him, they seemed odd, not to say bewildering. Belligerence, occasional charm and singular political ineptness were their abiding characteristics. Take Vincent Scully, member for County Cork:

Scully appears to have some wit – plenty of words – some astuteness – but no judgment. Irish to the backbone. The usual Celtic whine characterises his delivery.... Whether he is an earnest patriot at heart I cannot judge.[20]

Trelawny had a sharp ear for 'the regular Irish whine, plaintive even in good fortune'.[21] It became, indeed, an *idée fixe*. While asserting that the Irish were 'a body whom no Englishman can comprehend'[22] – witness one Commons evening when 'shillelaghs flew about indiscriminately in quite a comfortable manner'[23] – he nevertheless

believed that he had grasped their essential nature. It was that
tendency to trumpet complaint when they ought to have been
expressing gratitude.

Trelawny's caricature of Irish behaviour – brogues,[24] shillelaghs,
the whiff of strong drink,[25] the eye for the main chance – makes
picaresque reading; but it has a significance beyond entertainment.
His disposition to believe that grievances were contrived was doubly
unsubtle. On the one hand, it excluded the possibility of genuine
demands. On the other hand, it assumed that contrived (or, in the
language of the day, 'sentimental') grievances were not to be taken
seriously. This was foolish. Appetites remain appetites even if
irrational.

How did Trelawny view other denominational groups? They
stood equally condemned of bigotry and intolerance, but they had
characteristics of their own. The Irish were venal, low Protestants
merely vulgar. The Irish were humbugs, low Protestants genuine
zealots. Consider Charles Newdegate. A bigot and a bore, certainly:[26]
but he was also a man of principle, to be condemned not because he
made false arguments but because he made correct arguments
intemperately, thus exposing them to ridicule. At first Trelawny
thought Newdegate a figure of fun; he ended by taking him
seriously. Thus in 1862 he seemed no better than the Irish, reeling
'like a drunken man'[27] when infected by the virus of bigotry. In 1863
he considered him one of Disraeli's 'extreme men'.[28] Yet, though his
manner was idiosyncratic,[29] he had the merit of sincerity:

How he has improved! Recollecting his reception on many
occasions some 20 years ago, I shd. scarcely have believed that he
could ever have obtained the ear of the House. But time and
perseverance, with honesty of purpose & courage, effect much in
Parliament....[30]

Why did Trelawny warm to Newdegate? It was not because he
admired his consistency of purpose. It was rather because he agreed
with him on many matters. Newdegate was scared of the Pope; so
was Trelawny.[31] Newdegate detested the supposed immorality of
Catholic convents; so did Trelawny.[32] Newdegate despised priest-
craft; likewise Trelawny.[33]

The Irish were odd, Low Protestantism (as typified by Newdegate)
was eccentric but strangely impressive. What was the political impact of Nonconformists? As with the Irish, they wore grievances like

badges of honour and bored the House into resentment. 'This is the way Dissenters fail,' Trelawny suggested. 'They ride their hobbies too far.' They had a capacity for 'dog in the manger opposition'[34] which disgusted their friends and delighted their enemies. Worst of all, their appetite for agitation was undiscriminating. In highlighting grievances, any complaint would do, and better two complaints than one, even if that guaranteed the failure of both. Their perpetual failure to secure the abolition of church rates was the best example of this. They squandered their opportunities by a mixture of zealotry and tactical incompetence.

Here, then, was the context of the 'alliance' between Catholics and Tories in the late 1850s. Religious dispute was the chief characteristic of mid-Victorian parliaments. The Irish at Westminster were voluble but not especially effective. The same was true of Nonconformity. From the evidence of Trelawny, the strongest denominational interest remained Anglicanism: a fact not lost on its traditional ally, the Tory Party. It was, moreover, an Anglicanism conspicuously anti-Catholic in its expression. On the face of it, a rapprochement between Conservativism and Catholicism was likely to be ill-starred.

DERBY, DISRAELI AND THE CATHOLICS

Disraeli is the central figure of Edward Stanley's journals. This is how it should be. Stanley is too faithful an amanuensis to appear interesting in himself – a misleading impression, in fact. According to his editor, 'he was painfully and obsessively concerned with truth'.[35] The diaries are not, for all that, works of solemn self-analysis. 'Truth' in this case means 'accuracy'. Of what world are they an accurate representation? That of high-principled man:

> His diaries show a politician who is not an 'operator' ... his motives will usually surprise the student of politics by their unaffected absence of deviousness. Stanley give us a combination of commitment to politics as a vocation ... with a singular aversion to politics as politicians normally practise it.[36]

According to Stanley, Disraeli did not approve, still less did he join, the No Popery of 1850–1. Papal aggression held few terrors for him:

Disraeli treated the present agitation lightly – thought it would end as quickly as it began suddenly ... [37]

Years later, by his own admission, the episode seemed ridiculous, the British public in one of its fits of morality. In 1878, when 'Beaconsfieldism' was under attack, he could write thus to Viscount Barrington:

It is very disappointing that the country should go mad about Afghanistan but I have lived through more violent gusts. It's useless, I believe, to argue with the country when it gets into one of these quandaries, e.g. Cardinal Wiseman and Q. Caroline.[38]

The unflappability is too self-conscious to be wholly convincing, but at least he recognised 'No Popery' for the bubble it was. He was not alone in this. Others shared his embarrassment at politicians pandering to crude Protestantism. For him, the issue in 1850 was not religion but the proper relationship between high politics and low, because he was uneasy about parliamentarians legislating to control the subterranean world of ephemeral religious passion. There is thus no evidence here of especial sympathy between Tories and Catholics; evidence only that Disraeli was more temperate in private than others were in public.

Derby found it easier than Disraeli to get worked up about Catholicism, but he agreed with him that 'No Popery' in 1850 was manufactured by Russell for political gain.[39] But Russell was a humbug, nothing more. Anti-Catholicism was an political duty performed to keep supporters happy, acceptable as a 'cry', dangerous as a crusade. As Stanley himself later put it, referring to the notoriously sectarian General Election of 1852:

Protestantism has done good and harm. Our taking it up was looked upon – not unjustly – as rather a case of playing to the pit: but reasonable people are tolerant of such manoeuvres at election time, and the unreasonable are mostly with us.[40]

Notice, in passing, what this does to the claim that Stanley was averse to the seamier side of politics. He could play to the pit as well as the next man, indeed better than most. His tone does not suggest a 'natural alliance' between Catholic and Conservative.

We can make this point go further. For political purposes there were two types of 'No Popery' – one's own (acceptable) and the opposition's (understandable: 'reasonable people are tolerant of such manoeuvres'). There were also different ways of behaving like a statesman. Derby revealed them. In 1851 he knew public opinion to be overexcited. In 1853, he himself had a fit of morality. The occasion was the reluctance of the Aberdeen ministry to prosecute certain Irish priests for alleged electoral malpractice. Derby, seeing opportunity in the government's timidity, was indignant that they had been cowed by the anger of Irish public opinion:

> I am inclined to think that the non-prosecution of the [Irish] priests is a subject we shall do well to take up seriously. I believe it to be a gross case of truckling to popular clamour, and of sacrifice of justice to notions of mistaken political expediency.[41]

The shift is worth noting. To yield to a 'Protestant' cry was sensible; to yield to a Catholic one, cowardice. It may be countered that the two were not comparable; that Ireland was not England; that justice was with English Protestants in 1850–1 and not with Irish Catholics in 1853; that the rule of law must obtain. But at the level of intuition these considerations were secondary. Derby found it easy to acknowledge Protestant grievances and to doubt Catholic ones. It would be surprising had it been the other way round.

Derby's assumptions about party management and the politics of religion bear reflection. The willingness to play to the pit suggests electoral politics in which sectarianism was a constantly exploitable device, with the decision to exploit in the hands of the men at the top. Sometimes, it seemed, religious enthusiasm could be turned on and off like a tap.[42] The danger was that the tap was easier to turn on than off. Such was a risk of the game. Throughout 1854, for example Disraeli's denominational politics turned sharply Protestant, in an effort both to shore up his 'ultra' support and to embarrass Russell, who had softened his 'No Popery' of three years before. When the latter proposed a single parliamentary Oath of Allegiance, making it easier for both Jewish and Catholic MPs to swear loyalty to the Crown, Disraeli was quick to quote his words against him. The Papacy, he reminded Russell, was a 'vast conspiracy ... against Protestantism in general and this country in particular'. Papal designs were not as fickle as English ministers:

Has the Papacy changed its tactics or become decrepit? Has it renounced its ancient and energetic ambition?... Sir, this is not the time ... to relax the securities you already possess and weaken the bulwarks of the religion we profess to venerate....[43]

This was shameless. In reality, Disraeli felt no such outrage. It was also ill-judged. Stanley later warned him that – his own metaphor – he was playing with fire:

In the summer of '52 you repeatedly told me that our chance at the elections had been ruined by our taking up high Protestant politics. I agree with you then, as I do now. Shall we gain in '54 by repeating the mistake of '52?[44]

He had good reason to be concerned. Disraeli had chosen the wrong time to play the Catholic card. Stanley later complained that he had been 'sedulously ... blowing up the extinct No Popery agitation', impenetrable to the pleas of his colleagues.[45] But the error was simply one of inopportuneness. Why did Stanley resist another 'No Popery' cry? Because of its 'utter hopelessness', not because it was wrong in itself. Playing to the pit required an interval between performances.

There is another point to be made. Tories can be convicted of cynicism or bigotry, but not both. By its nature, their cynicism was itself unsectarian. Stanley noticed Disraeli's 'open ridicule, in private, of all religions'.[46] Stanley recognised the danger of 'that infernal Protestantism'.[47] So did his father, for whom all zealotry was a bothersome complication of parliamentary management.[48] Thus Catholics who believed in a 'natural' Tory alliance deluded them-selves not because they thought that *Catholics* were more favoured than others, but that *anyone* could be. To think otherwise was sentimentality.

However, some Catholics persisted in thinking otherwise. When Wiseman invited his flock to vote for the Tories in 1859 he was advocating Toryism *faute de mieux*, an expression of preference, not enthusiasm. This was how it should have been. Derby's main virtue was that he was not Russell, Disraeli's that he was not Gladstone. Unfortunately the political language of many Catholics was de-signed to express enthusiasms of every colour. The rhetoric of the *Tablet* was the rhetoric of moral certainty; Wiseman's vocabulary knew dogma better than it knew doubt. Thus Catholics were 'conviction' politicians, even when their position held little conviction, or none at all.

This was bad politics: not only did it make Catholics see virtues in allies who had none, it also repelled potential friends who disliked being made to feel so indebted to their votes. Indeed, 'conviction' politics encouraged, by making political partners into moral heroes, a mentality of ultimate betrayal. Think of the frequency with which Catholics felt themselves abandoned: by Russell in 1851, Gladstone and Palmerston in 1859, Derby in 1865, the Tories in 1868, Gladstone again in 1874. Statesmen were naturally suspicious of sectional interests which tried and discarded parties with such ease.

The language of Tory politics bears comparison. Wiseman's support of Derby was a rational calculation of the odds, however highblown the vocabulary of endorsement. In 1859 Tories were making their own calculations. Stanley, for example, could write to Disraeli about the proposed Catholic university in Dublin in a way which demonstrated the precariousness of the partnership:

> If the University were really powerful, and likely to be permanent, any step which gave Govt. a hold over it ... might be politic. But if it be likely to die out, are we wise in interposing to keep it alive?.... the unpopularity among English Protestants of such a step as you suggest I should be ready to face, with a sound or Liberal object in view: but I do not, as at present advised, see any public benefit likely to arise from strengthening the hands of the priests as educators of the richer classes in Ireland. As to Parliamentary strength ... I incline to think we should lose more on one side than we should hope to gain on the other. As to satisfying the Irish sacerdotal party, it is simply out of the question....[49]

There was no cynicism here, merely an understanding of the practical limits of the new alliance. Even so, Stanley's analysis contains an irony. There would be no benefits, he said, in strengthening priests as educators of the richer classes in Ireland. One so educated was John Pope Hennessy, who may be introduced here and considered in detail later.

John Pope Hennessy was a passionate Derbyite, later (and for the rest of his life) a passionate Disraelian. He became an MP in 1859, 'a notable accession of strength to the Derbyite Tories', according to Acton.[50] There were some unusual features here: he was only twenty-four, had no money, virtually no profession, and, most surprising of all, called himself an Irish Catholic Conservative. Coming from the commercial middle class, brought up to believe in his own worth, convinced that he was born for better things than Irish provincial life could provide, Pope Hennessy knew the English in Ireland humiliated those who could have helped them most – the 'richer classes' of whom Stanley wrote, and the socially aspirant like himself. To him, the governance of Ireland betrayed stupidity rather than malice. Witness an early entry in his diary, the same diary that recorded his admiration for distant Disraeli:

> Walked through Lisnegar before Mass. Parish Priest reading out the names of the people who gave *nothing* at Christmas. Probably interesting to a resident in the parish, but a very stupid bit of scandal to me. Made a very affecting speech; it clearly came from his heart. Pity that misgovernment and ignorance should force an educated gentleman to make such an exhibition. As policy and justice, the RC [Church] should be endowed, I always said. This little scene confirms that opinion.[51]

Pope Hennessy was able to see behind an impoverished priest the impoverished imagination of those who governed him. He was also able to see himself – an educated man who deserved better of the world. This was why he persuaded himself that he was a Tory. Yet how was his passion rewarded? By Stanley's weary rationalism. In sum, in 1859, the year apparently of its greatest strength, Tories were much cooler about the Catholic alliance than Catholics themselves. The latter brought quite different types of passion to bear in politics; a fact which formed the basis of much future misunderstanding.

Catholics were enthusiastic Tories in 1859, in Ireland and in England. Unfortunately the enthusiasm was a kind of innocence. Their bishops, for instance, especially Irish bishops, did not understand how politics worked, a fault which irked Stanley. He had strong doubts about the alliance on that account:

> I beg you earnestly – though I dare say it is quite needless – not for the sake of the Irish alliance to give any countenance, direct or indirect, to the move of the RC bishops against the National System of primary Education ... I am satisfied they have gone too far to succeed – *that they will have raised against them in England, and especially in Parliament, a feeling of which they do not know or have forgotten the strength* ... I see that the Irish party reckon on a good

deal of Conservative support and found their hopes on the *supposed* inclination we have shown to negotiate for their alliance. *It will not do to have a No Popery cry raised against us, and to be wrong, at the same time....*[52]

Stanley's reservations were predictable. Catholics regarded their alliance as a charity on their part to Lord Derby; Tories saw it as a marriage hardly of convenience, let alone of equals.

Catholic innocence was obvious even in trivialities. Disraeli, for instance, got fan mail from his Catholic supporters, which had all the qualities of the genre – at once intimate and obeisant, polite but pushy. As often as not, it was also vastly off the mark. Witness this effort by Lord Arundell of Wardour:

> I am flattered by the expressions which you indulgently use with reference to a letter of mine, which I had no right to expect would excite more than a local interest ... I have just admitted that I have been strongly influenced by your writings, but looking deeper into the matter, I think that we have both been influenced by the Catholic sentiment, and by this I mean the sentiment which the indirect influence of the Doctrines of Catholicity have introduced into the world. Of course, we have been influenced in a different manner. In any case there is no intellectual merit in recognising certain matters because it is mere instinct, but you can only have arrived at them by the force of intellect.[53]

Disraeli must have found this hard to take. We need not accept either Stanley's sceptical view of Disraeli's religious opinions, or Monypenny and Buckle's fanciful one,[54] to find Arundell's sentiments over-expressed. He never knew what Disraeli never forgot: that similar letters arrived all the time from Protestants, who likewise created a hero in their own image. Arundell may have been right, but the likelihood is against it. Disraeli was temperamentally unable to take anything too seriously. Being on the side of the angels was religion enough for him. Catholics had appropriated the public man and made him their own, a theft which he found distasteful.

It would be wrong to think, though, that the Catholic-Tory alliance was a one-way affair. Tories knew that Catholics, especially old Catholics, were odd,[55] but thought them worth cultivating nonetheless. Stanley appreciated the value of promoting one or two, the outward sign of the inward harmony which was supposed to exist between Catholicism and Toryism. That was the theory. In practice, patronage merely exhibited on the smaller scale of local interest the same tension which was clear in the larger scale of parliamentary alliance: a need not to offend Protestants by Catholic jobbery, a desire to please Catholics without ever giving them very much. This was most apparent in Ireland, where (according to their own supporters) Tories were notoriously mean with jobs.[56] (Lord Eglinton, writing to Derby, nicely demonstrated the practical difficulties of Irish Toryism: 'there is a tremendous howl from the Protestants at the promotion of O'Loghlin ... I wish you could make it clear to Disraeli how difficult it is to find any R. Catholic that I can take up, and how unwise it is to go so far in appointing political opponents as to disgust our friends'.)[57]

Ireland was exceptional, but similar considerations obtained in Lancashire, where there were lots of Catholics to please and even more Protestants to annoy. Stanley noticed Disraeli's desire to bring forward the talented Sir R. Gerard, but thought him 'unlikely to succeed, being a Catholic'.[58] He himself suggested a place for Lord Normanby 'to satisfy the Catholics',[59] even though he was not a Catholic, merely someone disliked by Irish Protestants. Eglinton was right: it was more prudent not to promote a Catholic than to offend Protestant friends. Catholics were a constituency to be pleased only in so far as no harm came of it. Derby likewise regarded such patronage as a supernumerary exercise from which the party may or may not have benefited. For example, he appointed Lord Gainsborough to the Lord Lieutenancy of Rutland because 'he has a good property, is a good friend, and will be the only R.C. Lord Lieutenant in England'.[60] The sense of afterthought is unmistakable. Once jobbery became contentious, its value diminished. As Derby observed when appointing Gainsborough, 'it will not do to buy new friends at the risk of alienating old ones'.[61] Tory loyalties clearly ran deeper than Rome.

Patronage of this sort was a thin fuel on which to operate any alliance. It is therefore no surprise that the Tories were phlegmatic about its end. Two things hastened the divorce – Derby's public association with Garibaldi's visit to England in 1864, and his 'muzzling-the-Catholics' speech in 1865. As for the first, Disraeli, perhaps aware of Catholic sensitivities, did not join the lionising when Garibaldi came to town; but Derby and son thought nothing of it. As for the second, Derby loudly protested that he had been misunderstood, as indeed anyone would who had blundered in the middle of an election.

He was right to protest: the undramatic truth was that he hardly took Catholics seriously at all, let alone worried about the danger of unmuzzling them. Anyway, the embarrassment was only temporary. By the time the election was over, gloom replaced remorse as his dominant mood. He doubted whether he would ever hold office again. Yet in the midst of his pessimism the perversity of Catholic behaviour cheered him up:

> Looking to the past, I do not think that the result could have been altered; and though my unlucky reference to Kennedy's metaphor of 'muzzling' *may* have cost us some votes, our chief losses have been where such a cause could not have had any effect. In this county, Lancashire the stronghold of the RCs, we have held our own, except in the S. Division, which we lost by Conservatives (!) splitting on Gladstone. There was indeed an RC lady who would not allow her servants to vote for us, because I had met Garibaldi at dinner! and so she insists on returning Gladstone!![62]

Derby's bemusement about Catholic rationality was justified. The *Tablet* insisted (its own counter-examples notwithstanding) that the Catholic Tory vote still mattered. It was 'by no means true', it pleaded, that Derby's speech had converted every Catholic into an implacable enemy of the Tory party.[63] Even curiouser was the case of Edward Ryley, a prominent Catholic Tory and self-appointed adviser to Disraeli on Catholic affairs. After an election in which his political leaders insulted his religion, he could still write to Disraeli thus:

> Other Catholics, both Whigs and Tories, estimate the bad effect of Lord Derby's speech last session as much greater than I do. I have always defended the speech and professed gratitude to Lord D. for having saved us from so objectionable a bill ... [64]

Not even Derby could have predicted such an attitude. He had merely hoped that his remarks had not done too much damage; here was evidence that some Catholics welcomed them.

THE CATHOLIC CONNECTION: EDWARD RYLEY AND DIS-RAELI

Ryley's unshakable Toryism reminds us that the links between Catholicism and Conservative politics need to be investigated at the level of individual lives. Not to do so is to get an unbalanced picture. To read only Catholic journalism is to be removed from how political decisions were made; to read only the intimacies of high politics is to risk an unsceptical acceptance of the principle of scepticism – though with Derby, Disraeli and Stanley it is hard to do otherwise. They necessarily dealt in caricatures, reducing complexity – how party, country and Catholics were likely to behave – to easily-managed simplicity. But how did politicians react to individual Catholics? Were the caricatures confirmed or confounded? How did Catholic Tories get on with their political leaders? Do their lives give any clue to the fundamental question: why be a Catholic Tory in the first place?

Two candidates propose themselves for this examination: John Pope Hennessy and Edward Ryley. Both were strong Disraelians; both presumed an intimacy with the great; both have sunk almost without trace.[65] Ryley largely deserves anonymity. Pope Hennessy is still remembered as the man who beat Vincent Scully in the famous North Kilkenny by-election of 1891 (Parnell's nemesis), but otherwise he is known only to his native Cork and, of all places, Hong Kong.[66] Yet for a while both occupied a place in the firmament of Catholic public life. It is important to see why.

Ryley was a Catholic professional and a professional Catholic: he earned his living as an actuary and by virtue of his religion was able to aspire to social circles otherwise closed to him. When he died, in 1896, nearly thirty years after he had withdrawn from public life, he still managed an obituary in the *Times*. It suggested a career of dull decency: a conscientious campaigner for equal rights for Catholics in prisons, workhouses and the army; a frequent contributor to the *Tablet*; a layman honoured by a synod of his church; a friend of Cardinal Wiseman; an anti-Liberal in politics and religion. There was only one hint of an existence beyond the monotonously conventional: 'Mr. Ryley, though on terms of personal friendship with him, was not a *persona grata* with Cardinal Manning.'[67] One is left to wonder why; perhaps he found Ryley's odour of sanctity faintly oppressive.

If Ryley ever did good, it was not by stealth. He was a born organiser of other people's lives. He enjoyed committees for their own sake. Letters to the editor came naturally to his pen. Delegations to politicians appealed to him. It was in this capacity that he came in contact with Derby and Disraeli. Disraeli knew him to be a friend of Lord Arundell – a questionable recommendation, perhaps. (However flattering Arundell may have been about Disraeli's spirit of Catholicity, Stanley dismissed him as a 'simple-minded bigot entirely in the hands of his priests'.)[68] Ryley induced greater respect. He was regarded in Tory circles as a man of ability and a useful contact with the English Catholic community. Reciprocally, Ryley regarded himself as a person the Tories ought to cultivate – talented, well-connected, an ardent advocate of the view that the English Catholics were all natural Conservatives. Ryley had a dream: a marriage between Catholic interests and Tory politics, at which he would be best man.

Ryley's arguments for a Tory alliance were precisely those which Lords Stanley and Eglinton had found so difficult to accept – that the Tories needed only to distribute patronage more intelligently, and listen to priests more attentively, for the Catholic vote to be theirs. This was especially true in Ireland, where the Whigs were winning Catholic sympathy only by default:

> If the next Conservative Government would frankly give up the task of educating Catholic children to the hands of Catholics, and by their dispersal of patronage would convince Catholics that they need not be Whigs to get a chance of employment and promotion, there would be an end of Whig domination for many years to come ... if the Irish landlords will protect the religion of their tenants, the Catholic Priests will be a Conservative police who will keep the Queen's peace in Ireland better than 20,000 troops.[69]

This was grandiose thinking. How many troops did Ryley have? In Ireland, by his own argument, not very many. But England, he claimed, was different. There, the Catholic forces were already mustering. He wrote to Colonel Taylor, the Conservative Whip, in a style full of the pathos of provincial self-importance:

> What I have now to communicate is that we have just received a letter from Nottingham informing us that in accordance with our advice, they have got up a Catholic Conservative Association there. Our correspondent writes: 'We find that all the Catholic

electors, with about 3 exceptions, are unanimous in their condemnation of the present government & are determined to oppose the
upholders of it at any further election ... we have examined the
register and find 103 Catholic electors on it on whom we can
depend & that there are twenty-five Catholics unregistered who
are qualified.
It would perhaps be as well to make a mem. of this ...[70]

Taylor did indeed make a mem. of this, and sent it to Disraeli. He
found Ryley's grand manner curious. There is no evidence that he
worried too much about the misled Nottingham three, or the
unregistered twenty-five.

Disraeli later experienced the grand manner for himself. In June
1865 William Monsell proposed an Oaths Bill, which would have
freed Roman Catholic Members from the supposedly offensive
obligation to swear loyalty to the Established Church. Disraeli, in a
notably conciliatory speech, opposed this. It was a jesuitical performance. The 'unmistakable tendency' of recent years, he argued,
had been to treat Catholic claims 'in a spirit of rational conciliation';
the papal aggression of 1851 had been badly 'mismanaged' by
Russell; there was nothing in the existing oath which an honourable
Catholic could object to; it would be 'a very great error' for Roman
Catholics to attack the Established Church; it was similarly erroneous
for Catholics to place their hopes in a Whig alliance which had for
thirty years done them no good; no-one, apart from the extreme
Protestant party (who believed that 'every Roman Catholic is a
Jesuit'), seriously doubted the loyalty of Her Majesty's Catholic
subjects; indeed, historically, the Catholic gentry had shown 'illus-
trious instances of loyalty' to their sovereign; and – the crucial point
– to alter the oath would make Protestant fears more likely and thus
'prevent the passing of measures ... of practical advantage to the
Roman Catholics'.[71]

This was an attempt to dish the Whigs. Ryley, however, saw in it
not calculation but idealism. He wrote to his hero a humble letter of
'thanks ... and admiration' from one who had 'for years' in his own
'small way' laboured to inculcate in his Catholic friends Disraeli's
advice about the Established Church. (For years, too, Ryley had
regarded Monsell as a typical product of the 'villainous, democratic
& socialistic school [which had] been springing up under a Whig
cloak': it was hardly a surprise that *he* should be the author of a Bill
which merely relieved Catholics of swearing that they were not

rogues or murderers.)[72] This language may have caused Disraeli a moment's unease. Someone had believed every word he had said. The Bill passed through the Commons but was defeated in the Lords and that, for the moment, was the end of the matter.

By February 1866 circumstances had changed. An Oaths Bill was again under consideration. This time it was sponsored by the government (now led by Russell), and was moved by Sir George Grey. He expressed the hope that a uniform oath might be made agreeable to all Members, and proposed a simple form of words.[73] It was opposed by Newdegate and other members of the Protestant party, who argued that the time was not right, Fenianism in Ireland being rampant, to tinker with the Oath of Supremacy. Nonetheless, the Bill received a Second Reading with only five dissentient voices. It seemed as if the Tories did not intend to resist the proposed alteration to the Oath.

Then came a surprise. Disraeli proposed two amendments in committee, 'one recognising the Act of Settlement, which ministers accepted as harmless: the other asserting the Supremacy of the Queen in language, which though not offensive, was obviously pointed at the Catholics and sure to be by them resisted'.[74] This amendment read as follows:

And I do further solemnly declare that Her Majesty is, under God, the only Supreme Governor of this realm, and that no foreign prince, prelate, state or potentate, hath any jurisdiction or authority in any of the courts within the same.

There were telling objections to this formula: it was incongruous, unnecessary, abstract, and it possibly limited the Queen's jurisdiction. It was defeated by fourteen votes.

What was Disraeli up to? Stanley thought it obvious: he had been pressurised by Protestant supporters who had persuaded him that muzzling the Catholics should be the best option for the party. By any standards it was a notable *volte-face*, the more so as he seemed adamant on the subject. As Stanley recorded,

I discussed this matter with him, and objected to his proposed oath, but he would listen to no argument, and I saw plainly that he felt himself pushed by a certain section of this party.[75]

But as to the shadowy pressure, Stanley gives no clue.

It is arguable that it was the Catholic, not the Protestant, section of the party which had spoken. Ryley's name must be re-introduced. He corresponded with Disraeli throughout the course of the Oath Bill and organised a deputation to see him and Derby to discuss Catholic responses to the measure. The whole episode is highly revealing of the Catholic Tory mentality. Notice, for example, the desire to please. As one member of Ryley's delegation, Francis Wegg-Prosser, wrote to Disraeli,

> The English Catholics are the last people in the world who ought to be loaded with unnecessary and unmeaning oaths in order to prove their loyalty, for if they have had any fault [!] it has been that of entertaining what some would consider an *exaggerated* idea of loyalty. Their adherence to the Stuart family (as long as the Stuarts were alive) was surely of that character ... I say nothing of the advantage to be gained by the Conservative Party if they act in a graceful and conciliatory spirit towards the Catholics ... I will only observe that many new elections may take place, and the harm done at the last election may be in some degree remedied now.[76]

Here was standard Old Catholic special pleading, combined with typical anti-Irishness,[77] a combination Disraeli knew well, and one which he dreamed of exploiting.

Ryley's delegation met Derby and Disraeli on 27 February 1866 – that is, before Disraeli proposed his amendments, but well after it was clear that the Tories would be in difficulties over the measure with their Protestant support. Many leading Catholic laymen were included, among them the Liberal, Charles Langdale, Lord Denbigh, Wallis (the devious editor of the *Tablet*), John Pope Hennessy, and Lord Arundell.

The next day, Ryley wrote Disraeli a long letter in which he summarised the conclusions of the meeting, and suggested future strategy. It provides insight into the world of Old Catholic Tory politics. The tone is important, as of two co-equal conspirators playing the party machine – Ryley's incorrigible fantasy. But the argument is important too. He wrote to Disraeli as Tory to fellow Tory, advising how best to win Catholic support for the cause. One way was deception. By meeting with a few Catholic Liberals he could appear statesmanlike and dish the Whigs all at once:

> I left with Mr. Langdale and Sir G. Bowyer. Both were fully

satisfied and the adhesion of Mr. Langdale is of more importance than that of any one other man – I spent an hour with him in the evening, and he ran over with a certain amount of glee the points in Lord Derby's speech – he was especially tickled with Lord D's exclusion of the converts from the sympathy and friendship he professed for the Catholic body. He was also much pleased with Lord D's frank avowal of his own Protestantism, and seemed to think it a great point that he was ready with such prejudices, to do so much.

Mr. Langdale's adhesion is all the more valuable because Dr. M[anning] is the lion in our path. He affects Lord Petre, Lord Edward Howard, Mr. Monsell, and Mr. O'Reilly.

He *says* that no-one knows his political leanings, but it is patent to all of us that he is a bitter Whig. He will checkmate us if he can. If he does not ... it will be out of deference to Mr. Langdale & the old Catholic names on our side ...

We see another difficulty. No doubt at all by the mouth of Sir G. Bowyer in the Commons and by Lords Denbigh and Arundell in the Lords we can signify a sufficient *acceptance* of Lord Derby's amendments, but how are we to get Catholics on a division to carry their adhesion to them so far as to vote *against the Government Bill* which is a satisfactory one ...

This difficulty might perhaps not arise by the Govt's acceptance of the amendments when suggested by you and supported by Bowyer, but if it came to a hostile division I am afraid we could do but little in obtaining votes for the amendment as against the Bill. But if the worst comes to the worst a great deal of good was done yesterday in strengthening the sympathy between Lord D and his Catholic supporters. Lord Denbigh's open avowal of unqualified adhesion ... was worth having, but the chief point is the extent to which we have committed Mr. Langdale....[78]

This letter opens a number of important possibilities. (It also illuminates, by the way, the obituarist's mysterious reference to Ryley's being *persona non grata* with the Cardinal: neither could abide the other's politics.) It reveals the strength of feeling which divided Catholic Tory from Catholic Liberal. Catholic Tories took their politics and themselves very seriously, and wanted other people to know it. The *Tablet* with its tone of defiant self-pity spoke for all of them:

> We are not unreasonable, and we don't ask much. All we desire is,
> that when Catholics claim or accept credit on the ground that the
> Catholic community in the empire has renewed its alliance with
> Whig-Liberalism, an exception may be made of those, who, like
> ourselves, persevere in Independent opposition to 'Liberalism, to
> progress and to modern civilisation'.[79]

Ryley's letter has a more important implication. It answers Stanley's
difficulty about Disraeli's seeming deliberately to offend the Catholics. On Ryley's evidence, this was a virtual impossibility. They
practised the politics of self-emasculation: the politics which welcomed 'with a certain amount of glee' unfavourable remarks about
one's co-religionists; the politics which preferred its leaders to insist
on their own Protestantism; the politics which could exonerate
Derby for his 'muzzling' speech; the politics which conceded that 'if
the worst comes to the worst' the sympathy between Derby and his
Catholic supporters would remain unimpaired. The paradox may be
offered that Ryley, far from fulfilling his mission of bringing
Catholics closer to the Conservative Party, merely enabled the Tories
to be anti-Catholic with greater impunity.

From Disraeli's point of view, Catholic criticism of him could not
have been more innocuous. But *why* were some Catholics so willing
to see things from a party perspective? Was it simple altruism? Once
again, Ryley suggests an answer:

> I am so circumstanced as to ordinary engagements that I am very
> frequently compelled to forgo what I perceive to be a very
> useful line of party action because I cannot with sufficient personal
> convenience move in it – the machinery of action is too much
> cumbersome, and the necessary preliminaries take up too much
> time, e.g. I want to come to an understanding with Mr. Whiteside,
> with whom I have always found a great facility of mutual
> understanding, or I want to communicate with someone about a
> pending or expected election – but I do nothing in the matter
> because it is too inconvenient to get at the necessary men.
>
> If you could get me into the Carlton, and then perhaps on to the
> Election Committee, I ... would ... count for several seats for you at
> the next election.[80]

As a begging letter, this was in the first division: the Carlton in
return for a few parliamentary seats, perhaps the occasional vote on

a division in the House. Ryley rated his value highly, in fact more highly 'than that of a single average MP'. His grandiose claims indicate that Catholic Toryism was a political world which was, like any other, held together by a network of patronage. Behind the lofty editorials of the *Tablet* lay an structure of favours and indebtedness, a web of petty jobbery. Ryley lived a life of dropped hints and nodded agreements. People wrote to him on their own behalf, or someone else's; he wrote to Disraeli in like manner – either for himself or someone else; Disraeli tested the machine to see what was available – all in the code language of political loyalty and service to the party. Catholic Liberals had their own network, with different people playing similar parts: Acton writing to Gladstone rather than Ryley to Disraeli. It was not for nothing that Ralph Earle could occasionally refer to 'our papists'[81] as if the other side had theirs, too; indeed they had. The *Tablet* occasionally sneered at the idea that there might be two parties among the English Catholics, but its editor knew that livelihoods, his own included, depended on it.

Men like Ryley were not insincere in their beliefs; on the contrary, only the sincere or the misled could have held some of the views he had. That said, political loyalty was a matter of finding a congenial patronage network, then sticking to it. In Ryley's case the system worked. He made it to the Carlton. What Disraeli got in return is less clear: much the same flattering advice, certainly, the conviction, perhaps, of a debt finally paid, but little more. Mainly, he received evidence of Ryley's bizarre posturing. By June 1866 Ryley had appointed himself the cloak-and-dagger man of Tory election politics:

I take the great liberty of sending you a sketch of such a letter as I want to receive from you. *If* there is a dissolution I pledge myself that by the limited and discreet use of such a letter we may gain from ten to fifteen seats.

I make this suggestion to you very reluctantly ... but the circumstances of the party at this moment seem to me to require that I should run some risk.

I know that with such a letter shewn only to people on whose secresy (*sic*) I can rely I can paralyse a Whig bishop here, and get the enthusiastic support of a priest there who can command the perhaps 15 to 20 votes wanted to turn the scale at a Borough election.[82]

Disraeli, it would appear, had found his Sancho Panza.

Ryley's ambition to wed the Catholics to the Tories was not entirely in vain. In October 1866 Disraeli made an important observation:

> My Roman Catholic policy, as distinguished from my Irish policy, has always been shaped with reference to the English Roman Catholics, a most powerful body, and naturally Tories. They have behaved admirably to us, and have much influenced the English elections in our favor (*sic*). They are generally speaking Ultramontane, but we never had, and we have not, better friends than Sir Robert Gerard, Lord Gainsboro, Lord Denbigh, Arundel (*sic*) of Wardour, and many others of that class.[83]

And so we return to the idea of a "natural alliance" between Catholic and Tory. Understanding Ryley, however, helps us understand the key phrase in Disraeli's statement – behaving admirably. Admirable behaviour, from Disraeli's point of view, was the ability to take almost anything lying down. He was right: he never did have better friends than his Catholics, and Ryley seemed to typify them – perversely loyal to the idea of an alliance which existed more in imagination than in reality. Disraeli himself – only a day after he had warmly praised admirable Catholic behaviour – hinted at the true nature of their relationship. Thus to Montagu Corry:

> Look well at the letter enclosed from a Mr. Ryley. He is a R. Catholic, a Tory much trusted by the English Caths. who, in journalism, are mainly represented by 'The Tablet' – the editor [is] Ryley's friend. He was for several years trying to connect himself with me, but I always fought shy. However, of late, I was obliged to see him only once. I have no reason to doubt his sincerity to us, from all I have heard of his antecedents, but I suspect him to be a Jesuit, and I think it is as well, without hurting his self love, I should keep him at arms' length. Earle knows him and all his entourage, and would give you advice if you require it. You had better write to Mr. Ryley and give him an appointment; the great pressure of affairs on me at the present moment rendering it quite impossible etc. etc. but expressing my desire that he should always communicate confidentially with yourself.[84]

This hit the mark: an entourage which had its uses but which needed to be kept at arms' length.

THE CATHOLIC CONNECTION: JOHN POPE HENNESSY AND DISRAELI

It was another begging letter which had provoked this observation. Ryley had asked Disraeli 'to do something for Mr. J-P Hennessy, who may perhaps fairly be called a personal follower of yours'.[85] This was understatement: Hennessy was devoted to Disraeli almost since boyhood. More than Ryley, who had to elbow his way into the company of the great, Hennessy was a figure in his own right. Indeed, he began his public career strikingly. A clever but improvident Irishman, he gave up, at the age of twenty-four, a junior clerkship in the Privy Council Office, to stand for Parliament. Astonishingly, he came top of the poll,[86] thus entering in 1859 the Commons as MP for King's County. He quickly made his mark as a man on the make, even appearing in a novel of the day, *Broken to Harness*, as the talented but priggish Mr. Hope Ennythink, a provider of diversion (if hardly of company) should the London season flag:

> After a lengthened period of inaction, there had been a fierce Parliamentary struggle brought about by that rising young gladiator, Mr. Hope Ennythink, who had impeached the Prime Minister, brought the gravest charges against the Foreign Secretary, accused the Chancellor of the Exchequer of crass ignorance, and riddled with ridicule the incompetence of the First Lord of the Admiralty. As Mr. Hope Ennythink spoke with a certain amount of cleverness and a great amount of brass, as he was thoroughly up on all the facts which he adduced – having devoted his life to the study of Hansard, and being a walking edition of that popular work – and as he was warmly supported by the Opposition, whose leaders thought highly of the young man, he ran the Government very hard and gave the Treasury whips a good deal of trouble....[87]

'Hope Ennythink' might pass as a generic for many Catholic place-hunters, from Ryley of the Carlton to Pope Hennessy of the Council Office, who could write to his father that 'the few acquaintances I have in London are all men who can be of assistance in pushing me on – I am determined not to make any other sort of acquaintances', or who felt 'pretty certain' that if he held a clerkship in the Privy Council Office 'and ... Disraeli's party got into power, [he] would be pushed up'.[88]

This was careerism of a conventional sort, not in the league of Tadpole and Taper, who aspired to twelve hundred a year, but bewitched nonetheless by politics as a channel of advancement. In Pope Hennessy's case, the careerism reflected necessity: he had come to London from Cork needing the money badly. Perhaps, being an outsider, he adopted the vocabulary of ambition too readily, as if mimicking the form of speech natural to all metropolitans:

> I was introduced to the Bishop of Southwark, Dr. Grant ... by Dr. Crookall a few days ago. I met them both by accident in the House of Lords.[89]
> My place-hunting prevented me from going down to Charles, but I intend going very soon.[90] My friend Keogh has the entrée at Cardinal Wiseman's and I am going to go with him to the next soirée of the Cardinal's.[91]

This romantic attachment to the world of 'affairs' found expression in the world of politics proper. Pope Hennessy was a 'natural' Tory because he was a natural snob:

> Nothing indeed makes one so ashamed of the so-called Catholics of Cork as the bold, positive and thoroughly Catholic spirit to be seen here [in England]. The English Catholics are ultramontane, that is they are bona fide Catholics, whereas in Ireland ... they appear to be half-ashamed of their religion.[92]

In the minds of Hennessy and Ryley, Ultramontanism, Toryism, and social self-regard were inextricably linked. That is why both were so passionate about their politics. Ryley had ranted against a 'villainous, democratic and socialistic school ... under a Whig cloak'[93] as if they were knocking down his door as he wrote. Likewise, Hennessy saw politics in stark, personal terms:

> Nothing has transpired yet as to what the Government will do [he wrote in April 1859, the Derby-Disraeli ministry having just been defeated on the question of parliamentary reform], but I strongly believe they are yet safe ... I hope they will dissolve parliament, if

it were only to get rid of some of the Irish *Cawtholic* Whigs. I walked to the Temple from the House on Friday morning with Bowyer. He was very much annoyed that not more than about half a dozen of the Catholics proved themselves to be honest men by supporting the Government. He thoroughly understands the relations that exist between the present ministry and the Catholic powers of Europe and says it is a most awful thing to think of a country like Ireland sending wretched Whig Catholics to Parliament to vote against such men as Disraeli and the present Cabinet....[94]

Hennessy and his like did not simply disagree with Whiggery in Catholics, they were personally affronted by it. This suggests a commitment to Toryism and Ultramontanism as social and emotional props as much as political and intellectual systems. Toryism lent moral dignity to personal antipathy; it made 'honest' the struggle against 'wretched' opponents, even though those opponents were fellow Catholics. Toryism made contempt legitimate; it thus appealed to the socially aspirant like Pope Hennessy.

Hennessy's decision to stand for Parliament was the act of an adventurer. Only he expected victory. Friends were less than encouraging; Alfred Austin (who had introduced him into Ultramontane Tory circles in London) told him he would 'die in a ditch'.[95] As it turned out, Hennessy scattered his enemies. The electors of King's County took immediately to this self-contradiction – an Irish Nationalist Conservative. So, too, did the House of Commons – at least according to family myth and later reminiscence. Justin McCarthy, a benign memoirist, recalled in the 1890s the world of the late 1850s:

At that time the Catholics of England and Ireland were much displeased with the Liberal, or should I rather say the Whig, party, because of the Ecclesiastical Titles Act, and were well disposed towards a sort of alliance with the Conservatives. John Pope Hennessy created a new character in politics – the character of an ardent young Irish Catholic and Nationalist who was also a devoted member of the Conservative Party. The new character took immensely.... There was something quite new to the House in the presence of a young Nationalist Irishman who made no pretence at floridity of eloquence and talked as if talking were a practical business and not a declamatory art.... He had an audacity

which nothing could possibly dismay or even discourage, while at
the same time he never seemed intrusive or overbearing....[96]

Hennessy was thus the linch-pin of the Catholic-Tory alliance; and
the burden of McCarthy's pen-picture is the special relationship
which the young man had with Disraeli.

What did Hennessy actually *do* as a House of Commons man and
scourge of the Whigs? First of all, he fantasised about his own
political importance – understandable enough in a young MP who
had quickly made his mark. The romance of politics besotted him:
Ralph Earle became not simply a colleague but 'a great political ally
of mine';[97] Disraeli, once a distant idol, now became a familiar face;
even the Emperor Napoleon (a man 'just like any mortal', he
noticed)[98] sought out the advice of the visiting Pope Hennessy in
1863. It was more than enough to turn the head of an £80-a-year
clerk. Still, Pope Hennessy *was* active in the Catholic interest, as a
maker of speeches and a poser of questions on Catholic education,
Catholics in prison, Catholics in Poland, Catholics in the civil
service. He even recorded some successes. As a champion of the
Polish provinces of Russia, whose insurrection had been ener-
getically stamped out by Tsarist troops, he proposed a Humble
Address to the Crown – warmly supported by Tory as well as
radical opinion – and became for a week in 1863 a national hero in
Poland. He obtained an amendment of the Irish Poor Law. He
argued against the 'anti-national' system of Irish education. He
successfully proposed amendments to the Mines Regulations Acts.

He was also the proposer of the Prison Ministers Bill, 1863, later
adopted and modified by the Government, which empowered local
authorities to appoint Catholic chaplains to prisons, and to pay for
them out of the rates. As an example of Disraeli's political skill, this
is worth a mention. The Bill as modified by the government was
supported on the Liberal side on the grounds that it was a necessary
policing device. On the Tory benches, however, there was division.
The Protestant party – Newdegate, Gore Langton, *et al.* – opposed
the Bill on grounds of unnecessity (in this they were wrong) and
religious principle. The Establishment was being threatened; worse,
the Bill was dangerous to the Protestant spirit of the country.

Disraeli's response revealed the illusory nature of his Catholic
alliance: he supported the Bill, thus pleasing 'his papists', but did so
for purely Protestant reasons. The Established Church was threatened? Not so, he said, by a minor act of justice to an obvious

minority. The Protestantism of old England was in danger? Surely not:

> Why, it is only recently that they [the Catholics] have had conclusive experience of the power of the Protestant spirit of this country. [Why was it, he asked, that there was only one English Catholic MP?] ... because those who advised the Roman Catholics of this country took a course ... which was supposed by the Protestant people of this country openly to outrage or cunningly to circumvent the Protestant feeling of this country.[99]

Indeed, Protestants had a *duty* to themselves to permit Roman Catholic chaplains, because without them, Catholics would be as dangerous to the community on leaving prison as they had been on entering it. It did not say much for a Catholic-Tory alliance if the best arguments for it were designed to appeal to the 'No Popery' school.

Pope Hennessy was actively Conservative as well as actively Catholic. This had paradoxical consequences. As an Ultramontane, he had no difficulty in accepting the principle of Establishment, however much Ultramontanism may have rendered him politically suspect. Ironically, the best proof of both his Catholicism and his Toryism was an ability to mimic the Anglican accents of the party. This was illustrated in 1861, when the Church Rates Bill again gave the Tories their favourite cry – 'the Church in Danger':

> I was travelling in the East of Europe, when I received from Colonel Taylor ... an intimation that an attack was about to be made in the House of Commons on the Church of England. By travelling night and day, I managed to reach England an hour or two before the division. Two hundred and seventy four members voted against the Church, and two hundred and seventy four for the Church. The House being equally divided, the Speaker cast his vote with us; and that evening Mr. Disraeli said to me 'the fact that you travelled all this distance to add your vote to the two hundred and seventy three members of the Anglican Church, who were thus enabled to resist successfully the attack of today, is a significant event in your career' ... [100]

How significant remained to be seen, but it added greatly to Hennessy's romantic self-importance. And with reason. He had proved to Disraeli, as Ryley did later, the practical value of his

Catholic alliance: that Catholic Tories could always be relied upon to come to the aid of the party, no matter how seldom the party came to the aid of them.

Did Disraeli make good his implied promise to Hennessy that his 'career' would benefit from this and other such actions? By the end of the Parliament he had credit to his name – a Bill, a few amendments, an Address to the Crown, an intimate knowledge of *Hansard*, a page in a novel, a trans-European dash, an ability to score points off Palmerston and Gladstone. He seemed a worthy candidate for a junior ministry.

It was not to be: the Liberals won the election, and, worse, he lost his own seat. In fact, the first of these was a greater disaster than the second, for six years as an MP had left him massively in debt: in 1865 he still owed money for the jaunting cars from which he had campaigned in 1859. A tactical retreat from the *beau monde* would have done him no harm. But with Disraeli out of office, the patronage-machine died. He could not write to his leader, as unblushing Ryley did, '[as to] patronage I would say with Poor Jo in *Bleak House*, "Please write it werry large sir"'.[101] Disraeli, in 1865, was only in a position to write it very small, if indeed at all.

Hennessy had to wait until June 1866, when Derby and Disraeli once again formed a ministry, for his material prospects to improve. What happened to him captured the doubtful value of Catholic Toryism as a network of jobbery. Disraeli shared Ryley's vague desire to 'do something' for Hennessy, if only to be rid of his embarrassing obsequiousness.[102] But the 'something' turned out to be a post wildly disproportionate to Hennessy's notion of his own indispensability – the governorship of Labuan, a malaria-drenched island off the coast of Borneo with a white population of forty. At first Hennessy accepted this with impecunious, ignorant alacrity. Only gradually did he discover the mistake he had made, and when he did, the elaborate formulas of politeness evident in his previous letters gave way to querulousness:

> You must not think I am inclined to grumble, but the more I find out about Labuan the less I like it. I now hear that the late governor ... resigned from ill-health, and the few white inhabitants ... are constant victims to the jungle fever. My Catholic friends in the Conservative Party express the greatest regret at my acceptance of such a post. Lord Denbigh ... said that that section of the Catholics who have regarded me as their political leader anticipated that

one who had done so much for the Conservative interest among the Catholics in England ... should receive a good post at home where he could continue his labours, and not be sent to a sort of penal servitude in Borneo.[103]

Time and again he repeated this theme: that special consideration for Catholics meant, in practice, special consideration for John Pope Hennessy. It was merely a more advanced form of the political solipsism many Catholics in England exhibited: the next step after overrating the importance of the Catholic 'vote' was to overrate one's own importance in marshalling it. In other Catholics this was intellectual insularity, but in Hennessy there was an element of vanity too:

It would be madness to ... [go] to such a dreadful place as Labuan. Even if Queensland [another Governorship] cannot be promised, I heard today at the Colonial Office that Western Australia (£1,000 a year) will be vacant in a month or two. *Between ourselves*, the permanent officials at the Colonial Office were astonished at the Duke [of Buckingham] having thought of giving me such a small place as Labuan. Pray try to send me some assurance that I may get a better place. P.S. The Stafford Club Catholics were about holding [*sic*] an indignation meeting if I took Labuan.[104]

It was at this point that the Catholic connections, so sedulously built up, began to break down. Hennessy seemed not to realise the weakness of his case. Alone, an indignation meeting of the Stafford may not have achieved a great deal, but there was the hierarchy to enlist, too. Belying the pose of political neutrality which necessarily they adopted in the Catholic press, the bishops were as interested as their flock in the distribution of patronage:

A few nights ago I met Dr. Grant, the Bishop of Southwark, at dinner, and he spoke very seriously about the exercise of Government patronage in my case. I hear he intends to write to me on the subject, but without waiting for his communication I think it well to mention to you the substance of what he said. He was pleased to say that I was the only Tory who sat in the House of Commons who commanded the confidence of the Catholic prelates; that they still regarded me as the only link between the Tory party on the one side and the Irish and English Catholics on the other, and that, especially in the future relations of the Irish Catholic body and the State, they anticipated from my presence in a future Parliament some advantage both to themselves and to the Government; but that their faith in great ministers would be shaken if, in the meantime, I was kept at the coal-fields of Labuan.

Strange to say I have heard somewhat similar language from the strongest Protestants of the North. I understand that some of the Ulster MPs got up a kind of memorial or protest to the effect that I ought to have received the Government of Queensland, but ... found on enquiry that it had been already promised to some-one else.

I did not see this paper ... [105]

From one who prided himself on the subtlety of his political skills, this was crude. Special pleading which promised so much – the Irish Catholic vote, the English Catholic vote, the loyalty of the Irish to the State, the unshaken fidelity of the English bishops to the Tories, even a renewed support from Ulster Protestants – merely drew attention to the miserably small object of the pleading: something better than the jungles of Borneo. Nor was Disraeli likely to feel threatened by the dinner-party anger of the Bishop of Southwark, a charming man but a political lightweight.

The more Pope Hennessy argued his cause, the more he proved its weakness. Initially, Disraeli had been well disposed towards him. 'He has served us well and ought to be well rewarded,'[106] he wrote to Montagu Corry. It did not take long – in fact only two days – for this patronly benignity to pass. The reason was 'another ... indiscreet letter from Hennessy':

He criticises our electioneering tactics, but the only instance in which he had the direction of our affairs in that way, in the famous ... Cork Election, in which he induced the present Lord Gainsboro to be the candidate under his management, he made the greatest *fiasco* on record; not only lost a seat which might have been won, but nearly ruined Lord Gainsboro by the wildest, most reckless, and most foolish expenditure, in which a candidate was ever involved.

I fear his professional status would not justify an Indian judgeship, but if so it would be well thus, when we can, to provide for him.[107]

Hennessy had a knack of antagonising people at the wrong moment. Ryley had the same skill, encouraging Disraeli to think him a Jesuit who had to be kept at arm's length a day after he had mused that Catholics were his closest political allies. This suggests not Disraelian double-dealing (others shared his reaction to Hennessy to the extent of using almost the same words to express it)[108] but rather a capacity to wake quickly from the dream of getting Catholic support without having to pay for it. Hennessy reminded Disraeli that although his deisre for Catholic votes was genuine, it was not, for all that, very earnest. It took the self-love of Ryley and the careerism of Hennessy to suggest a paradox. The price of Catholic support was to take Catholics seriously, yet the nature of that support (letters of congratulation on the 'muzzling' speech, gleeful approval of Derby's strong Protestantism, excessive enthusiasm for the Established Church) made taking them seriously very difficult. There is no better example than Pope Hennessy. Despite his high indignation, his dark threats about the Stafford Club and the furious Bishop of Southwark, his gloomy warnings of Irish disloyalty, Ulster displeasure, and English disbelief, he ended up in Labuan nonetheless. Did this kill off his enthusiasm for Disraeli? Not at all. All the warnings were forgotten as he shipped himself off to his penal servitude. Within a year he was once again writing in the intimate mode, describing his reforms on the island, and suggesting that they were important enough to warrant a knighthood.[109]

1868 AND ALL THAT

Ryley and Hennessy on the one hand, Derby, Disraeli and Stanley on the other: inhabitants of separate worlds, linked only by that which defined the distance between them – an ability to say what they did not mean and mean what they did not say. Although their language proclaimed otherwise, Ryley and Hennessy thought that Catholicism was a help to their social advancement, not a hindrance. The rhetoric of minority, oppression, inequality, persecution, concealed a conviction that their denomination was a badge of distinction for which they deserved reward. Politics made them sectarians by showing them that denomination was a card to be played. Their Toryism was flawed by contradiction: by the argument on the one hand that Catholics were a harmless minority who were owed an historic debt which could best be paid in terms of personal patronage; by the pretence on the other that they were so important that no party could afford to ignore them.

Likewise with Derby and Disraeli. What was said was never meant and what was meant was never said. Catholics misunderstood what Derby said about their 'natural' alliance. Any 'muzzling', stirring up of 'No Popery', loyalty to Protestantism or Protestant voters, could be made acceptable to them in the name of party pragmatism. Thus the paradox: it was his so-called Catholic alliance which enabled Derby to be as Protestant as he was. It allowed him to persuade Catholics like Ryley and Hennessy that *his* Protestantism was in *their* best interests. The *Tablet* got it right, without realising how self-denying was the argument:

> His support of any Catholic claim was all the more valuable to us from the fact that his proved and notorious devotion to the opposition of Protestant bigotry.[110]

Derby convinced Catholics that he was their best Protestant friend and so used their political paranoia to his best advantage.

So did Disraeli. He talked about a Catholic alliance, publicly and privately, without infusing the words with political meaning. Indeed, to *dream* of such an alliance was to admit of its impracticality: politics reduced to the hope that Irish Catholics would vote Tory, that Ryley be not such a Jesuit, Hennessy not such a slippery customer. The idea of a Catholic alliance was a piece of Disraelian escapism.

This day-dreamy approach to Catholic politics came to an end in 1868, Disraeli's *annus mirabilis*. When Derby resigned and Disraeli succeeded him, there was nothing to suggest that Catholic-Tory relations were moving towards as decisive shift. Derby was dispatched handsomely by the *Tablet*[111] and even Manning welcomed Disraeli's ascent of the greasy pole. The Archbishop was never as intimate with the new Prime Minister as he had been and was to be with Gladstone, but they corresponded with more than formal civility on personal as well as political matters. The signs therefore did not point towards any especial difficulties between Catholics and Tories.

How did the amity end? Gladstone, Manning, and the question of Irish university education had much to do with it. Most of Manning's correspondence with Disraeli before he became Prime Minister had been devoted to Ireland. Fenianism worried him deeply: 'Nothing will lessen it but a large and adequate policy for Ireland.'[112] For a long time he argued that a charter for a Catholic university in Ireland, or failing that a more just recognition of the existing Catholic university, was 'the Chief object of desire'[113] of the Irish bishops, and of the Irish people. This did not mean that the church and land questions were irrelevant; only that the education question was easier to solve and therefore should be solved first. He went so far as to write on one occasion that a solution was 'practicable and even easy'.[114]

Manning had forgotten about the unlikelihood of English Protestants seeing the world the way he did. Even so, he gave Disraeli the impression that a charter for the Catholic university – rather than merely the Queen's University with modifications – would assure the Tories of the support of the Irish and English bishops.

This charter scheme was part of a long-term 'package deal' which included the concurrent endowment of the Roman Catholic and Presbyterian Churches in Ireland, designed to spare the feelings of the Anglicans by levelling up, not levelling down. Whether anything would have come of it cannot be known. A few days after the new university was proposed (10 March), the plan went badly – from Disraeli's point of view, disastrously – awry. On 16 March 1868, Gladstone announced that it was his intention not to tinker with the Anglican Establishment in Ireland, but to do away with it altogether.

This had several immediate consequences. First, Disraeli lost the political initiative, and Gladstone gained it. Secondly, Gladstone, not Disraeli, became the focus of Catholic hopes – or at least of Irish Catholic hopes. As Blake has noticed, Manning ceased communication with Disraeli the very day of Gladstone's declaration, and the resumption of correspondence, nine months later, was chilly.[115] Finally, the university scheme collapsed, its back broken by the excessive and impolitic demands of the Irish hierarchy.

This left Disraeli with the conviction that he had been stabbed in the back by the Catholics. He was a fatally weakened Prime Minister whose only reason for staying in office was to enable a new electoral register to be completed. His sense of desertion was captured two years later when English Catholics, appalled by Newdegate's campaign for an inquiry into the state of their convents, appealed to him for help. It was not forthcoming. Cashel Hoey's account of the reason for this – given in a letter to the Earl of Mayo – has a melodramatic ring:

About a fortnight or three weeks ago, the Duke of Norfolk and Sir Charles Clifford waited on Mr. Disraeli in regard to the pending motion of Mr. Newdegate about our convents.

Mr. Disraeli said that it was impossible for him to give any help to Catholics in matters affecting their political interests – that when in office he had made certain propositions, and that on the score of these propositions certain Catholic leaders had given him an undertaking of support – that that understanding had not been observed but had been betrayed – in consequence he had felt impelled to place his resignation in the hands of Her Majesty, and would have done so but that superior considerations of public policy intervened ... and in fine that he no longer possessed the confidence of the party on Catholic questions. The Duke and Sir Charles withdrew, but he followed them to the head of the stairs and said that it was to Archbishop Manning that he particularly referred, and that he wished what he had said to be communicated to his Grace.

Very soon after the negotiations touching the grant of a charter to the Irish Catholic University proved unsuccessful, a rumour spread in London that Mr. Disraeli attributed its failure to the Archbishop, and that he had even said that the Archbishop had stabbed him in the back. The phrase in due course reached the Archbishop's ears ... [but he] felt that the rumour attributing this very violent phrase to Mr. Disraeli was a mere scandal. [Now it appears that it was not]. [I shall do my best to ensure that this does not become public] though the story would certainly shed some light on the prolonged intellectual incubation which has resulted in the production of *Lothair*.[116]

The phrase 'stab in the back' is notable. It became part of Disraeli's Catholic mythology. Years later, it was still used – by his associates as much as by himself – as if it distilled the received and unarguable history of his relations with Catholics.[117]

Yet there is irony here. The events of March 1868 had the effect of *increasing* support for Disraeli among Catholic Tories. For the *Tablet* it was Gladstone who was the villain of the piece, a shameless opportunist using the pretext of Disestablishment to gain office.[118] Moreover, his Erastianism was as objectionable as his hypocrisy. Disestablishment, it was argued, was merely the first step towards complete secularism. Thus though Disraeli abandoned the Catholics, not all of *them* abandoned him.

What Disraeli's 'stab in the back' mythology ignored was that if he did have to be stabbed, it was lucky for him that it was Catholics who did it and not Protestants. To judge by the advice of his colleagues, anti-Catholicism was the perfect cry for 1868. Colonel Taylor proposed a straightforward dumping of the Catholics to win the Protestants. 'You should let the Catholic College go if you possibly can – it is the only drawback to the Protestant feeling in our favour.'[119] Derby, dismissing disestablishment, captured in a sentence the politico-religious priorities of a lifetime: '[You run] the risk of mortally offending the Protestants without at the same time satisfying the R. Catholics...'.[120] Corry, much cheered by the prospect of Liberal divisions, believed 'the Protestant cry will land Ministers with a triumphant majority at the General Election'.[121] Humbler supporters thought likewise: 'Your programme is admirable – resistance to Romanism in its attempt to tyrannise over us – rejection of Ritualism and sham Romanism in our church – opposition to rationalism.'[122] William FitzWilliam Dick, an Irish follower, reported a conversation with the Bishop of London: 'Let ... Mr. Disraeli ... declare the realm of England shall not be ruled by High Church Ritualists or Irish Papists, and he will have such a following thro'out the Empire as no minister has had for the last half century.'[123] If Disraeli could command such support, it may be that Manning had done him a good turn: stabbed in the back, yes, but only with a rubber dagger.

The initial disposition of Disraeli's Catholic followers had been to applaud him for upholding Catholic as well as Tory principles. This was in March 1868. In April, however, he went further. It was then that he made his famous accusation that 'the High Church Ritualists and the Irish followers of the Pope have long been in secret combination, and are now in open confederation' to destroy the link between church and state.[124] Did this offend his Catholic support? The *Tablet* reported the speech but professed puzzlement that people should have been so annoyed by it. 'We do not know what Mr. Disraeli meant by the assertion ... but what of it?' It is hard to think of a more amenable response: if he wanted his 'No Popery' cry, there were some Catholics happy to let him have it. For Wallis, editor of the *Tablet*, Disraeli was 'guiltless' of the charge of anti-Catholicism.[125] Lord Denbigh was anxious that he might allow the 'apparent exigencies of Party' to lead him into 'No Popery' but never thought that he would. After all, there were so many reasons for 'the Catholic body to come to [the Tories'] aid – not for Party purposes, but in interests of the moral welfare of this country'.[126]

The *Tablet* had an answer to any fear that Disraeli might foment 'No Popery' for party purposes. It was that if there *were* such a cry, it would not be Disraeli's fault, but Manning's and his brother bishops'. One of Wallis's last editorials, written as the Liberals were achieving their victory, made this plain:

> What is certain is, at the beginning of this year the Tory party were offering to the Catholics such concessions, as a few years ago would have been thought astonishing, that our Catholic leaders preferred to repel their overtures, and to join in an attempt to Disestablish and Disendow the Protestant Church, and that when the Tories tried to defend their Church, the Catholic leaders accused them of getting up a No Popery cry. Our opinion is, that that was most unwholesome and discreditable, besides being most unwise and impolitic. If the Tories now fall back into their old attitude of hostility to Catholic rights and interests, because they are satisfied that no behaviour on their part can win Catholic support or disarm Catholic opposition, Catholics will have little reason to congratulate themselves....[127]

This was remarkable. Wallis in his valedictory leader admitted that under his editorship there had been those who felt that the *Tablet* had exhibited 'a maximum of Toryism and a minimum of religion'.[128] It is little wonder.

The *Tablet* did appear to have mapped out a reasonable and intelligent political position, but the realisation that Catholics often only had themselves to blame for the antipathy of Protestants was achieved only by default. The irony is that even when Catholics admitted that they, too, might be responsible for anti-Catholicism, they still held that they *were* specially favoured. They could never shake off their self-importance, even when they were self-abasing. In its account of the political position of Derby and Disraeli the *Tablet* fortuitously got it right. They were non-Catholics operating in a non-Catholic world. To understand that was the beginning of wisdom.

3

Catholics and Tories 1868–74

CATHOLICS AND DISRAELI UNTIL THE VATICAN COUNCIL

Disraeli discovered in 1868 what Gladstone realised only in 1874: that Catholics lived in a world where political common sense was a rare visitor, and a generally unwelcome one. The dates tell why. For the most part, it was the experience of office which opened eyes. What Disraeli endured at the hands of Manning and the Irish bishops in April 1868, Gladstone endured at the hands of Manning, Cullen, the infallible Pope and his international conspiracy of Jesuits throughout the whole of his ministry. The quixotic behaviour which Derby had noticed in 1865,[1] Granville noticed in 1870. The one-sided favouritism expected only briefly of Disraeli eventually drove Gladstone – who had done his best to please – to reject a Catholic vote which cost more trouble than it was worth. Both men in short felt themselves used and abused by Catholics whose support they had never fully understood. Both had imputed their own political rationality to a group happy with a more innocent vision of the world. Both had imagined that Catholic support could be had without much trouble from their respective Protestant flanks. And both reacted to their disillusion in characteristic ways: Gladstone wrote a tract and Disraeli a novel.

For Disraeli, opposition brought respite from Catholic claims but not release. As usual, defeated supporters required the consolation of patronage just as the well was drying up; as usual, many of them contrived to make their leader feel, along with their constituents, a shared guilt. Note, for instance, the anguish and guile of George Bowyer, the most doughty of Catholic Tories, who had lost his seat in Dundalk:

> The Whigs made such a *dead set* at me, that nothing could stand it. Gladstone and Bright sent a joint letter *denouncing* me, and they used every influence against me ...
>
> My *not* supporting Gladstone on the motion on which he resigned was *fatal* to me, as I told you I feared it would be, when

you pressed me not to vote.... and Archbishop Kiernan ... declared
that after *that*, he *never would support me again*. And he allowed his
curates to canvass against me.[2]

A week later, insidiousness had replaced excitability:

Knowing how chivalrous and true you always are to your friends,
I do not hesitate to say that I have a strong claim on the consideration of the Government.[3]
    During my whole career I have given valuable independent
support to the Conservative Party ... I was always an obstacle to
Palmerston and Gladstone and Russell; who I moreover made
unpopular in Ireland by denouncing as enemies of the Pope.
If I had not had the fear of my constituents, I could have ... *greatly
hurt* Gladstone's resolutions [on the Irish Church] ... If I had *not*
done what you pressed me to do ... I should now be MP for
Dundalk ...

There was a self-contradiction here typical of many Catholic claimants: at one moment, Bowyer was triumphant, proclaiming himself
the papally-approved hammer of the Whigs; the next, he was
dashed, a fearful victim of constituents who – only a sentence before
– were supposed to act according to his dictation. He made matters
worse by showing Disraeli a letter he had received from Bishop
Moriarty of Kerry, in a last effort to prove his political worth.
Moriarty's advice to him had been clear:

No statesman before Gladstone ever acknowledged the rights of
Ireland. You should have, in the present circumstances, joined his
standard. Our people are persuaded you are a D'Israelite. With
that condition it would be impossible to return any man – the Pope
included – for a liberal Irish constituency.[4]

These were words of doubtful comfort to a defeated Prime Minister.
They suggest an irony: just as it was Gladstone's Catholics who
unwittingly persuaded him that the Catholic vote was lost, so too
was it Disraeli's Catholics who convinced *him* that he had lost *his*
Catholic support. Acton showed Gladstone how ultramontane
English Catholicism had become; Bowyer explicitly told Disraeli that
the Pope himself could not make Tories out of the Irish.
    For Disraeli, opposition also brought renewed interest in Roman

affairs. The Vatican Council impinged upon Tory thoughts as well as Liberal, though not, as with Gladstone, to the point of obsession. As Gathorne Hardy[5] noted laconically in his diary,

> I ought not to omit another event which may (one wd. think must) have important consequences – the carrying the vote for Infallibility ... on Wedy last.[6]

There was no Gladstonian passion here. Nor, a year later, was the pose of uninvolved chronicler dropped: 'Yesterday, the Pope's Jubilee and the Triumph at Berlin – great events in their way.'[7]

The insouciance was typical of the party as well as the man: it was Gladstone's overreaction to religious matters which Tories regarded as the main political advantage to be derived from the Council. They found it easy to convict him of 'Enthusiasm', and his response to Infallibility was taken as further evidence of it. They privately nicknamed him 'Monsignore'[8] – shorthand expression for religious humbug – and considered his anti-papal fervour altogether excessive. After all, his leadership of the Liberal Party – dictatorial but crafty – suggested Vatican metaphors closer to home. Some of Disraeli's more bellicose supporters therefore saw in the religious events of the early 1870s not a threat but a political opportunity. Consider the views of one self-appointed adviser:

> I hope you will work Gladstone on this Popery move. It will explode the whole pack by and bye. For the country is becoming restive and will not stand it much longer.... Depend upon it, there is a reaction going on – and a break up may soon be anticipated.[9]

The 'Popery move' was the repeal of the Ecclesiastical Titles Act, and the correspondent, G. R. Badenoch, an evangelical Protestant from Liverpool whose Toryism – at least in his letters to Disraeli – consisted of anti-Popery interspersed with frequent avowals of patriotism. Badenoch may have been unsophisticated, but he was not unorthodox: it was obvious Tory wisdom that the Liberals' Catholic difficulty could be their Protestant opportunity. Gladstone and Granville themselves thought so. They were convinced, for example, that Lord Cairns had been sent to Rome in 1870 as a Tory *agent provocateur*, seeking party advantage only.[10] Perhaps so: but as they also interpreted the Vatican Council in terms of party gain or loss, they could hardly complain.

Other Tories thought of the Council in terms not of party but of personal gain. George Bowyer was one of them. Deprived of his licence in Dundalk, he set up his stall in Rome, trading in Catholic inside information. As supplier to the Party of gossip, sacred and secular, his intention was to suggest indispensability, but the effect was to indicate eccentricity. In a world in which 'contacts' were all, Bowyer had one upon which he battened shamelessly – Cardinal Bernardi, the Cardinal Prefect of Propaganda. He quoted letters from him like gobbets served with the ritual of high-level espionage[11] and claimed that his own letters 'had a great effect' on the Cardinal's thinking.[12] Disraeli knew the idiom well: Bowyer, once the publicity-officer of a Pope, now styled himself the confidant of a Cardinal. The Opposition Leader was meant to feel a debt of gratitude. But Bowyer was not venal; he wanted merely to be taken seriously as a political figure, the spokesman of a distinctive point of view. That is why he also approached the Whigs, writing for example to Lord Granville in the grand style:

> As I devoted many years in Parliament to the defence of the Holy See, and I thereby excluded myself from all those objects of honourable ambition which are the rewards of Parliamentary life, I think I have a right to address you and Her Majesty's Government regarding the momentous events which are taking place in Italy.[13]

This was a classic statement of the Catholic political myth. It contained three elements. In the first place, Bowyer believed, though he pretended otherwise, that Catholicism was a card to be played, not hidden. In the second, it was disingenuous to claim that his denomination had denied him the objects of honourable ambition. It hardly seemed like that when he wrote to Disraeli. Thus, thirdly, Catholicism was the perfect justification for favouritism and the perfect explanation if the favouritism was not forthcoming. Events like the Council did not embarrass Catholics so much as provide them with opportunities to prove either their value or their virtue.

Bowyer had about him a whiff of desperation. His tone to Granville (an unlikely correspondent) was of a man for whom any audience would do. One reason perhaps was that he had rivals for Disraeli's ear. Other Catholics were anxious to advance themselves in the party by claiming denominational deservedness. One was Lord Robert Montagu. Montagu's career exuded disappointed enthusiasms. He was MP for Huntingdonshire (1859–74) and then for

Westmeath (1874–80). Twenty years in the House showed him the emptiness of his heroes, Disraeli in particular, with whom he had a notable falling-out in 1876.[14] This propensity to disillusion had its religious aspect as well. In mid-career Montagu became a convert to the Church of Rome, thereafter displaying a zeal proverbial to the point of parody. It took the usual forms: proclaiming to the tract-reading world his former error, his new-found freedom; telling his new co-religionists how to behave; pestering political colleagues about the treatment of Catholics; addressing public meetings. Montagu's light – which was smaller than he thought – was never hidden under a bushel. There was something feverish about this – Gathorne Hardy once complained of 'that half mad Robert Montagu'[15] – and eventually he felt himself abandoned by the Church he had once embraced. He therefore left it, and – the double-zeal of a double-convert – began to attack it with the passion once reserved for defence of it. Thus the author, in 1873, of *Register, Register, Register! An Appeal to Catholics* was also responsible, in 1888, for *Whither are we drifting? or The Progress of England Romewards*; illustrating, one may suppose, that those who live by exclamation marks shall die by them.

Montagu's reputation for instability was long-standing, but Disraeli came into closest contact with it between 1870 and 1876. His political style was in the manner of Edward Ryley: ever at his master's service, ever ready with Catholic information, ever able to put a Tory construction on it. It is therefore as a correspondent from Rome that he has his greatest interest. He went there in April 1871 and had several meetings with Vatican officials. The most important of these was with Cardinal Antonelli, the Secretary of State, to whom he delivered the usual Catholic Tory line on Ireland:

> I began by remarking ... that all over Europe, except in Ireland, the Liberals were the natural enemies of the Catholics; but that in Ireland the opposite was the case. I mentioned the cause: ... that the road of the Catholics and road of the Liberals had been parallel.... Those roads were no longer parallel; the Catholics had obtained all that the Liberals would ever consent to give, and that which they now desired was Denominational Education ... I then said broadly: that the Bishops and Catholic people of Ireland had fought against the Catholic Church & had established the unity of Italy & imprisoned the Pope in the Vatican.[16]

Here was standard fare: even after the events of 1868, even after

Newdegate's convent-campaign, even after *Lothair*, Montagu stuck firmly to a 'natural alliance' theory of Catholic-Tory relations. Temperamentally, he had little alternative: any Liberalism which disestablished and disendowed a national church was socially anarchic and self-evidently impious. Like many Catholics, Montagu could not abide a party, still less a Cabinet, which contained John Bright. If the price of religious equality was parity with secular nonconformity, Catholic Tories did not want it.

Montagu conformed to Catholic Tory type in another way: he expressed preference in the language of enthusiasm. Disraeli was his leader, but he had to be his hero as well. He believed, with prelapsarian innocence, that Disraeli's every public utterance formed a pattern:

> Cardinal Antonelli ... spoke very warmly of your policy as having always been favourable to the temporal power of the Pope; and of your speech on the Irish Church in 1844; and assured me that they entertained *very* friendly feelings towards you ... I then said that you had always been consistent in your policy, as announced in every speech & conveyed in every novel you had written, but you felt you had been betrayed and stabbed in the back by Cardinal Cullen and the Catholics....[17]

The reference to Disraeli's novels – he had *Lothair* in mind – bears examination. The novel recounts the adventures of the empty-headed Lothair, an orphan who inherits a fortune on his twenty-first birthday. Moving in aristocratic circles, he is exposed to conflicting attractions: romantic revolution in the form of Theodora, ceremonial and cerebral Catholicism in the form of Cardinal Grandison and assorted clerics, courtly love in the form of Lady Corisande. Grandison, a manipulative ascetic clearly modelled on Manning, urges Lothair to conversion, promising that Catholicism shall bring him pre-eminence in this world and bliss in the next. Unpersuaded, he follows Theodora to Europe to fight the reactionary forces of the Pope. Theodora is then killed in battle, he seriously wounded. Lothair is restored to health in the care of Catholics in Rome, who employ various devices, all dubious, to convert him to their creed. In the midst of this travail, the dead Theodora appears to him in a vision to remind him of his proper loyalties, and this prompts him to escape from the city and its proselytising clutches. He returns to England by way of Syria, and satisifies his romantic and religious yearnings by marrying Corisande while at the same time becoming an Anglican.

Much may be learned by considering reaction to *Lothair*, Catholic and otherwise. Its publication was as much a political as a literary event, as any *roman à clef* by a former Prime Minister must be. But it did more than provide London society with its chief talking-point of the season,[18] or Manning with a grudge against its author, or Lord Bute (its clear object), with a source of holy confusion,[19] or the Tory Front Bench with evidence of their leader's frivolity,[20] or certain bishops with a new and unlikely hero who had shown the 'hollowness of modern Romanizing, and the dangerous drift when we leave the old Reformation moorings'.[21]

Disraeli certainly knew the political appeal of the old Reformation moorings. *Lothair* astonished parliamentary colleagues[22] who, though seeing little reason to love Catholics, saw none to insult them gratuitously; but it cheered Disraeli's Protestant support in the country, weighed down by Gladstone's Erastianism and the prospect of years more in opposition.[23] For the same reason, it scandalised Catholic Ireland and this, in turn, further delighted those Tories who, released from the strain of courting Irish votes, could gladly abandon them altogether. One correspondent thought that Disraeli might be 'glad to read' of 'the rampant indignation' of Irish Catholics against *Lothair*, an indignation which extended far beyond press or pulpit:

> A friend of mine told me the other day that her maid (an R.C.) said to her, 'Oh, mam, have you read *Lothair*?' 'No,' was the reply. 'Oh then mam pray don't read it, for everyone says that it is the most awfully wicked book that ever was written, and that it was written by a pagan and an infidel.'[24]

Perhaps the writer intended irony. It was lost on the Orange wing of the party, always glad to read of Irish Catholic indignation.

Such might have been predicted, but the effect of *Lothair* on Catholic Tories is arresting. So far from angering them, it confirmed some of them in their Toryism. Consider George Bowyer, writing to Disraeli in the year of *Lothair*'s publication:

> I wish we had a *Conservative* Government now. But the *Standard* which raved about the robbery and sacrilege of disendowing and disestablishing the Irish Bps is now furious to disestablish and

disendow the Holy See and it exults over the approach of the
Revolutionary King to the Conservative City of Rome. He is to
have the Quirinial Apostolic Palace which he will convert into a
brothel. And moral England will applaud and call it progress!... I
fear the Council and the Infallibility complicate the position. I have
always *feared both*. If you had been at the head of the Government
you might have prevented the War. Gladstone and Granville were
not equal to the occasion.[25]

Some Catholics were evidently prepared to applaud *Lothair*'s treatment of the revolution and ignore its treatment of themselves.
Alfred Austin – hopelessly besotted with Disraeli – wrote to the
author to congratulate him on a work of genius.[26] A precedent
suggests itself: Edward Ryley's gleeful enthusiasm for Derby's
'muzzling the Catholics' speech of 1865.

If the reaction to *Lothair* convinced Disraeli that some Catholics
were uninsultable, Montagu's despatches from Rome indicated that
others were anxious to please to the point of self-emasculation. If
Catholics were to be condemned, Montagu was happy to oblige. His
conversations with the Secretary of State confirmed it:

> [Cardinal Antonelli] again spoke very warmly of you; and I said
> 'Mr. Disraeli is, I feel sure, anxious to continue the policy of Pitt &
> to support the Temporal Power; but the fact is that he cannot trust
> the Catholics.'[27]

Disraeli's thoughts exactly. Like Ryley, Bowyer and Hennessy
before, Montagu's technique was to establish his own merit by
proving the demerit of his co-religionists. The risks were obvious.

Montagu's *naiveté* lay not in his failure to recognise that Disraeli
had a Protestant flank to keep under control. It lay in his belief that it
was easily controlled, and in the conviction that the anti-Catholic
elements of Toryism were preferable to the anti-religious elements of
Liberalism. He even lectured the Pope on the subject, showing His
Holiness how Disraeli was a better friend to the Church than
Gladstone:

> I explained that there were bigoted Orangemen on one side, who
> were an obstacle to the policy which Mr. Disraeli desired; but that
> on Gladstone's side there were 160 Red Republicans who were
> atheists & these were Mr. Gladstone's obstacle; that the bigoted

Orangemen were more stupid or more easily 'managed,' as they had no principle clearly defined before their minds; while the Radicals or Red Republicans knew very well what they wanted to do; so that I supposed that Mr. Disraeli was more likely to carry out his policy than Mr. G....[28]

Bigot-management was less mechanical than Montagu imagined. He forgot that Orangemen were more easily managed precisely because it was easier to be anti-Catholic than not. Montagu always ignored this simple if unappealing logic of Protestant politics.

CATHOLICS AS PATRONS AND CLAIMANTS

These networks of information prompt reflections. It is striking how all of Disraeli's Catholics, both individually and as it were cumulatively, either told him what he knew already, or what he knew to be untrue, or what he wanted to believe but could not, or what he wanted not to believe but had to believe. Disraeli knew Ultramontanism to be an opportunity to revive his Orange support, but it was important to have Bowyer confirm it. He knew that Irish nationalism was not the result of misdirected patronage (though he once thought it was) but it was revealing to see Montagu and Bowyer try to argue otherwise. He wanted to believe that those Catholics who were Tories by conviction were so because their convictions were Tory; but Hennessy's nostalgia for the 1840s, Bowyer's narrow Ultramontanism, and Montagu's belief that Catholics should establish their own party[29] indicated not. He wanted not to believe in the strength of unsophisticated Orangeism, personally, because he disliked fanaticism, politically, because it required of him the performance of unnatural acts such as enthusiasm for the Bible; but it was an exploitable device and it was suggestive that Montagu tried to argue it away.

Catholics thus convinced Tories that they had a distinct voice, but that it was distinctly self-defeating. Let one example stand for many. At the height of Newdegate's convent-campaign of 1870, Montagu Corry confessed himself 'somewhat surprised to find how deeply the country is taking to heart the convent inspection question'; as if this hoary Protestantism, with its quasi-sexual obsessions, were a thing of the past. The reason why it was not soon came to him:

'mainly (as I believe) owing to the agitation the Papists are raising, which seems very likely to destroy its object'.[30]

Perceptions like this diminished official sympathy for the Catholic cause. Catholics failed to realise that deputations to politicians (to which they were much given) and other instruments of self-advertisement were often a waste of time. If they wanted badly enough to prove their influence over politicians, politicians had a sixth sense which told them to resist. It took a long time for Catholics to realise this, if, indeed, they ever did.

What may also have lessened sympathy was the suspicion that many Catholic grievances, however well-founded, seemed contrived. Bowyer, as he confidentially expressed to Disraeli his fears of Infallibility, failed to suggest a man who had been losing sleep. Montagu, as he complained that Catholics were artificially divided into Tory and Liberal camps, hardly disguised that his career as a sectional spokesman depended on it.[31] Denbigh, as he urged defence of 'all those Constitutional & Religious foundations ... so dear to the heart of every Catholic' seemed to thrive on any 'anxiety'[32] which enabled him to reiterate his Toryism. This is not to impute insincerity; only to notice that the obverse of 'Enthusiasm' was indignation, and that Catholics were much given to both.

English Catholicism in sum was a self-absorbed world with several layers. These networks of information were networks of patronage as well. Catholics depended on one another for jobs. That is why the *Tablet*, Manning, Vaughan, even Newman, like to see Catholics do well in public life. It meant that there might be more jobs to go around. Think of Pope Hennessy. Small in Disraeli's world, he was big in his own; indeed, was probably more begged against than begging. No one was embarrassed about asking him favours, however lowly the object,[33] and even distinguished figures – Lord Arundell of Wardour, for instance – wrote to him in supplicatory mode:

> I beg to enclose a letter from Mr. Welman respecting his son Henry Welman. I shall feel much obliged if you can see your way to doing something in the matter without inconvenience.... I think ... we have known each other sufficiently to ... ask anything in the way of mutual accommodation.[34]

Arundell was a Tory writing to a Tory, but his subject was non-political. There also existed, however, political jobbery with Hennessy at its centre. One example is provided by the former editor of the *Tablet*, John Wallis, who was in the mid-1870s more stridently Tory than he had been in the late 1860s. Wallis regarded Hennessy as a fellow-soul, but also as a useful friend in high places. He was obsessed by the world of affairs – the obsession which comes from exclusion.

> If you get a chance, you would be doing us here a good turn by recommending the F.O. to appoint Sir Philip Francis, now Consul General and Judge at Constantinople, to succeed General Stanton here as agent and Consul General. Stanton is retiring on his pension as soon as he has done the honours to the Heir Apparent. Then if Francis gets in the place, Cookson will succeed him, and I shall succeed Cookson at Alexandria.[35]

Such was the mentality which had charge of the *Tablet* for so long. Wallis had an eye for the main chance so sharp that it could see round corners, but even Newman could write to Lord Ripon, when he was Viceroy of India, in worldly terms:

> That you are doing great work in India, none of us doubts, and it is selfish to complain you are not doing work at home, but be sure some Catholics here all feel how much you would be doing for us if your duty did not call you away. Especially do I often think how many young men there are, of position and with a future, who are sadly [deprived] of what you can do for them.[36]

Newman did not try to disguise that this was the role of Catholics in politics. No wonder the less saintly were more cynical.

TORY REALISM AND CATHOLIC ROMANCE:
ANTI-CATHOLICISM AS A POLITICAL TACTIC

In the first half of the 1870s, Catholicism was a political smear with which each party attempted to besmirch the other. Tories seemed to have the better of the argument. The vulnerability of the Liberals was obvious. Had not Gladstone come to power with the help of massive clerical intimidation in Ireland? The same Gladstone who disestablished the Irish Church and stole its property to pay his debts; who was secretly a Jesuit or lover of Jesuitry; who waited breathlessly upon the good opinion of a Cullen or a Manning; whose whole Irish policy assumed that law-breakers were to be pleased, not punished? Rhetoric like this came easily to Tory lips, and occasions which justified it were seized upon.

The Galway by-election of 1872 was one such. The Home Rule candidate, Captain John Nolan, won the seat with much clerical influence and was later unseated at the recommendation of Judge William Keogh. Keogh used the occasion to deliver a judgment which has been described as a 'vituperative masterpiece':

> F. Lavelle is still an officiating priest, who goes to the altar, and who ... does not perform but desecrates the renewal of that *tremendum mysterium* which was consecrated upon Calvary ... As to Revd. Peter Conway ... what an odious exhibition he made of himself ... as he swelled and fumed, talked and raged ... [Dreadful was] the organised system of intimidation which has pervaded this county in every quarter, in every direction, in every barony, in every place.[37]

Perhaps the judge was unhinged: he certainly became so later.[38] But he had identified a serious abuse and – worse – embarrassed the government who wanted to shelve his report so as to appease their Irish support.

Here was an episode custom-built for Tory opportunism. Derby – sounding like his father twenty years before, for whom the non-prosecution of priests was a subject 'we shall do well to take up seriously' – was gleeful:

> I am told – not as a certainty, but as a thing believed by Gladstone's friends – that he will, on some excuse or other, avoid taking action of any kind on the Keogh report – so that perjury and intimidation are to go unpunished, because committed by priests! You know better that I how far any such story is likely to be true. If it should turn out so, what a position! We should have against him the justice of the case, the Liberal feeling against priestly power, the English feeling against lawless & violent proceedings, and the irritation which is produced among honest people when they see an obviously partial exercise of ... judicial powers. This is so obvious that I should have thought the Cabinet must see it – but the Cabinet is Gladstone, and Gladstone loves a priest. It really looks as if there were a possibility of effective action.[39]

Derby gave voice to instincts which were purely partisan. Lord Claude Hamilton did the same. 'The whole affair is such an admirable card for us to play that we should lose no chance of making the best of it.'[40] As a tactic this was reasonable, in that it was justified by success: Gladstone *was* embarrassed, and the trial of Bishop Duggan of Clonfert for electoral malpractice – he was acquitted – destroyed the last vestiges of Liberalism in Ireland.[41]

Judge Keogh's condemnation of clerical electoral abuses deeply angered Irish Catholics. Tory readiness to exploit both it and the government's delinquent response indicates not only the value of Catholicism as smear but also an inclination to write off, indeed to be rid of, the Irish Catholic vote.

A year later, the tendency was even more marked. Consider this robust communication from a Disraeli supporter in, of all places, Rio de Janeiro. His purpose was to congratulate him on refusing office in 1873, after Gladstone's Irish University Bill fiasco:

> The Irish Roman Catholics are never to be depended upon – their own interests and principles must ere long withdraw them from the radical ranks – *and* Roman Catholicism is daily becoming more abhorrent in England from its assumption of a political position....[42]

With the congratulations – Irish University reform was Gladstone's mess and he should clean it up himself – came a warning: beware of Catholic votes, even if offered.

The writer from Rio was not singular in his philosophy. Tories could never be sure whether Catholics were as good as their word. But of one thing they *were* sure: they had no wish to be associated in the public mind with the Catholic cause. Consider their claims to Protestant support. *Lothair*, the Keogh case, opposition to disestablishment, anger at disendowment, nodding assent to convent investigations, triumphant visits by Disraeli to Lancashire, official links with Orangeism, refusal of office in 1873, would all be undone if it were thought that the party was secretly sympathetic to Catholic demands. Witness the anxieties of one of Disraeli's correspondents:

> ... any suspicion of Conservative sympathy with Ultramontanes will be a serious injury to our party: and I am more convinced of the necessity for great care by the circumstance that, during the

autumn, in private intercourse, I have found symptoms of an unexpected willingness on the part of Liberals to break with the Roman Catholic party whilst their local organs in the press endeavour to associate them with us in the public estimation.[43]

There was no reason for Liberals to characterise the Tories as Ultramontanes unless some people would believe it. This was not a forlorn hope, because however well tethered to the 'old Reformation moorings', Tories had areas of religious vulnerability. One was ritualism. As a rule of thumb, no more, ritualists were to the Tories what nonconformists were to the Liberals:[44] an important component of party support, but at times an embarrassing one. It is no coincidence that the passage of the Public Worship Regulation Act (1874) was as fraught for Conservatives as had been that of the Education Act for the Liberals four years before.[45] The party's dependence on anti-ritualist support was complicated by the High Churchmanship of leading figures such as Salisbury and Carnavon. Tory ritualists embraced their religion with a conviction which was altogether too serious for politics. Derby's complaint about Salisbury, for instance, concerned less his beliefs then the narrowmindedness with which he held them:

> I don't imagine that Salisbury is exactly a 'Ritualist': in fact he makes no secret of his opinion that that party are bringing their cause into contempt by their follies: but he sympathises with a good deal of what they teach, and (*like Gladstone*) *he attaches more importance, personally, to that class of questions than to all political or national considerations.*[46]

Disraeli needed little reminder of how troublesome Ritualism could be. For years at Hughenden he had been plagued, and for years more he was to be plagued, by local objections to the Romish practices of the rector there.[47] High Anglicanism, therefore, though not a gaping wound, was a nagging sore of which the Tories were made constantly aware.

The other area of religious vulnerability for Tories in 1874 – one which made possible the Ultramontane smear – was that, by the election, they were indeed the party to which many Catholics were giving public support. Catholics shared in the general 'reaction' against the Liberals, and had their own reasons for doing so. Some held that Liberals had betrayed a trust which should not have been theirs in the first place. Others claimed that a party supported by secular Nonconformists was no place for them. Even Manning distanced himself from Gladstone on grounds of his reliance on Nonconformity.[48] Yet more were reluctant to abandon the Liberals because they doubted if the Tories would be much better. There were those who felt that at best Disraeli would be the lesser of two evils. Better 'a little tyranny' from him, Bishop Vaughan suggested, than a greater one from Gladstone.

These were grudging endorsements. Catholics such as Bowyer, Pope Hennessy and Denbigh were much more enthusiastic. Bowyer had long claimed that the Irish representation in the Commons was 'so bad that the Irish members are themselves ashamed of it, and many of them will be turned out at the next election'[49] Pope Hennessy had maintained for thirty years that Catholic and Tory were natural allies.[50] Denbigh had pointed out in 1868 the imposture of a partnership between the Liberal Party (radical, republican and secular) and Irish Catholicism.

Such proclamations of loyalty were important for two reasons, both linked: first, because Conservative Catholics took too much credit for the party's electoral success; second, because this implied that they were owed a debt. In January 1874 a supporter warned Disraeli, 'in the interst of the Conservative Party',[51] to have nothing to do with Catholics. Two months later, Denbigh argued the reverse:

> I hope you may be able to find time to cast your eyes over a copy of the *Tablet*. I send you this by post, as it contains a good deal of information ... which is carefully kept out of sight by the ordinary Protestant papers ...
>
> PS I hope you have seen how much the Conservative successes have been helped by the votes of Catholics throughout the country.[52]

Did Denbigh delude himself? Not entirely. Tories were sufficiently gracious to acknowledge some debt. As Lord John Manners wrote to Pope Hennessy in 1874:

> It was, I need hardly say to you, most gratifying to us to witness the cordial support rendered in most English constituencies by your co-religionaries to the Tory candidates, nonetheless so because it was avowedly based on an agreement on principle on the question of Education....[53]

This was genuinely meant, but not very remarkable. More interesting is how things stood a year later. Manners wrote again, and gently reminded Pope Hennessy of reality. 'It may, I think, be a little open to doubt whether you have not a little overestimated the influence of the RC voters on the English majority ...'[54]

The conclusion is plain. In 1874 Catholics were elaborately rejected by the Liberals and were embraced – so they thought – by the Tories. The truth is that they did the embracing, not the Tories. The party which they had abandoned in 1868 was no different from the one they rediscovered in 1874. In 1874, *both* parties, not the Liberals, tended to write off the Catholic vote. This was a political isolation of which Catholics had little inkling. Voting for a principle, not a party, was, the *Tablet* suggested, 'the glory of the Catholic community'.[55] From the perspective of the Tory benches, it did not seem like that. Derby was there, writing strong despatches to the Spanish government because 'it would please the Protestant throughout England';[56] Disraeli was there, refusing to make royal appointments which would be 'dangerous to the Protestant religion';[57] Cairns was there, 'absolutely under the influence of Roundell Palmer and Roundell Palmer [was] another Gladstone – and dangerous';[58] Manners was there, politely but firmly disputing Catholic claims of serious political influence; and behind them all, the Queen, than whom nobody could be 'more opposed ... to the doctrines of the Roman Catholics'.[59]

4

Lord Ripon: A Catholic in Politics

THE 'PERVERSION' OF LORD RIPON

Distrust of Catholics was general in 1874 in a way that it had not been since 1850, at the height of Russell's contrived 'No Popery' agitation. Nor was it a suspicion born simply of broken trust and undelivered votes. Catholics spoke a different language from their contemporaries; never more so than when they were trying to say the same thing. Consider loyal toasts to the Crown. Somehow they came out garbled, as if delivered by mouths impenitently clenched in honour of a better dispensation. Lord Denbigh, Disraeli's plaintive correspondent of 1868, was a past master at the art. Nobody understood better the bizarre grammar of Catholic patriotism, or spoke it to more baffling effect. One example may stand for many. Speaking in the Town Hall, Wednesbury, Staffordshire, in 1874, he proposed first the health of the Pope, explaining that Catholics 'adopted the principle of "Church and State", the Church coming first...'. The present Pope, he continued, had long outlived St Peter and was especially worthy of good health:

> The Pope at this time of the world stood before all. He was the cynosure of all eyes. He was the object of admiration, both of angels and men.... It was not for nothing that Almighty God had permitted the Pope to pass the years of Peter. Although they knew not the exact moment, the time would certainly come when those who now appeared to be doing the Devil's work would be trodden under-foot – when they had done their work of clearing away the dross of the Church....[1]

Not until this vision was proposed did the Queen get a mention.

Protestants despised a loyalty which, it seemed, only Jesuitry could call forth. For them, affection for the throne was expressed by cheers, not footnotes. Catholics, it was clear, took too much pleasure in trivial differences. Denbigh, for instance, 'could not see why a person could not be a good Catholic without losing half his English nature'.[2] Without realising it, he had answered his own question. He could not see how foreign to the English mind was all his talk of angels and Devil's work. That, more than anything, *was* the mark of Catholic distinctiveness: a failure to understand how self-defeating were protestations of a loyalty which ought never to have been in doubt.

In an obvious sense, though, Denbigh was right. It was otiose to imagine that Catholics were somehow less than English. On the contrary, they seemed to overdo their conformism. The debate about Catholic representation at Oxford and Cambridge is an example.[3] So, too, the ethos of the Catholic public school. How different from Eton and Rugby were Ampleforth and Stonyhurst? Was Latin verse the better construed for its being done *ad majorem Dei gloriam*? Was Benediction any less a chore than Evensong? As a manual of all things English, there were pages of the *Downside Review* which were beyond parody:

> An English school without cricket is an anomaly that we trust has never yet been attempted. A thoroughly national sport, it not only enters into the national life but is an important factor in the formation of national character. To face without flinching a persistent bombardment at twenty-two yards, implies pluck, a cheerful acquiesence in a long course of leather-hunting ... develops dogged determination and perseverance; the military obedience to the captain, the ready acceptance of the umpire's decision, the emulation, and, we may add, the nascent consciousness of personal superiority, all contribute to the building up of a true Briton.[4]

The *Downside Review*'s evocation of manly summer days, like Denbigh's weird cosmology, was mere device, but both had a purpose: the one to loosen the pockets of nostalgic Old Boys, the other to give heart to a community under attack as it had not been for some time. Denbigh's words, spoken in the autumn, were a response to a strong resurgence of anti-Catholic feeling which had been sparked by the most dramatic Catholic event of the year: the conversion of Lord Ripon.

Ripon was received into the Church in September 1874. In the lists of Victorian sensations, this ranks honourably high: less melodramatic than Jack the Ripper, less beloved of the music-halls than the Tichborne claimant, less lewd than Sir Charles Dilke's commodious bed, but still a worthy portrait in the hall of scandalised Victorian smugness. Editorials were devoted to it, conversations on trains dominated by it,[5] letters to friends full of it, entries in commonplace books shocked by it. It was, as Gladstone noted, a 'very startling intelligence'.[6] Opponents of Popery needed no more striking illustration of its advances in England than the fact that the son of a Prime Minister – a man, indeed, born at No. 10 – had embraced the Scarlet Woman. Arthur Helps, long one of Ripon's most trusted advisers, captured the mood of delicious shock. Thus to Disraeli:

> Were you not astounded at Ripon's 'version'? I use the word advisedly. *Convert* is too flattering: *pervert* too condemnatory: *vert* is the proper word, especially for statesmen and official men, who delight in compromises and ambiguous sayings. Not that you do; but our clan does generally.[7]

Helps' astonishment was shared by the rest of the political world, and was anticipated by Ripon himself, who had written almost tearfully to former colleagues telling them of the painful outcome of a *crise de conscience* of whose existence they had not, until then, been aware. Their replies were models of decent embarrassment. Only Granville managed to imply, even then with impatience which soon passed, that Ripon's conversion could have been prevented by sensible precautions. 'I have recd. the news with some surprise, as I did not know you were inclined towards Roman Catholicism, and have never for a moment felt able to believe in its doctrines.'[8] Kimberley, too, regretted being 'so widely separated from an old friend' in matters of religion; 'but disapproval or blame do not enter my thoughts'.[9] Lord Aberdare, the former H. A. Bruce, was more expansive. Equally repressing an urge to sit in judgment, he did his best to offer comfort:

> I do not pretend [that your conversion] did not cause me a sharp pang & that it will not long continue to be a subject of grief to me. But I have learned during life a lesson of profound humility with respect to the convictions of others. Especially in matters of religious faith do I shrink from assuming that my opinions ... are the only right ones ... [10]

Others were less hesitant, but Aberdare's tolerance, so different from Gladstone's bruised indignation, repays examination. Ripon's 'perversion' has often been seen as an episode of outraged Victorian Protestantism. This is misleading. Aberdare's caution was ambivalent in a way that Gladstone's bluster was not; a good example, in fact, of the lapidary compromises, the 'ambiguous sayings', of his profession. Why feel grief over matters avowedly open to disagreement? This was untroubled latitudinarianism: beyond the humility lay boredom, beyond the diffidence, indifference. Here indeed was the problem: why abandon a political career, Aberdare seemed to imply, merely at the promptings of a mistaken religious conscience? Granville and Kimberley likewise regretted less Ripon's decision – Catholicism, after all, left them cold – than his transformation from pragmatist to idealist. Granville was especially insouciant, having grasped nothing of the real nature of Ripon's turmoil:

> In many ways it must be a wrench for you – and you make some personal, social and political sacrifices.[11]

Here was the off-the-cuff reaction of one who had never given such matters a moment's thought. Like Lord Halifax, who regretted that Ripon had taken 'a step which must impair the usefulness of your public career',[12] the primary sorrow was for a talent wasted, not a soul doomed.

It is too simple, therefore, to imagine that Ripon offended the religious sensibilities of political contemporaries. On the contrary, his only eccentricity was to take religion too seriously, forgetting Lord Melbourne's phlegmatic view that it should not be allowed to invade the sphere of private life. We do well to remember – never more than when considering the fanciful reaction of Catholics to the conversion – a passage in the *Personal and Literary Letters* of Lady Betty Balfour. Lord Lytton, writing to her in 1874 of an encounter with Sir William Harcourt, was

> impressed with the cynical light-heartedness revealed in the conversations of those whom he had hitherto looked upon as serious politicians. The time previous to the meeting was spent ridiculing the fine things they intended to utter from the platform, after the meeting in laughing still more heartily at the fine things they *had* uttered.

Lytton helpfully records where this encounter took place: 'at Lord Ripon's'.[13]

It would hardly do to convict Ripon of frivolity. His reputation for earnestness, for a Victorian high seriousness, is well established and wafts from the pages of his two biographers[14] like the scent of strong carbolic soap. But Lytton glimpsed a world in which public opinion, a troublesome paymaster, had endlessly to be flattered. Halifax's regret – like Granville's, Kimberley's and Aberdare's – was that Ripon could no longer bring himself to flatter it. Regret, and perhaps a momentary fear: any fall from grace was a reminder that they, too, might offend, in ways unknown, that excitable but exigent audience.

No such considerations seemed to weigh with Gladstone: for him, Ripon's offence was real, not notional. He had accepted the moral and intellectual serfdom of Rome. Thus it was a matter of relief that his public career had come to an end. The two men exchanged letters still painful to read: Ripon, all anguished simplicity, Gladstone unrelentingly logical in pursuit of his quarry. He, indeed, had the better of the argument, but only by being clinical where others would have been compassionate. Still, his logicality was never redundant when there were Denbighs around to propose the principle of Church and State, 'the Church coming first'. To such priorities there could only be one reply, and the *Times* provided it:

A statesman who becomes a convert to Roman Catholicism forfeits at once the confidence of the English people. Such a move involves a complete abandonment of any claim to political or even social influence in the nation at large, and can only be regarded as betraying an irreparable weakness of character. To become a Roman Catholic and remain a thorough Englishman are – it cannot be disguised – almost incompatible conditions.[15]

Ripon – whose inclincation was to keep out of the public prints on the matter – had an answer for such fits of spleen. He simply denied it. He wrote thus to Gladstone after the latter's *Political Expostulation*, which had argued the same line:

I utterly deny that by becoming a Catholic I have become one whit less loyal or dutiful as a subject of the Queen, & I have served Her Majesty too long and am too grateful for her many acts of gracious consideration for me to allow you, who are my political chief & who were so recently the head of a Cabinet of which I was a member, to say or imply without protest from me that I have done

or am likely ever to do anything inconsistent with perfect loyalty
and duty to her.[16]

Gladstone demurred:

> I hold by my words ... By 'Rome' ... I meant to mark out what
> Dante, 550 years ago, blasted in his immortal and priceless poem,
> the Roman or Popish element in the Western Church: much more
> virulent now than in his time, since the convulsions of the 16th
> century unhappily brought into being the order of the Jesuits. You
> are bound to obey whatever the Pope enjoins, under the name of
> moral duty, even if it be, according to your judgment and mine, in
> the domain of civil loyalty....[17]

Gladstone refused to yield his notion of Catholics as dangerous
subversives, Ripon his of men honourably untroubled in the service
of two masters. Neither made any sense to the other. Such is to be
expected when a bad argument is made well and a good one made
badly.

There the matter deserved to rest, but Gladstone's disagreement
with Ripon was a public, not a private matter. *The Vatican Decrees and
their Bearing on Civil Allegiance* and, later, *Vaticanism* became hugely
popular and were distasteful in the extreme to English and Irish
Catholics. In Ripon's case the distaste was accompanied by bewilder-
ment. Why, he wondered, had his 'old chief' gone to such lengths to
hold him up 'to the distrust and contempt' of his fellow countrymen?[18] It was a good question, for the works seemed disproportionate to their task: the conversion, *sub specie aeternitatis*, was a
small nut, the response, a heavy sledgehammer. In truth, Ripon was
unfortunate in his timing: Gladstone, released from the silence
imposed by office, could expose to the world his long-held belief in a
Jesuit conspiracy; Ripon, the wrong man in the wrong place, got six
years' anger in six weeks.

The anger was great. Even Gladstone's Catholic advisers were
astonished by the ferocity of the attack. Acton was aghast, though
nobody had advanced himself better than he (except perhaps Odo
Russell) by confirming Gladstone's prejudices about Popery. Suddenly, Acton found his own arguments used against him. The
'tremendous No Popery cry'[19] which, he had warned Gladstone,
would be the result of Infallibility was being instigated *by* Gladstone.
This in a way was poetic justice. Acton had been a sparring partner

for Gladstone on Catholic affairs. It is difficult to sympathise with one so incompetent as to get himself knocked out.

The same applies to others. The writer Ambrose de Lisle, a second-division Acton, had also made a career out of telling Gladstone what he liked to hear about Catholics. (He had written to him, at the height of his disillusion with his Irish followers, of the 'Machiavellian' plans of 'our Catholic MPs to ditch the Liberals in favour of the Tories' – 'a horrible disgrace';[20] he had even helped in the preparation of the Ritualism tract.) De Lisle realised too late the dangers both to Catholic and Liberal interests of Gladstone's outburst. As he wrote to Bishop Vaughan:

> The results may be serious to us, and for himself it puts him (I should say) in a false position, as a sort of unwilling leader of the No Popery Party. I should think too it would hopelessly damage any chance of a return to office.[21]

This was unrealistic. The idea was common, particularly among Liberal Catholics, that Gladstone's anti-Popery stemmed from his own Catholicism. He was Catholic, the argument went, but not Roman. Thus his reluctance to lead a 'No Popery' party. Nothing could have been further from the truth, indeed self-evidently contradictory. Gladstone's only reluctance was personal, that an unpleasant subject had recurred. (The religious turmoils of others – Manning's and Ripon's most obviously – he understood largely in terms of the 'pain, sometimes [the] agony'[22] that their decisions had inflicted on *him*.) Otherwise, he knew exactly the political conse-quence of his action, and anticipated it with relish. De Lisle's premise – that Gladstone had blundered into anti-Popery – was as false as his conclusion – that this position guaranteed perpetual opposition. Gladstone saw it differently. Thus to Granville:

> Suffice it to say that I have thought as well as I could about the party, to which I am sanguine enough to think that it might be rather beneficial than otherwise. We have had since the Irish measures were completed, no hold whatever on the RCs, except a handful.[23]

Granville, too, recognised party advantage:

> As a party question, it will of course set the whole of the Catholics

against us (including Ripon, of whose openness to reason on religious questions, I have given up all hope). Acton's friends are a mere handful. He could never raise the number of subscribers to the *Home and Foreign* beyond a thousand. On the other hand I have no doubt your pamphlet will give great pleasure to a large majority of the country.[24]

Gladstone's pose of spiritual anguish was therefore only half the story. The other half was that the 'great pleasure' of millions held more votes than the cries of a few thousand. Granville, it is true, ritually condemned 'the monstrous assumptions of the present papacy',[25] but that phrase had been battered to death through years of over-use. More important was Irish ingratitude, English Protestant impatience, and the political *naiveté* of English Catholics, of which de Lisle's analysis was another example. For Granville, the 'sensation' was a political stunt, not a moral crusade. This was because he kept his religion and his politics separate; precisely what 'poor Ripon' had failed to do.

The same was not true for Gladstone, whose anguish at Ripon's 'perversion' was genuine, though puffed up for political ends. His reaction exhibited not hypocrisy, but extreme sanctimony. Such is apparent from the welter of rationalisations, some of them contradictory, which accompanied his central justification for *The Vatican Decrees*, the belief that 'the effect on the Liberal Party ... [would] be good'.[26] Thus at one moment he claimed to be writing for the good of Catholics, to encourage 'discussion' among them;[27] the next, to teach them a lesson, by putting 'a spoke in their wheel' or by setting 'people like Ripon a little on their guard for the future'.[28] The reasoning, sometimes emollient, sometimes offensive, may suggest that zeal for religion got in the way of competence for politics, whereas Granville (so the contrast might go) was sufficiently indifferent to soul-craft to remain level-headed.

This is mistaken. Gladstone calculated the odds perfectly well. 'No RC vote is to be had except for a price';[29] 'for each RC vote gained we lose several Protestants':[30] these were not the considerations of plain piety. Moreover, Gladstone's political instincts were sound in a way that Granville's were not. He gave the public what it wanted because he wanted it himself. Who has ever heard of 'the people's Granville'? In the same way as 1874 anticipated the fully-fledged Gladstonian populism of 1876 and 1879 on the Eastern Question and 'Beaconsfieldism' respectively, so can it be said that it was precisely

Granville's refusal to get worked up about theology which deadened his political sense. He hoped, for example, that were Gladstone to write another anti-papal tract, it should be bland:

> I should make it as short as possible, & ... get some [one] like Acton to mark unmercifully anything that would touch the corns of the Catholics.[31]

There were times for caution and this was not one of them. It was absurd to envisage a 'No Popery' cry designed to please everybody, the Papists included. By this stage, corns were beyond pain; the jugular had been gashed.

The consequences were curious. Patronage, for example, became scarce. Witness a passage in a letter of Ambrose de Lisle to Newman, revealing how Catholic preferment depended on subtle changes of public mood. Noticing how low the Catholic star had fallen, de Lisle remarked that one light had been Newman's reply to Gladstone[32] – and even that might have been dimmed by contributions from their own side:

> I believe 'the vacant Thistle' never would have been given to Lord Bute but for your noble reply to Mr. Gladstone. He (Ld. B) said the other day to my daughter Margaret that he quite dreaded [Manning's] pamphlet (before it appeared) lest it should mar the enormous effect produced by your own ...[33]

It is salutary to recall a world in which vacant Thistles, and the knighthoods of a few Catholic worthies, depended on public understanding of scriptural exegesis.

Bute's anxiety about advancement was significant because by it he recognised that 'No Popery' cries were only worth talking about as public spectacles. No one expected that minds would be changed by the arguments; but there was a dramaturgy which both sides understood, perhaps enjoyed. Even the theologically sophisticated relished the theatricality of a debate as joust. 'I wish I could live to see,' wrote one of Newman's friends, 'a fight between Church and State represented by Manning as Pope and Gladstone as English Prime Minister.'[34] Denbigh, more fatuously, emptied the argument of meaning by regarding it as a private performance for his own benefit:

It is quite amusing to see the impotent and ignorant rage of the organs of world, and is additional proof, if proof were needed, of the rectitude of ... [Ripon's] step.[35]

This was a characteristic response to *l'affaire Ripon*. Catholics were determined, come what may, to make the best of a good catch – 'rising statesman, a nobleman of the first rank, a gentleman of wide popularity',[36] as *The Tablet* described him. *The Tablet* missed the point. Unlike Denbigh, who was at least conscious of the ignorant rage of the world, it welcomed 'with feelings of joy' this 'distinguished accession to the ranks of the Catholic Church ... because it cannot fail to mark some further diminution of anti-Catholic prejudice...'.[37] A comparison with Milton is irresistible. Consider the drunkards of *Comus*, unaware of how they appear to the rest of humanity, and English Catholics after Gladstone had finished with them:

And they, so perfect is their misery
Not once perceive their foul disfigurement
But boast themselves more comely than before.

This distorted vision of comeliness led Catholics to believe – *pace* the man himself – that Ripon's career was not over. On the contrary, they rejoiced at the prospect of having one of their own at the political centre, the better to prove a civic worthiness which, ironically, had only been rendered doubtful by the very extravagance of their pleasure. The anger of Protestant England was to many of them nugatory. Writing before the storm had fully burst, Lady Anabel Ker conceded that a Catholic in politics might experience difficulties, but her reasoning was innocent:

I do believe that Catholics of Liberal opinions (I use the word entirely politically) have uphill work nowadays, and the great cause for the uphillness is the favour they are looked on with by Protestants, who think ... they are not altogether loyal to the Church.[38]

Ripon was in no danger of being killed by kindness. Lady Anabel nonetheless wished to see him remain a statesman:

My love for the Church prompts me to wish that the *reason* of your public life should be that you are a Catholic, that every public word or action on never mind what subject should be prompted by the desire to forward the interests of the Church and not as might be the case with some men in your place, by the desire to maintain as much as possible of their old position in spite of being a Catholic.[39]

Let this be the text by which to examine Ripon's career as a Catholic in politics.

RIPON'S EARLY CAREER

What was the public life whose end was confidently presumed in 1874?[40] Ripon was born in 1827 during the brief premiership of his father, Viscount Goderich. He was a solitary child, educated private-ly, almost autodidactically. Possibly from formidably wide reading, or *noblesse oblige*, or priggishness, his earliest political excursions were radical. In the winter of 1851–2 he supported, with proper Christian-Socialist conviction, the Amalgamated Society of Engin-eers in their dispute with their employers. His views on education were also advanced; too much so even for F. D. Maurice.

Goderich entered Parliament in July 1852 for Hull, second in the poll. He won 2258 votes.[41] This owed nothing to his family (they had no wish to subsidise his bland form of Chartism) and too much to J. J. Bezer, his election agent and publisher of the *Christian Socialist*. Bezer had been excessively generous with electoral favours, and as a result Goderich was unseated for corruption in March 1853.

This setback was short-lived. He was returned for Huddersfield – vacant because of another unseating – in April 1853, after a campaign in which, according to a recent biographer, he had given a 'crucial' account of his political principles. Professor Denholm makes much of these, but most were unexceptional: commitment to 'liberal and enlightened progress'; opposition to 'taxes on the food of the people'; hope that 'all classes ... may go forward in steady and glorious progress'; support for 'a large extension of the franchise'; abolition of the 'unjust' privileges of the Established Church – church rates and Easter dues; belief in the gospel of self-help.[42] It is Denholm's contention that these were ideas from which Goderich never deviated for the rest of his life. This is an unusually large claim. Further examination may modify it.

Goderich's early parliamentary career followed a pattern. The Commons were treated to his views on profit-sharing, limited liability, the need to encourage 'the combination ... of skill, labour and capital', the absence of adequate trades union legislation. They listened respectfully but were not persuaded. Unabashed, he extended his range to include army and administrative reform, this latter a defining interest of advanced young politicians – Henry Bruce, Austen Henry Layard, Danby Seymour, Edward Horsman, and a few others – collectively and self-consciously known as the 'Goderichites'. He supported open examinations for the civil service. In June 1855 he seconded Layard's motion deploring the sacrifice of 'merit and efficiency ... in public appointments to party and family influence ...'. Only by recognising merit, Goderich argued, only by forsaking the 'manifold evils'[43] of jobbery, could the country be rid of that narrow class prejudice which led in the Civil Service to blind inefficiency, in the army to gross unfairness in promotions, and in politics to unthinking and vicious favouritism.

These attacks on 'the most obnoxious system of patronage' came to little but they enhanced the reputation of their author to the point where he began to be talked of as a future 'advanced-liberal Prime Minister'.[44] This was optimistic. His oratory was unspectacular: like the virtues it extolled, it was solid, efficient, workmanlike – no crime in the leader of a ginger-group which despised the flashiness of the old guard. At any rate, he began to get the feel of the House, preaching to it less, cultivating the arts of party management (even if his coterie hardly deserved the name) and discovering in the process that vested interests did not reform themselves simply because they lost the argument. He became, in short, a practical politician.

By 1859, Goderich had become Earl de Grey and a member of Palmerston's administration. He was in office for seven years: as Under Secretary for War from June 1859 to April 1863 (except for a period at the India Office) and thereafter as Secretary of State for War until February 1866, serving both Palmerston and Russell. He did not waste this opportunity to implement ideas for reform of the army. Necessarily modifying his early idealism, and inevitably failing to shift every vested interest, he nonetheless justified his historical reputation as precursor of the Cardwell reforms of Gladstone's first ministry. He promoted improvements in army education; attempted to restructure the War Office itself; encouraged the formation of a volunteer army. (This last was a particular dream of advanced liberals, who had hopes of civilising the working classes by putting them into uniforms.) In all these endeavours de Grey showed his qualities: administrative ability, political skill, common sense, awareness of the possible; idealism tempered by office but not tarnished.

These credentials suited him to be a member of Gladstone's great reforming ministry. He was Lord President of the Council from 1868 until his resignation in 1873. In Gladstone he found a hero: one whose politics combined moral commitment and administrative intelligence. Gladstone, for his part, recognised in Ripon (as de Grey became in 1871) a fellow soul. He was firm in his support of Irish Disestablishment, which appealed to every facet of his political personality: his Christian-Socialist sense of justice, his administrator's sense of efficiency, and his Whig sense of reform in installments or, in this case, at a distance. Indeed, it has been argued that Ripon's support for Irish disestablishment was greater than Gladstone's, for he persuaded the Prime Minister not to abandon the Bill in the face of hostile amendment from the Lords.[45]

Other measures followed. Ripon was instrumental in persuading the Lords to approve the secret ballot in parliamentary and municipal elections. After the experience of Hull he could speak authoritatively about the 'illegitimate influence' of employer or landlord which could corrupt 'honest, high-minded men'.[46] His outstanding contribution to the ministry was, however, in education, notably in the preparation of Forster's Act of 1870, but also in the passage of the Endowed Schools Act of the previous year. His political intimacy with Forster was striking: together they persuaded Gladstone out of his preoccupation with Irish land reform to take their schemes seriously. Certainly their plans were ambitious – they wanted a system by which 'the means of elementary education may reach every home, and be brought within the reach of every child in the country'. They were also adventurous, for elementary education was a defining interest of every sectarian group in the country. Ripon's ideas are therefore of particular significance for the future.

The details of the 1870 Act are well known. It established a system of districts under the auspices of a Board of Education inspectorate; it afforded financial assistance from public funds for those existing voluntary schools which agreed to inspection and to a conscience clause; children not of the faith of the denominational school could withdraw from sectarian religious instruction; local school boards were to provide schools on the rates, with each board empowered to choose its own form of religious instruction; boards were empowered, if they so decided, to make attendance compulsory between the ages of five and thirteen. The Act thus provided for a two-way system of elementary education: rate-financed board schools teaching the Bible; publicly funded but privately managed voluntary schools which were clearly denominational. The compromise was obvious: complete secularism along the lines of the Birmingham League was no more acceptable than out-and-out voluntaryism. But it was a compromise which appealed to Ripon. He believed strongly in the principles that informed the Act; it will be interesting to see his position when he himself became the spokesman of a sectional interest.

Ripon had one final achievement which should be noted, not least because it earned him his Marquisate in 1871. He negotiated the Treaty of Washington (1871) which, *inter alia*, settled the *Alabama* case. It was, Professor Denholm says, his finest hour; this notwithstanding the collapse of the original agreement, the isolation of its author in the Cabinet, the humiliation he suffered when he presented it to Parliament. Denholm does his best to talk it up, but his peroration has a feeble ring:

> The whole story of the negotiations revealed de Grey's ability to see the other side's point of view, and to resolve differences by discussion and compromise.... These are the hallmarks of a 'liberal' attitude ... [47]

Such was the career ruined by Rome.

RIPON'S RETREAT FROM POLITICS

Ripon returned in 1874 to an obscurity the more marked for the extravagant belief of Catholics that they had found in him a new political leader. For them, if for no-one else, conversion worked wonders for a political reputation: a man could become a hero on Monday who had not been heard of on Sunday. When the *Tablet* saw in Ripon the Catholic a statesman 'of the first rank'[48] it did well to forget its earlier description of de Grey the Protestant as 'modest and sensible enough not to exaggerate his own powers', a man with no 'particular aptitude'[49] for high office. When Bishop Vaughan wrote of him as if he were a secret weapon (a new discovery to be held back 'for a year or two'[50] to cause maximum surprise when eventually unveiled) he forgot his own observation that he had come from a party so steeped in secularism as to make Tory tyranny acceptable by comparison.[51] Rarely did official Catholic opinion evince a grasp of reality. A few did not share the optimism but they had the better of the argument:

> If half the House of Peers submitted to the Church, England would still be far from the Catholic faith.... When we hear of a Catholic movement among the English dissenters, or when some dozen shopkeepers in London or Liverpool seek to be received at the nearest Catholic chapel, I shall begin to believe in the conversion of England. Until then, the less we pride ourselves in conversions, the better.[52]

This corrective suggests another. Professor Denholm has it that politics were the poorer for Ripon's going. It did not seem like that at the time. Colleagues regretted the departure but they did not mourn it:

> Lowe has returned in a more irritable state.... He seems dissatisfied with the colleagues ... whom he met at Osborne. 'Ripon affectionate and sentimental, Bruce exuberant in spirits. Everyone thinking of himself and of no-one else.'[53]

And outside the Cabinet, Lowe's end-of-term impatience found ready echoes:

> I had a long conversation with Delane after dinner yesterday [about the Government changes].... He thought Ripon no loss ...[54]

This which may explain the especial ferocity of the *Times* a few months later, Delane being its thunderous editor.

There was a real sense in which Delane was right. What loss was Ripon to a party which contained the Gladstone of *Vaticanism*, and William Harcourt who 'hate[d] the Pope, as Nelson did a Frenchman, like the Devil'?[55] It was a party which included MPs who preferred 'the ordinary Englishman' to 'the Tories and Papists and Publicans',[56] and supporters who detested 'in the Ritualists ... their false doctrines and their symbols of Popery'.[57] What place had he among the 'able, temperate, rational Protestant leaders' that one MP hoped to follow?[58]

Ripon's retreat from politics seems an act of common-sense. The years between resignation and rehabilitation are therefore crucial in understanding his return. They require more investigation than his biographers give them. It is not enough to say that he 'contented himself ... with travel abroad, the domestic pleasures of Nocton and Studley Royal, and the study of religion and politics'[59] as if, like *Adam Bede*, his life has chapters 'in which the story pauses a little'. The interval was four years 'of quiet contemplation and study', when he 'painstakingly' concluded that 'in spite of the *Syllabus Errorum* and the Vatican Council, there was no conflict between [his new religion] and his old political beliefs'.[60] In fact, the retreat was not so complete as it appears, the resumption not so firmly based upon first principles. Ripon's sabbatical was spent in the discovery that, Catholic or not, his reflexes were still those of a Liberal politician. His painstaking conclusion owed little to enlightened speculation: Ripon was no Acton.

How was this made manifest? Among his new Catholic friends Ripon found it difficult to abjure the habits of a lifetime, so that even social occasions were placed in a political context. 'Dined at the Oratory,' he told his diary; 'found the Fathers very Tory.'[61] Many Catholics were, indeed, very Tory. Ripon, when he converted, gained a new circle, and its members – Denbigh, Norfolk and their like – took their politics from a different source. He had to treat carefully. This presented difficulties. Ripon was expected to pay a full role in Catholic public affairs, to become part of the fabric of a Catholic establishment. He was not prepared to do this. Only Norfolk could afford to support every imaginable Catholic enterprise: Catholic book-clubs, working-men's colleges, trades unions, even Catholic banks.[62]

Such was the small-change of public life; a more serious encounter came in 1876, with the Eastern Question. Denbigh summarised neatly the political services expected of Ripon by his coreligionists:

> My dear Ripon, Will you join the Committee in aid of the sick and suffering soldiers in the Turkish field Hospitals ... I had a talk with the Cardinal about our support of the Turks in their opposition to the Russian aggression and he feels that on Catholic grounds we ought to do all we can to oppose the insidious advances of Russia towards Constantinople, where, if she was once established, the same treatment of the Oriental Christians would take place as the poor Poles have experienced....[63]

This captured the four essential elements of the Catholic reaction to the question of the East:[64] sympathise as they might with the agonies of the Bulgarians, the first duty of Catholics was to co-religionists in the Ottoman Empire; despite its claims as protector of persecuted peoples, Russia was no friend to the Church in the East, as its supression of the Polish revolt (1863) showed; third, a reputation for butchery notwithstanding, the Turks had acted within their rights, for (in the unlovely formula of the *Westminster Gazette*) 'sharp government is necessary for Eastern races – these things must not be gauged by Western tests';[65] finally, Bulgarians had only themselves to blame, because it was they who had started all the 'burnings, butcheries, ravagings and other abominations'.[66]

Behind this strong feeling lay an *eminence grise* – Manning – and behind him, the Pope. English Catholics responded to the Eastern Question by following a line dictated to them by the Vatican, which had been hostile to Russia since well before 1863. Gladstone complained that 'the Turk ... has two special allies, the Pope and the English Government'. He also maintained that the Pope's 'wretchedly false position' was the work of the Curia which had 'betrayed him and with him the Roman Church'.[67] This view rested upon two false assumptions: that the Pope was open to persuasion, and that Manning was the most likely persuader. When Ambrose de Lisle, acting for Gladstone, asked Manning to soften the Vatican line, he received a peremptory reply:

> I am not aware of any position 'wretched' or otherwise taken up by the Pope. It is clear to me as day that to light a fire against atrocities is the way to make smoke.[68]

Manning's second sentence was as important as his first: Catholics objected as much to the form of the anti-Turkish agitation as to its substance. Mass demonstrations, huge petitions, populist pamphleteering (of unhappy memory in Ripon's own case) seemed to them inflammatory. They had no desire to have a fit of someone else's morality. To do the Liberal Party's work for it was to them unpalatable. Catholics owed Gladstone no debt.

It has been argued that the Eastern Question represented 'another step in the long struggle for the soul of the Catholic Church in Britain',[69] a grandiloquent way of saying that it made Catholics into Tories. This is procrustean. To say that the Eastern Question deepened a relationship with the Tories which 'had been apparent for about a decade' is to injure the facts. Apparent since 1866? Since 1868? Surely not. The point about Catholic political relationships was their precariousness, as Gladstone and Disraeli had cause to know. It is therefore unhelpful to talk of 'trends' which take a decade, even two, to work themselves out; to say nothing of a 'process' which was 'speeded up' by the Bulgarian atrocities. This makes little sense. Consider the conclusion it generates:

> This process [of Catholic Toryism] culminated in the naming of Henry Matthews as the first Catholic member of Salisbury's Conservative cabinet. This trend had predated the Eastern question, but that emotional issue speeded up the process.[70]

Any trend which culminates in Henry Matthews is a trend not worth talking about. Those who know anything about that confused appointment[71] will not recognise in it the final enactment of a 'process', least of all one which began about 1866. The Eastern Question, it is fair to say, reveals Catholics in a Tory mood, but should not be made to bear every burden of interpretation placed upon it.

Where stood Ripon? Denbigh's request was not welcome. Articulating a specifically Catholic line made him uneasy:

> I cannot, I am sorry to say, comply with your request ... I am heartily anxious that Russia should not get Constantinople, but I have no sympathy with the Turks (except such as one must feel for any sick or suffering fellow creature) and I cannot do anything that would involve direct or indirect support of them.[72]

Ripon's first instinct was thus to avoid contact with his new political family. This he justified on grounds of tactics, but he had no wish to be associated with any kind of theodician politics. His impatience with Catholic unsophistication was hard to conceal:

> I have thought it right to keep myself clear of both sides in this hot controversy so as to preserve the power of unfettered action in Parliament.... It seems to me very important not to give the Turkish govt. the slightest reason to suppose that if they refuse to accept the joint proposals of the great powers they will have the support of this country.

The moment is very critical; Lord Beaconsfield's speeches (forgive me for saying so) have done great mischief ...[73]

Ripon wanted nothing to do with exclusively Catholic pressure-groups. He wished to be unfettered – a suggestive metaphor – to attack Beaconsfieldism as he saw fit. It is hard to credit the argument[74] that his refusal to become involved reflected a desire not to do Gladstone's dirty work for him; harder still to understand that it has been made on the basis of this letter.[75] On the contrary, however much he may have resented Gladstone's anti-Turkish tracts, Ripon saw no reason why they should make him a Tory. His silence was an attempt to suggest the same to his voluble co-religionists.

The Eastern Question was not the only occasion when Ripon found himself at odds with English Catholics. One of the unhappier consequences of conversion was the political companionship of Lord Robert Montagu. Denbigh's demands were polite and naive: Montagu's were preposterous. He was, in all probability, unbalanced.[76] Montagu's chief activity of 1876 was to lead a campaign to secure a greater support for Catholic elementary schools. This involved proposing two amendments in committee to the Sandon Education Bill. According to Professor Denholm, 'Ripon took a prominent part in the education controversy in 1876 on behalf of Catholic schools',[77] the one occasion in his four year sabbatical that he returned to the political fray.

This is to simplify. It wrongly assumes an undifferentiated Catholic response to the question of schools. In fact, the point of Ripon's intervention was to educate Catholics to a more sophisticated reading of contemporary politics. This was a matter of tactics – telling them when to propose an amendment, when not – but tactics also implied an need for political self-knowledge. As he wrote to Manning:

I cannot think that Lord R. Montagu's motion is well timed. Both its wording and the time which it is to be moved (on the second reading of Lord Sandon's Bill) give it the character of a censure on that measure. The Government must therefore necessarily oppose it; it will undoubtedly be also opposed by the whole body of the opposition & the result will be a very large majority against it, which may be understood in the country as if it were a majority against religious education, or at least may be used in that sense by the Secularists.[78]

He hoped to suggest that the tactic was wrong because the strategy was wrong, being founded on the false premise that the Education Act of 1870 could be improved.[79] If Catholics demanded too much, he assured the Cardinal,

> the only result would be a speedy reaction, the swing of which would overthrow not only any such temporary gains but the social advantages we now possess.[80]

Montagu forgot – if he ever knew – the danger of Catholics pushing their luck. And Ripon went further: he showed how unfriendly was the world in which they had to move. The denominational dynamic of Liberal politics derived from the tension between two sections of the party, both quite indifferent to Catholic claims:

> ... the left wing, who are in favour of undenomintional ... or ... secular education & the right wing, who, with Forster, uphold the present grants to Denominational schools & respect for the free choice of parents. In this state of things, it is our policy to keep these two sections *apart* & never ... to make them vote together.[81]

Montagu's motion threatened just that.

Ripon's cleverness was to establish the pitfalls of Liberal politics, then demonstrate how Liberals were nonetheless the Catholics' best friends. In this he acted (though he pretended otherwise) as a Liberal partisan, seeming to take the Catholic side against the party. Letting Catholics think they could exploit Liberal divisions had the paradoxical effect not of increasing their threat to the party but of neutralising it:

> So long as we take our stand on the Act of '70, as a *fait accompli*, and claim that it shall always be impartially administered as between Denominational and Board Schools, we shall have a hold on the members of the late Government, which it will be very difficult for them to shake off; we have Forster with us by conviction and we have an *argumentum ad hominem* against his less favourably disposed colleagues which they will not find easy to answer. Abandon this ground and your hold is gone. The nonconformist

pressure, which is always difficult for the Liberal leaders to resist, has full sway, and it will be hard even for Forster to stand up against it.[82]

It was skilful of him to bind his co-religionists to the party by pretending to distance himself from it. He was less adviser to Catholics than anaesthetist.

Ripon was consistently cleverer than Catholics who tried to coax him into their schemes. Consider the skill of his refusal when, in 1877, Lord Petre asked him to chair a Registration Committee of the Catholic Union – the perennial object being to get more Catholics to vote. Having no wish to be associated with a sectional interest, Ripon managed all the same to imply that there were good Catholic reasons for his non-involvement. Was it not a principle of the Catholic Union, he argued, to have 'nothing to do with party politics, and that consequently the new Registration Committee [should] be absolutely cut off from all connexion with them'?

> What then could be more strange [than] to select as Chairman of that Committee a decided Party man, intimately connected with the leaders of the Opposition, sitting on the opposition front bench in the House of Lords and likely at any moment to make a strong party speech or to give a distinctly party vote?[83]

Ripon could not object to the *principle* of Catholic registration; but even there he foresaw dangers. Was the intention to register Irish Catholics, for instance? That would merely help the Home Rulers, who were no friends to English Catholicism:

> If I were to appear as the head of the Registration Committee, it is not reasonable to expect that the Tories would resist the temptation, after an election in which the Home Rulers had made themselves troublesome and unpopular, of attacking me for the sake of getting at my political friends, and of charging us with all sorts of intrigues with the Home Rule Party.[84]

Of all people this sounded most like Gladstone who, it will be remembered, had a whole armoury of devices to 'keep the RCs in order', one of them the hint that though they might not get all that they wanted from him, the alternative was considerably worse.[85] Ripon likewise kept Catholics quiet by hinting that his caution was better than their zeal. He wanted to do more, in fact, than ensure that Catholics understood the consequences of their actions. He wanted also to lessen their political embarrassment to him. When warning of the difficulties of Registration, he implied that his embarrassment was theirs also:

> If I were Chairman of the new Committee it would be almost certain that, at the next General Election my political friends would come to me and say, 'You are head, we hear, of a Catholic Registration Society; what can you do for us?' I should, of course, refuse to do anything, but I should be placed in a position of no little difficulty, and surrounded, you may be sure, by suspicions of every side.[86]

Here was an astute prophecy of future electoral behaviour, but for the moment it is enough to note how Ripon had avoided Petre's clutches: suggesting that *he* was the potential political embarrassment, not they; implying that the greater the stridency of English Catholicism, the greater the likelihood it would be adversely confused with the Irish version; hinting that if he kept a safe distance from Catholic organisations, they, in turn, would be protected from the vote-hunger of Liberals; arguing, in short, that with Tory cynicism on one side, Irish radicalism on the other, and Liberal opportunism on a third, it was best to leave politics to the politicians. To let, in other words, Ripon do what he liked.

Thus did he use his sabbatical. Far from four years of inertness he was still acutely political in his responses, still distinctively Liberal in his sympathies. More than that, he gave the first indications of a political relationship with Catholics which was subtle, shifting and fraught with significance for both the Catholic world and the Liberal.

RIPON'S RETURN TO POLITICS

In 1878 Ripon returned to the inner circle of Liberal Party leaders, largely because he shared their anger at Disraeli's conduct of foreign policy. The war in Afghanistan renewed his conviction that Beaconsfieldism was profoundly immoral: not simply cynical, but pagan to its very core. Only Gladstone, of his former colleagues, got so worked up about it. The others – Hartington, Forster, Aberdare – agreed, but without the same depth of feeling; the reason, Denholm argues, why Ripon grew steadily disillusioned with Hartington's leadership and actively supported Gladstone for the premiership in 1880. There was more to it than that,[87] but Afghanistan did offer him the opportunity, gratefully accepted, to return to the centre of affairs. 'I am inclining more and more to the opinion,' he told Forster, 'that the time has come for bold action ... It is most gratifying to me to feel that we shall fight side by side'.[88]

By this he did not mean a return to office. Though he thought opposition to Disraeli's foreign policy would ensure a 'real and reliable' election victory, he specifically ruled out (as late as December 1878) 'any chance of a return to office' on his own part.[89] Did this self-exclusion reflect altruism? Professor Denholm thinks so:

> In an age threatened increasingly by the disruptive forces of nationalism, imperialism and Marxism, he sought to restate an old truth for himself, that men of all conditions could be brought together in the love of Christ through his Universal Church.[90]

This is uncritical. So, too, is the view that Ripon's attitude towards the O'Conor Don's Irish University Bill (1879) was 'but another example of [his] conviction that political decisions should be based upon morality, not expediency'.[91] Let us examine this. Does Ripon require the services of a hagiographer? That decisions should be based on morality does not itself amount to very much: many believe likewise but stress that the word 'should' gives, as it were, a casting vote in favour of expediency. Denholm's own example makes it plain that Ripon thought so. Consider his account of a meeting of the Liberal leadership on the issue of the O'Conor Don's Bill. He noticed that 'everyone in the room, except Hartington and possibly Granville, were in favour of the Bill on its merits; but the question of right and wrong was pushed aside, and the lower ground examined'.[92] Five days later, he recorded a meeting with Forster. 'He is,' he wrote, 'in favour of the University Bill, but annoyed, *as well he may be*, at the prospect of a new difference with his Non Con constituents.'[93] A month later, he described another

> long discussion on the Irish University Bill. Hartington said he should vote for the 2nd Reading – the fact was that they felt the strength and justice of the Catholic [case] but had no enthusiasm for the measure & felt the difficulties it might raise with the Non Cons – *this is natural* – but I think the action taken will be right.[94]

In other words, the conviction that decisions should be moral amounted in practice to a belief that it would be preferable if they were made for the right reasons, but that interests existed and it was acceptable for politicians to acknowledge them.

These views are significant as they relate to matters of Catholic concern. There is no evidence that Ripon's Catholicism impaired his political judgment, or that he was notably vocal in support of a Catholic measure. His own account shows this:

> Then the matter was discussed simply as a question of party tactics: were the Catholics or the Non Cons the most powerful? which of them could do the Liberal Party most harm?[95]

'What will the Non Cons say?'[96] he used to confide to a diary amply familiar with his political caution on religious matters. His co-religionists were not so circumspect, but it was a necessary question. To participate in the Liberal leadership was to understand the varieties of religious experience. If the best that Ripon could say of Hartington was that his views did not arise 'from anti-Catholic feeling', they must have seemed like that to those not in the know. The best that could be said of Harcourt was that his bark was worse than his bite. (Ripon and he got on surprisingly well,[97] in fact.) As for others, in so far as Catholicism ever touched their lives, it was to add a bizarre quality to them. Consider an episode in the life of Lord Spencer (the Red Earl) whose uncle, a convert-priest, was a member of the Order of Passionists, with the adoptive name of Father Ignatius of St Paul:

> In 1862, shortly before his death, Father Ignatius was invited to Althorp to a grand dinner for the Volunteer Corps, where he sat next to this nephew. At Spencer's insistence, and in full Passionist habit, he delivered a speech to the assembled guests.[98]

This confirmed a view of Catholicism in which its adherents were even physically different from the rest of humanity – dying monks, brutish Irish, smooth bachelor priests. (Manning's preternatural gauntness was a case in point; decisive evidence of the oddity of Romanists.) Ripon's colleagues had an impression of his religion which was a jumble of all these things; and they were only more articulate, not more enlightened, than the people they represented.

As for the enlightened classes proper, Carlyle seems typical. Witness his opinion of Manning – 'the most entirely complete representative of humbug we have in the world – Yon beggarly bag of wind'.[99] Such were the attitudes Ripon confronted. He had every reason to worry about 'what the Non Cons would say'.

Yet this world rehabilitated Ripon as if it had never spurned him. Moreover, he was not brought back because he kept quiet about religion. On the contrary, he was still a prominent Catholic: leading and receiving delegations, attending meetings, dining with priests, persuading Newman to accept the Cardinalate. Thus his expectation that, back in favour or not, he would not again hold office. Still, before that possibility could arise, an election had to be won. Ripon's role in securing victory was a model for the future.

RIPON AND ELECTION POLITICS: 1880

A notable feature of the election of 1880 was a nasty scrap between Gladstone and Lord Bury concerning the civic loyalty of Catholics. Bury was a convert and a minor member of Beaconsfield's government: double qualification for an appeal for Catholic votes. He therefore wrote to the *Tablet* reminding Catholics that Gladstone doubted their loyalty, a letter which brought immediate and indignant response. Gladstone wrote to him demanding evidence which would substantiate the claim. To this he received a reply written on the back of his first letter, promising that proof would be soon forthcoming. Gladstone refused to wait. He wrote back, informing his correspondent that 'under the circumstances' he had answered his charge 'through the columns of an evening newspaper [*The Echo*]'[100] and had asked that a copy be forwarded to him; an action, Bury thought, 'hardly in accordance with the usual courtesies of correspondence'.[101] This complaint left Gladstone cold: with the election half over, and with a 'monstrous assertion' roaming unchecked, there was little time for the usual courtesies, particularly as Catholic votes were shifting to the Tories. At any rate, *The Echo* was treated to a sterile debate, with Gladstone, in a welter of self-quotation, showing himself a firm believer in Catholic loyalty, and Bury in reply telling him not to dissemble. As Gladstone must have realised, the damage had been done by then; it had been done, indeed, some years before. All the same, the fight concentrated minds on the direction of Catholic votes, and gave the impression that both parties were prepared to cultivate those whom they had once condemned.

No mind was more concentrated than Ripon's. The election was for him a time of intense activity, which he summarised thus:

> Sunday 11 April 1880. From the last date [Thursday 18 March] till now I have been so busy chiefly in an endeavour to counteract a tendency among Catholic Liberals to leave the Party that I have not kept up this journal. This tendency appears to be the result of some intrigue, of which I have not yet got to the bottom. I have, I think, been able to do a certain amount of good, and could have done more if I had known sooner what was going on; but the affair was very secretly conducted. I think I carried Meysey Thompson's election at Knaresborough and was useful at Bath and perhaps elsewhere. G. Blount was particularly helpful and Pollen worked very hard. Since the last entry, the Conservatives have been utterly overthrown ... [102]

This intensity of feeling derived partly from heightened responsibility (he was the Liberals' best hope for Catholic votes), partly from close involvement in a small number of campaigns, especially in South Lancashire and South Wales. That he was regarded by colleagues as a channel of Catholic votes is clear:

> Wrote a letter to the *Tablet* criticising Ld. Beaconsfield's letter to the Duke of Marlborough. Called on Granville and showed it to him. He approved.[103]

Well might Granville approve. In it, Ripon gave his clearest indication that one Catholic, at least, would not 'abandon, in ungrateful forgetfulness, the party to which English and Scotch Catholics owe a long series of measures of justice and relief'.[104]

However, this bid for Catholic support had the defiance of defeat about it. For example, it provoked a reply from Bury (the one that so annoyed Gladstone) which convincingly showed how many Catholics had abandoned the Liberal Party:

> The Catholic vote turned the scale in favour of the Conservatives in Southwark. If the public prints are to be trusted, the highest authorities of the Church view the Conservative cause with no disfavour. The House of Howard, till lately Liberal, has now, with

the Duke of Norfolk at its head, become Conservative. A member of that House, the only Catholic who is contesting an English seat, Lord Edmund Talbot, fights as a Conservative. Lord Beaumont and the eldest son of Lord Petre, both Liberals, have joined the Conservative ranks. So, I am told, has Lord Mowbray and Stourton. Mr. Weld Blundell, of Ince, representative of one of the oldest Liberal families, is working for the Conservatives in Lancashire. There is every appearance that the Catholics of the Western Constituencies of the metropolis will do as Southwark has done.[105].

There was force to this head-counting which Ripon was hard-pressed to rebut. Behind the scenes he therefore spent his time not in arguing the case for historic gratitude to Liberalism but in trying to poach Catholics back from the Tories and ensuring that others did not join them. The way he did so says much about the workings of Catholic politics.

One of the recruits of which Bury boasted – Thomas Weld-Blundell – was the kind of Catholic both parties hoped to attract. The name will be familiar to chroniclers of Lancashire recusancy, and the type to students of local political influence: the Weld-Blundells dominated their territory, though on a smaller scale, as the Cecils ruled Hatfield and the Howards, Arundel. In both instances, the tenantry took their politics and their livelihood from the big family. This being so, political apostacy was a serious event. Local Liberals were worried enough to write to Ripon for advice, who replied *in extenso*.

The concern was two-fold: first, that Weld-Blundell's Toryism endangered the whole Catholic vote, both because he set trends and, presumably, reflected them; second, that he had deserted the party because he had been 'fixed' by the Tories. Monsignor John Fisher, Catholic Provost of Liverpool – all the while denying he was meddling in politics – detected Tory conspiracy:

My dear Lord Ripon, You will have seen from the *Times* that the Catholic vote of this county which with the exception of Lord Gerard's tenantry has always been with the Liberals is now given over to the Conservative Party. I confess that I am much surprised, and it seems to me there must be something in the background quite unknown to me. If it be thought best to support the present Government there must be some understanding which is hidden from me. Lord Molyneux and Mr. Rathbone are the candidates for this division of the county in the Liberal interest. Mr. Rathbone I know well and I know his father – the Catholics of L'pool never had such friends as the Rathbone family ... I am sorely afraid if the Catholic vote is given to the Conservatives, the Liberals will be last. Could anything be done with Mr. Weld Blundell ... to induce him to change ... ? I feel certain that some pressure or some promise has been made through some high quarter to induce him to think that Catholic interests are safer in the hands of Lord Beaconsfield than in those of his opponents. The Earl of Gainsborough wrote to me some time ago to support Mr. Whitley [the Tory candidate] against Lord Ramsay, which I did not do, and this circumstance leads me to suspect that there has been some intrigue.[106]

These assumptions were the commonplaces of local political management: where the tenants of a Catholic Tory voted Tory, and of a Catholic Liberal, Liberal; where it was assumed that enlisting the support of the clergy would ensure the votes of the flock; where – a particular version of the general argument – gratitude was owed to families who favoured Catholics as well as to governments who did so.

Fisher's calculations did not, unfortunately, take into account one striking fact: Weld-Blundell was in Biarritz at the time. This added a proper touch of absurdity to a paranoia about plots whose *real* purpose was to explain the inexplicable (Catholic desertion to the Tories) and to forgive the unforgivable (Liberal failure to prevent it). News of Weld-Blundell's desertion triggered general panic in Liberal ranks. Granville wrote to Ripon asking if Lancashire Liberals were 'somewhat alarmed'[107] by the Catholic defection; Ripon telegrammed Rathbone pledging his full support, and drew his attention to his letter in the *Tablet* 'which may perhaps be of some use with the Catholic voters',[108] particularly if it were to be printed and distributed separately; he also wrote 'far and wide to intimate Catholic friends of my own who might be able to help'.[109] First among these was Lord Lovat, Weld-Blundell's son-in-law, a 'great friend' of Ripon, to whom he wrote 'very fully'.[110] The prospect was thus entertained that Weld-Blundell could be enticed back to the Liberal fold solely by the workings of the Catholic network.

Ripon was sure that conspiracy was afoot. He had no doubt that Weld-Blundell's action was 'the result of some secret understanding of which he [had] been made the victim'.[111] He was less sure, precisely for that reason, how best to deal with it. Tackling the victim head-on raised the possibility of doing more harm than good; travelling to Lancashire was equally problematic, 'as being a Peer I could do nothing publicly'.[112] For the moment, the best he could suggest was that Fisher write to Weld-Blundell

> explaining to him the strong claims which Mr. Rathbone has upon Catholic support, [being one] to whose family Catholics are so much indebted ...[113]

Why Fisher? First, because of the seriousness of the matter. With extreme embellishment, Ripon argued that 'no step has been taken, since Catholic Emancipation, so fatal for Catholic interests in this country, as this unhappy defection'. There was another reason why it should have been the Monsignor: 'Such a letter coming from you who are in no way a party man ought to have great weight'.[114] This was disingenuous. Ripon contended that 'party bias' had not entered his mind. Nothing was further from the truth. He knew that no-one did the party's work better than one who could pretend to be untainted by it. Fisher recognised this too. His support of the Liberals and his scorn for Beaconsfieldism were long-standing. But being a convinced party-man did not make him a subtle tactician. On the contrary, his information to Ripon suggested, by its circularity of reasoning, one who had failed to think hard enough about electoral politics. Thus, on the one hand, his fiction of a captive tenantry –

> If he will allow his tenantry to vote as they please ... many of them would vote for Mr. Rathbone and his colleague[115]

and, on the other, his contradictory realisation

> that the Catholic vote nearly all over England will be given in support of the present administration.[116]

There is irony in his delicate feeling of 'allowing his tenantry to vote as they please'. But his broader theme, that 'nearly all over England' Catholics were turning Tory, could only be maintained by positing 'some promise ... given by Lord Beaconsfield'.[117] The evidence was non-existent. Not that this mattered: lack of evidence proved the cleverness of the intrigue. The fiction had to be preserved that a vote against the Liberals was so out of character as to be explicable only as the result of dastardly plot.

The suspicion grows that what worried Ripon and Fisher was less the Toryism of the Catholic vote than the fact that it was becoming more difficult to control. Catholics resistant to overwhelming argument clearly had minds of their own. Failure to feel gratitude to historic Liberalism suggested a view of politics altogether more demanding than before. Faith in a flashy and shallow Toryism suggested dangerous credulity. Scepticism and credulity: this odd combination made electoral management extremely difficult. Fisher felt anxiety that old techniques ('I am trying to do what I can very quietly with others of rank and position in the county')[118] were losing their power. He could not repress nostalgia for a time when, '18 years ago', elections could be decided 'by the Catholic votes of Gerards and Traffords'.[119] The flock was more fickle now. The Gerards might still get the vote out (they were Tories after all: the losers' myth dictated that the winners be better organised); but Liberals feared that the Catholic public were bored with old tricks and wanted new ones.

In the absence of anything better, there was no alternative to paternalistic politics. The tactical discussions of Ripon and Fisher show this. Moreover, they reveal how misguided is the idea that the Catholic vote was unitary, national, and susceptible to 'processes' of change which Disraeli, and later Salisbury, manipulated better than Gladstone. This smooth texture disappears upon close scrutiny to reveal a reality altogether more complicated:

> I feel certain that the Catholics, except perhaps those under the influence of Catholic landlords will vote for the Liberal Party – with few exceptions. As for Lord Gerard, it is useless to write to him, the family have always been Tory, so have the Traffords, but they have not much interest down here. I am inclined to think that the feeling South of the Catholic Party (*sic*) is stronger against Liberal interest than in this quarter & I attribute this to the Duke of Norfolk and Lord Edmund Howard. I have not seen any statement of Lord Howard of Glossop, he was certainly a disciple of Lord John Russell.[120]

Ripon – or Manning, or Norfolk – could therefore no more deliver the Catholic vote than they could reasonably promise it; they might have been able to deliver Catholic *votes*, but that was a different matter.

Within that constraint Catholic politics were fought with an intensity which makes the *Tablet*'s fiction of harmony and piety seem quaint. Leaders of Catholic opinion regarded each other more as rivals than colleagues, and the smaller their world, the sharper its divisions:

> I regret as much as you do [Francis Stonor, younger son of Lord Camoys, told Ripon] the part taken by the Catholics; they naturally look to the Duke of Norfolk as their guide and he supports the Conservatives, and is even starting his brother as the Conservative candidate for Burnley. Then again, Cardinal Manning throws the whole weight of his influence into the Conservative camp, which is all the more strange as he is the Apostle of Temperance ... Lord Norreys at Townley is doing all he can for the Conservative candidate.[121]

The resentment is clear. All the same, knowing the opposition had the advantage of making tactics easier. However much he deplored Tory plots, Ripon was not averse to a little sharp practice of his own:

> I have every reason to believe that if it would be of any use to publish a statement that Cardinal Manning has 'made up his mind not to interfere at all even indirectly' in the present Election, it might safely be done without any fear of contradiction.
>
> The words between inverted commas were spoken by the Cardinal not to me, but to a person of great weight in the Catholic body.... They are now before me in his handwriting. As I saw a statement of an opposite character in a Liverpool Tory newspaper, I thought a contradiction if it could safely be given, might be of use; but my name should not be mentioned.[122]

This was the true Ripon: devious, plotting, secretive. Boxing Manning into a corner by publishing anonymously a statement which he could not contradict – as it were, interfering on behalf of one who refused to interfere – was a sort of political blackmail; it was not the behaviour of harmonious colleagues.

Ripon's mingled derision and disbelief at the thought of Manning backing the brewers was nothing to the astringency with which he greeted Norfolk's political activities. Norfolk-bashing was acceptable sport among many Catholics, who resented his powers of patronage and found it easy to dismiss him as a political light-weight. In truth, he was far from it, but reducing him to the status of misguided amateur was comforting. In the 1886 election, for instance, Ripon showed his colleagues how they could dish him:

> *English RCs are not an influential body* but we want every vote that we can pick up and now that the Duke of Norfolk has become such a desperate Tory it is important to counteract his influence. There is an opening for this just now as many RCs are shocked at his vehemence and especially at his taking an active party against the Attorney-General.[123]

Others did not hesitate to sneer at 'a certain noble duke who is better known for his association with the Primrose League (to say nothing of the Orange Society) than for his wisdom'.[124] Catholic politics had villains as well as heroes and not all of them were Protestant.

To return to 1880. From a Catholic Liberal perspective, the campaign was a shambles. 'Gladstone is the cause of all the defection among the Catholics and ... many of them say ... they will never support a party of whom he forms one.'[125] Ripon's letter to the *Tablet* started a row which did nothing but harm to the cause. Reminding Catholics of their debt to Gladstone was one hostage to fortune too many. The letter also created organisational difficulties. Being the chief weapon to attract Catholic votes, it was much in demand, and Ripon found himself posting and packing it to beleaguered constituency parties. Thus Aberdare from Wales:

> Did the *Tablet* publish your letter? and could you let me have a copy of it? The Catholics hereabouts appear to be going against us – at Cardiff no doubt Lord Bute's power over their leaders is considerable. I don't understand why in other places they should be so hostile ... [but] I believe that the publication of your letter might still do some good.[126]

A week later, from the same source, came evidence that Ripon had done his duty, and more:

> I have received large supplies of your letter to the *Tablet* & to Mr. Blount [which said the same things and was likewise written for public consumption] – this last much to the purpose at Cardiff

where there are 600 Catholic voters & where the Tories are repeating the tactics of 1874. I have also recd. this morning a stout packet of the same pamphlet – the 'Catholic vote.' All of these are on their way to Cardiff and Monmouthshire.[127]

Devotees of high imperialism might like to ponder that the year which ended with Ripon as Viceroy of India began with him surrounded by parcels, string and a list of addresses. We, on the other hand, can content ourselves with the irony that in the election Bute supported Disraeli and Ripon, Gladstone, each having been respectively slighted by them in the early 1870s on account of their Catholicism.

Aberdare was not the only beneficiary of Ripon's energy. Charles Dilke also had cause to thank him. The Ripon writ was not confined to Wales:

My dear Sir Charles, I hear that there are some difficulties with the Catholics in Chelsea ... [128]

Help was at hand, but only if Dilke were discreet:

It is, of course, a delicate matter for me as a Peer to meddle at all in an Election, but I know that I can safely rely on your discretion and I therefore write to say that you can make any use of my name which you may think judicious – and especially that you may say that I, who am Chairman of the Catholic Poor School Committee, the principal Catholic Educational body, am perfectly convinced that the Catholics have nothing to fear for their educational interests from the Establishment of a Liberal Government at the present time. I enclose a note showing my interest in your success, which you may show with due caution, where you may think it may be useful – but it must not, of course, be printed or circulated in any way.[129]

So much for Ripon's promise to Petre to 'refuse to do anything' if his political friends ever asked him to help them out.

These prodigies of organisation reflected rather than relieved the seriousness of the Liberal dilemma. Aberdare could not deny that any Catholic vote would be a bonus. Nor could Fisher conceal that Weld-Blundell was not to be persuaded out of his Toryism or, indeed, out of Biarritz. On the contrary, his name added ever greater lustre to the Tory cause.[130] Fisher was aghast 'that any Catholic, much more a priest'[131] should vote for the Tories. For this, he blamed Manning and Vaughan, implacable anti-Liberals, both.

Other explanations were less far-fetched, but all reflected the suspicion that Catholics were less susceptible than before to old methods of political control. To vote against Liberals despite all their 'good deeds'[132] suggested not only ingratitude but failure to recognise a debt at all, as if 'Catholic interests'[133] were no longer a determinant of political loyalty, or only one of many. Here was a crucial intuition. Secularisation, Lord Braye told Ripon, would make distinctively 'Catholic' politics an impossibility:

> You may think me a pessimist but it seems to me the accession of the Catholics to the other side is only one symptom of their gradual loss of influence in this country, of which another sign in a totally different direction is the fiasco at Kensington [the abortive Catholic university college] and a third ... is the practical loss of faith among the young men of some of the best families.
>
> Even the sort of *social* intercourse of English Catholics has now been absorbed into the general fashionable world.
>
> Something must be done ... [134]

He ended by regretting – an ominous phrase – the 'political warfare among Catholics'.[135]

Braye's analysis, in some respects acute, was in other respects amnesiac. He forgot that only six years before, the burden of Catholic annoyance with Gladstone was that they *were* absorbed into the fashionable world and should be treated accordingly. Catholic politics were more secular than sacred; Braye's mistake was to think they had ever been other. Elections had always been as much about patronage as about piety. Even unworldly Monsignor Fisher understood that. 'The Conservative Party will hardly make a Catholic magistrate, and certainly it is so closely allied with the Orange Party that there is little to expect....'[136] Jobs remained the most intelligible political language.

To conclude: Ripon had no need to be told how Catholics annoyed their neighbours, or how they needed, like any other group, their due share of political reward. He straddled two worlds, the Liberal and the Catholic, but his loyalties were not, for all that, co-equal. Political colleagues came first. They recognised how well placed he was to capture Catholic votes; he recognised it too, and acted accordingly. Nor was this a phenomenon of 1880. In 1886 and 1892 the story was the same. In June 1886 he recommended Henry Bedingfeld for a peerage because his 'assistance wd. be useful amongst Catholics', especially as 'we cannot afford, at this election to lose a chance of any kind'.[137] And in February 1892 he received a communication from Sir William Harcourt:

> You would be a proper person to express the indignation of the Catholics at [Lord Salisbury's portrayal] of them as the traditional enemies of their country. You could put the Duke of Norfolk and other Catholic Peers in a great hole, so pray prepare a hot oration on the subject.[138]

Liberal politics had come full circle. Ripon had been hounded out of the party in 1874 because of Catholicism. In 1892 Liberals were still hounding Catholic peers. This time Ripon was helping them.

5

Catholic Toryism during Disraeli's Second Ministry

Ripon was wrong to sniff conspiracy in 1880, not only because it did not exist, but because it did damage to the true nature of Catholic Tory relations during Disraeli's second ministry. No sooner had the curtain risen on that government than familiar actors took to the stage, speaking for the most part familiar lines: Denbigh quick to remind Disraeli that he owed his return to Catholic votes, Bowyer (even less wisely) that his own defeat in Ireland had been due to his powerful advocacy of the Tory case. And of course there was Pope Hennessy, with his usual brand of self-depreciating self-promotion:

It is with the greatest pleasure [he wrote to Lord Carnarvon] that I welcome you back as our Chief to the Colonial Service. If I may presume to say anything of Party relations, it is that your acceptance of office & that of Lord Salisbury are more gratifying to me than any other events in the recent Revolution. If you at all remember our conversations at Hatfield in 1867, and any incidents in my little Parliamentary career, you will know that I have always combined great affection for Mr. Disraeli with deep sympathies for you and Lord Salisbury.[1]

The Catholic search for place went on apace; invested this time with a little more subtlety. Threatening Disraeli in 1867 with the Bishop of Southwark got Pope Hennessy no farther than Labuan; in 1874, the lesson learnt, he chose a better code – elaborate enthusiasm for Salisbury and Carnarvon, the two most 'Catholic' members of the new administration. It seemed to work. Before the year was out, he had won the Governorship of Barbados and the Windward Islands; the result (he acknowledged) of a 'powerful word' spoken on his behalf by Disraeli:

But though that word and Lord Carnarvon's kindness have now

given me a first class Government and four thousand a year, I regard as far more precious than the high office and the salary, the evidence this promotion affords of your continued confidence in me.[2]

That confidence was always more political than personal: Hennessy knew the right things to say about Irish prelates and their perfidies. Disraeli never tired of hearing about 'the anti-Catholic conduct of those who supported Mr. Gladstone in confiscating Church property', so Hennessy never tired of telling him. Disraeli was pleased to learn that Hennessy, too, disapproved 'as a Catholic ... [and] a gentleman' of 'the blunders of the Bishops', the 'deliberate treachery' by which they had tried to 'serve the temporary interests of Mr. Gladstone and to damage you'.[3] The last thing, in other words, that the promotion of Pope Hennessy proved was that Disraeli felt an especial debt to Catholics.

Disraeli's return in 1874 gave heart to those exasperated by the advances of Whiggery in Ireland. They were much in need of it. For Catholic Tories, almost worse than being deprived of patronage was the thought of the enemy enjoying it. Jealousy was their abiding vice. Typical was Wallis, sometime editor of the *Tablet*, who, welcoming the new government because it would allow 'real' politics to begin, could not disguise simple pleasure that the 'outs' were in:

It is progress compared with the soul-destroying Catholic Whig era – when the mind of the people was completely averted from politics and Bishops, Priests, Lawyers and ... a score of placemen were the only persons who moved and they only at election time, and Monsell, O'Hagan, Cogan and More O'Ferrall were accepted by cabinets as the right persons through whom the Church and People were to be got at. And Paul Cullen spun his spider webs in the dark and Woodlock and Canon Farrell came over to London, like Roman Ambassadors, to bring messages to Mithradites – A. M. Sullivan is an improvement on that.[4]

Passion and patronage were thus the twin poles of the Catholic Tory world. Tory statesmen tended to understand the latter better. They thought – because generations of supplicant Irish Tories had taught them to think – that Whig passion would go once Tory patronage came. This was doubtful. More likely was that jobs would whet an appetite not wholly satiable. And there was another dif-

ficulty. Politicians too readily assumed that *everything* was a patronage question, all support explicable in terms only of preferment.
When Derby proposed that the government should give more
honours to scientists, for example, his reasoning had nothing to do
with science:

> Anything you can do in this line will strengthen your hands where
> strength is required.
>   Conservatives are numerically strong: they are weakest among
> the intellectual classes: as is natural. Science, like art, is very
> neutral: ready to speak well of any minister who does well to it.[5]

And when he suggested Carlyle for GCB and a pension, recognition
of merit was the last thing on his mind:

> Whatever you and I may think of his style, [he] is immensely
> popular and respected: he is, for whatever reason, most vehement
> against Gladstone, and well disposed towards us.... Anything that
> could be done for him would be really good political investment.[6]

Such calculation was the only way to make the system work:
sentimentality was the enemy of sense. The danger was that Derby
or Disraeli would dispense favour with such detachment as to forget
the eagerness with which it was sought. They were not to know, for
instance, that Pope Hennessy in Labuan and Wallis in Cairo (with
only the *Times* for company) sweetened their exile but soured their
politics by wondering which Catholics at home were getting which
jobs. Wherever the English newspapers are (in Egypt or elsewhere)
there shall always be political passion.

The same might be said, though Catholics did not realise it, of the
Queen. She was passionately 'political', and the passion was Protestant. Such was clear from the start of the ministry, when she
expressed herself 'glad' that Disraeli had not offered the Irish Lord
Lieutenancy to Lord Beauchamp. Indeed, she accepted him as Lord
Steward of the Household only on condition that he should 'under-
take not to take any prominent part in Church politics':

> It is very desirable that this condition should be clearly under-
> stood, as Her Majesty looks upon the view of the Church party
> with which Lord Beauchamp was connected as detrimental to the
> interests of the Church of England and dangerous to the Protestant

religion.

The Queen therefore could give no countenance whatever to that Party by admitting a prominent member of it into the Royal Household.[7]

This set a pattern for the rest of the administration: no ritualists in the palace, no Romanists at the gate. In matters of religion, the Queen as an eccentric, occasionally querulous task-mistress, constantly chivying Disraeli about appointments, threats to the Church, the dangers of Popery, and the like. For her, ecclesiastical preferment was miles removed from Trollope's little world of cathedral closes and minor jealousies. There were bigger battles to fight:

> The danger to the Church is *so great* that we must look beyond mere feelings of colleagues & votes in Parlt. which are *temporary* whereas the preferments in the Church are of *lasting effect* for good or evil; [we want more than the merely pious], we want talent and intellect to grapple with the dangers of Atheism and Catholicism.[8]

These dispatches were hard to ignore, even if the Protestantism was the kind upon which (in less elevated quarters) the Tories had always relied for electoral success. It was the regularity, as much as the substance, which was the problem: a reminder to Disraeli of the constraints within which all Church policy had to be formed. Her ministers were not allowed to forget that the Queen disliked Catholics; and occasionally this had implications for policy. One example will suffice. In 1875, as Manning was returning to favour with the government, being seen as a possible intermediary between the Pope and the King of Italy,[9] the Queen felt a need to

> call Mr. Disraeli's attention to the approaching return of Archbishop Manning & ... the possible attempt on his part to claim the rank of Cardinal here. It is a foreign title, unrecognized by us & the Queen trusts that the Govt will take care [of] this ... Of course R. Catholics may do what they like in their own houses among themselves, but no Protestant should give it him.[10]

Disraeli tried to ignore this, but the Queen persisted. (A week later: 'What has the Chancellor said about Archbishop Manning's rank?')[11] His answer was that all would be for the best, a *placebo* more readily acceptable from him than from (say) Gladstone. It says much about the imbalance of the 'natural alliance' that as many Catholics were moving towards Toryism, Disraeli (unbeknownst to them) was assuring the Queen that they would be making as little noise as possible. Disraeli's confidence was not misplaced. The likes of Pope Hennessy and Wallis had the nuisance value of claimants or job-hunters; otherwise they represented Catholicism quiescent. For them, Disraeli's reputation remained unimpeachable, the bishops' unforgivable. They clung, for instance, to a reading of Irish politics which would not have shamed a Liverpool evangelical:

> The sad fact remains that the Catholic Prelates of Ireland are the allies of liberalism ... I know some priests who would welcome the formation of a National Conservative Party; but they are afraid of their Bishops. If we have some little basis of union in this country to begin with, you may be sure Mr. Disraeli will move in the direction ... but he waits for the first step in Ireland itself.[12]

Disraeli could do no wrong, but the compliment was never reciprocated. There remained doubts about the reliability of such self-advancing loyalists. 'Two intriguers who understand one another!' thought Derby of Pope Hennessy and Gifford Palgrave.[13] He was right to be wary. Catholics had less to offer than they thought. Their 'natural Toryism' was, as natural things go, most peculiar.

FOREIGN AFFAIRS

It was well for the government that Catholics were so amenable. For one thing, it made foreign policy easier. In 1875 Derby viewed the political turmoil in Spain[14] – 'the present Spanish Government is thoroughly Ultramontane and reactionary ... we are bound to have trouble with Master Alfonso sooner or later'[15] – from the point of view of one unlikely to be embarrassed by Catholic complaints at home. Tories expected silence from Catholics and generally got it. Sometimes, in fact, it was an important consideration of policy. As has been noticed, one argument for ending the Jervoise mission to Rome was that it would be 'a slap in the face for the Ultramontanes ... exactly what the public wants'.[16] Likewise when the Protestant community of San Fernando was insulted by the Alcalde, Derby thought seriously about asking the Spanish government to dismiss him:

What are we to do now?.... Insist on the removal?... Reasons for [this] are – it would please the Protestants throughout England. It would show the Spanish Government that we are not to be bullied ... [17]

Even so, this cheap source of Protestant support represents only half the story. Precisely because it was foreign, foreign policy was the one sphere of government influence where Catholics could be courted with minimised risk of Protestant revolt. Disraeli understood the value of gesture. Witness his invitation to the Duke of Norfolk in 1879 to act as Ambassador Extraordinary to the marriage of the King of Spain. Norfolk declined, his wife being ill, his foreign languages poor.[18] Persevering, Disraeli then considered Denbigh. The reasoning, he explained to the Queen, was simple:

It [has] been intimated that if Lord Denbigh, a kinsman of the House of Habsburg were appointed by Your Majesty it would be deemed a very gracious act by the English Catholics who not all support your Majesty's Government ... [19]

But the Queen would have none of it. Indeed, she anticipated and repudiated Disraeli's specific argument. 'Strongly object,' she telegrammed, 'for reasons to be represented by Lord Denbigh.'[20] Better to have no delegation at all than to have him. But she suggested a compromise:

[Send] anyone not a Rom. Cath. or at any rate not a proselyte: Would Lord Napier of Magdala not do?[21]

Disraeli, his relief palpable, jumped at the idea:

Lord Beaconsfield with his humble duty to Your Majesty. The Embarrassment Extraordinary has been removed by Your Majesty's happy suggestion.[22]

That the Queen should have found Denbigh unacceptable need not surprise. Nor should the alacrity with which Disraeli changed his tune. Catholic Toryism amounted to little if Disraeli conducted foreign policy either to please Protestants or to do for Catholics abroad what embarrassment prevented at home; even less when he pursued the latter with feeble conviction.

THE DUKE OF NORFOLK AND SIR GEORGE BOWYER: TORYISM HIGH AND LOW

The connections between Catholic and Tory politics were not all negligible. The response to the Eastern Question has already been noticed; so too the impressive number of leading Catholics who sided with the Tories in 1880. Some of this *was* the result of conscious effort by the party. As Gladstone failed to cultivate Norfolk, so Disraeli succeeded. The putative Ambassador did not know how Extraordinary he would have been, still less that Disraeli's 'kind offer' was tokenism. Norfolk's capture nevertheless demonstrated Disraeli's command of the political arts. Minor kindnesses cost little and yielded much. In 1877 Disraeli attended Norfolk's wedding and elegantly proposed his health. (Afterwards he wrote a feline letter to Lady Bradford about it.)[23] In 1879 he wrote lines for a memorial cross to Lady Loudon, Norfolk's late mother-in-law, which the family recognised as a political act:

> I was glad to have met you on Saturday at Norfolk House ... not only as an old and attached friend of [Lady Loudon's] but as the Chief of that Party which we now hope the Duke will continue to support.[24]

This arch formulation was appropriate because the Duke's politics were still undecided. The family tradition was Liberal but the present disposition increasingly Tory. This caused embarrassment, evident in 1878 when Disraeli offered him the vacant Garter, a straightforward political overture. Norfolk declined, more regretfully than he had Gladstone's offer five years before:

> I am very sorry I cannot do what you propose. I have always thought that I should someday join the Conservative Party and it is easy to see at this time that questions may come up which would make me feel it to be my duty to do so at once. Were I to do this however I should be breaking from the traditions of my family and I think anyone so acting ought to take care that his motives be not misunderstood as mine would probably be if I became a

supporter of Her Majesty's Government within a short time of my accepting the Garter.[25]

This evinced a classic Disraeli response:

> Lord Beaconsfield with his humble duty to Your Majesty. This is a very singular and interesting letter from the Duke of Norfolk. His Grace declines the Garter, which he highly appreciates, because he is going to join the Conservative Party!!![26]

All the same, Disraeli did well to stifle his sneers in public: Norfolk's support, if not his political wisdom, was still worth having. Part of the problem was his extreme diffidence. Even when he had clearly become Tory, Norfolk shrank from embracing his new friends. A letter he wrote to Disraeli on behalf of his brother, Lord Edmund Talbot, who was hoping to stand for Burnley in 1880, was typical. Self-effacement was the Duke's trademark:

> [He] is most anxious to do whatever ... is ... the best for the Party ... and I therefore venture to ask you if you would view with favour his coming forward ... [27]

Disraeli seized the opportunity: a meeting between the three was hastily arranged, Disraeli ensuring that no-one else was present. ('His Grace is so shy that it is well that I am quite alone.')[28] Talbot was accordingly nominated, though he subsequently lost. So, after some difficulty, the Norfolk interest seemed secure for the Tory cause.

Other Catholics were less reluctant. Several rungs below the House of Howard was the House of Bowyer, a prize which glittered only in its own eyes. As a particular type of Catholic Tory – isolated by clerical radicalism in Ireland, ignored as provincial by metropolitan Toryism at Westminster, threatened by conventional 'No Popery' in his English constituency – George Bowyer seemed the personification of at least three lost causes; but without self-awareness, he continued to air portentous views. The fascination of his relationship with Disraeli is of watching a magician whose tricks resolutely refuse to work. Thus of the Irish University Bill of 1879:

> I then got the Pope to say that the question must be settled ... [29]

Of his ability to square any opposition to the Tory line on the Bill:

> I settled matters with ... the better class of my colleagues.[30]

Of his skill in controlling obstructionists:

> Manning helped me with them and at my request came down to the House repeatedly.[31]

Of his power over troublemakers:

> We silenced Monsell and kept him quiet.[32]

And his point?

> Without all this management your Bill would have been obstructed ... [33]

Disraeli did not take the hint. He ignored all pleas to find Bowyer a safe seat. And for good reason. Despite the wooing of Norfolk, and the occasional distant gesture in diplomacy, the Catholic-Tory connection remained, at constituency level, highly uncertain. In Bowyer's case this took the form of opposition from local Wesleyans and Baptists to his representing a town where his family had lived for three centuries. 'Without the Protestant prejudices,' he glumly told Disraeli, 'Abingdon would be mine.'[34]

As Abingdon went, so did the nation. Consider another episode in the election of 1880. When Monsignor Fisher of Liverpool suspected a Tory plot to capture Catholic votes, the only 'plot' in that city was intended to woo a quite different section. This was the appointment of Dr Ryle to the new Anglican see, an unblushing attempt to reinforce the Protestant vote. Even the Queen recognised that. When Disraeli wrote that

> The people of Liverpool are very anxious about their new Bishop. The Tories subscribed the whole of the endowment, built the 'palace.' Lord Sandon says his seat ... depends upon the appointment being made by Yr. Majesty's advisers. The whole city are most anxious that Yr. Majesty should appoint the present Dean of Salisbury ... [35]

she willingly approved

> as she is most anxious to do anything to please one to whom she
> owes such a debt of gratitude.[36]

Against such competition, Bowyer's tussle with Abingdonian dissent
could claim little attention. In the matter of preferments, it was as
much as Disraeli could do to plead with the Queen to appoint the
occasional High Churchmen; not because he cared for these 'con-
federates of Mr. Gladstone' but because patronage would deaden the
'intrigue & exaggeration & false representation'[37] by which they had
more than once defeated Tories in elections. Courting low Protestantism while placating high ritualism was hard enough without
having also to listen to the distant sounds of Catholic claims.

MANNING, DISRAELI AND 'NATURAL' TORYISM

If Norfolk and Bowyer personified phantom elements in the Catholic
Tory world, there was another of greater substance in Manning.
There is no better expression of the different levels at which Catholic
politics operated in the later 1870s than his relationship with
Disraeli, in which he revealed himself in at least five roles – jingo, self-
professing non-politician, anti-Gladstonian, putative Tory, pat-
ronage-seeker – all characteristic of the changes so disturbing to
Ripon in 1880. Nothing in their dealings at the end of the decade
suggested the embarrassment of *Lothair* at the beginning: chill had
been replaced, if not by warmth then by a kind of political intensity.
Manning found himself in vigorous agreement with much of what
Disraeli said. The question of the East contributed significantly to
this. He was quick to support the 'foresight and firmness of the
Government of the Eastern question';[38] and to imply that the Pope
thought similarly. Likewise with Afghanistan. While Ripon was
calling down thunder on Disraeli's adventurism, Manning was
showering blessings upon it. Writing in January 1879 before a
journey to Rome, he took the opportunity to state the vital importance
of the Prime Minister to the country:

> I hope you may have full strength to carry the country with you in
> firm and solid compactness which, with the continent before me, I
> believe to be vital to the safety of the British Empire.[39]

A month later the beginning of the Parliamentary session called forth another endorsement:

> The meeting of Parliament will not, I think, be brisk enough for the ABCDs, still less for the Liberals generally.... Health and strength for the work before you.[40]

There was serious intent, political and diplomatic, behind this intimacy. Manning travelled to Rome in 1879 preoccupied with Eastern affairs – hoping that England and France might regain influence over the Armenians at Constantinople and that the Latin rite might be established in Cyprus. His cleverness lay in implying that English and Catholic interests were synonymous:

> No-one among our statesmen knows better than you of how great importance the religious influences are in the East: and it seems to me that at Constantinople much may be done.[41]

This was the diplomatic intent. The political skill was to associate himself closely with the government, thereby acknowledging a debt and causing one. When he generously offered 'to make known to [Disraeli] certain matters in which the interests of the government may be affected',[42] he was positioning himself for his next request: the creation of a bishopric of the Latin rite at Nicosia 'for the Catholic residents of various nations, and for the Catholic soldiers of our army'.[43]

This was astute politics. However, Manning's sympathies were genuinely, not pragmatically, pro-government. The Beaconsfieldism was firmly held:

> I am no Politician but it is clear to me that, having an Empire, we must either give it up or keep it up. To give it up would be our extinction as a power in the world: to keep it up seems to me to demand and even to dictate the policy you have pursued.[44]

Given this conviction, Liberal opposition to Disraeli's foreign policy seemed almost treacherous. Even as he rejoiced at the recapture of Kabul, he noticed

with dismay the violence of passion and speech with which

everything, over which Englishmen ought to have been silent and firm, has been hailed and greeted.... It is strange that Frenchmen, Germans and Austrians can see what some Englishmen ... cannot.[45]

This was a reference to the Midlothian campaign, which, for all the vigour of its rhetoric, Manning considered a form of national cowardice:

Englishmen must give up trembling at dangers and puling about taxes. There is nothing imperial about such conduct.[46]

Manning stood for many. Jingoism was typical of most Catholics, still resentful of Gladstone, still mindful that they, too, had once suffered his demagoguery, still anxious to protect perceived Catholic interests abroad, still keen to prove their loyalty. Ripon was an exception to this; so too Newman, who in 1880 welcomed Disraeli's fall as if the country had been purged of a great tyranny.[47] Most Catholics preferred to think, with Lord Bury, that 'Lord Beaconsfield has kept us at peace, has upheld the dignity of England, and added not a shilling to the national debt'.[48] These were the comforts upon which Catholic Toryism was built.

It was built on patronage too. Manning's brought deserving Catholics to Disraeli's attention, cleverly making it appear that *he* was doing the favour. Thus of Lord Beaumont, a thirty-year-old Lancer who had served in Africa:

He has now decided to give his support both in and out of Parliament to the Government ... I believe that ... taken under wise and kind political guidance [he] could be made a useful man in public life. It is with this in mind that I have urged him to speak to you ...

And there were plenty more where he came from:

Many of our young men stagnate, or waste their life ... from want of encouragement and a definite aim.[49]

Disraeli may have resisted as improbable the notion of a pool of Catholics through which he needed only to trawl a net to land himself permanent support; still, he could hardly complain of the Catholic desire to please.

Jingoism and jobbery can only explain so much. There was another reason for Catholic Toryism. Catholics disliked Gladstone's bluster, but even more they resented his party's secularism. In matters of education – to Ripon's intense puzzlement – they preferred Tory Establishmentarianism to Liberal Erastianism. Lord Bury reminded *Tablet* readers that the Liberal Party was steeped in irreligion:

> The reason is not far to seek – it is that fierce dogmatism of the Radical, and not the milk and water 'toleration' of the Whig, is the force which has to be reckoned with in the future. The Board School, with its secular education and its legal prohibition to pronounce the name of God in school hours, will be the fate of our children if Mr. Gladstone is returned to power. The Conservatives have at least this in common with Catholics, that they dread the complete secularisation of education.[50]

Ripon resented the implication that the party of Granville had become the party of Bright, preferring Catholics to remember that it was still the party of Ripon. In 1880 they were not persuaded.

Education revealed the conviction of Catholic Toryism, but it also revealed its vulnerability. Look, for example, at how paltry a measure from a Catholic point of view the Irish University Act (1879) turned out to be. Better still, look at the bizarre arguments used by Catholics to urge Disraeli to take it up. Lord Denbigh, claiming that education (both in England and Ireland) had been the key factor in detaching Catholics 'from their Liberal ties and caus[ing] them to rally round the Government',[51] insisted that Liberal measures were therefore all the more to be feared. If Gladstone should offer more to Catholics (by supporting the O'Conor Don's Bill)[52] than Disraeli, the damage would be severe:

> For, if once the Catholics return to the side of their old Whig Patron, they may not be so easily detached again.[53]

This was self-emasculating: it suggested a commitment to Toryism which was immune to Liberal counter-inducements, indeed fearful of them. Denbigh's adverb gave the game away. Catholics, he let slip, might not be so *easily* detached from the Whigs in future. In other words, education was a cheap source of Catholic votes for the Tories and should be cherished.

This plea demonstrated the unbalance of Catholic Toryism: Denbigh was sufficiently Tory to support the party even when the Whigs promised more; but he feared that the party was reluctant to reciprocate:

> I wish you to call the attention of such of your colleagues who might hold back from the fear of awaking Protestant bigotry and perhaps endangering one or two elections, that there are two sides to be looked at, ... that ... Catholic support is not lightly to be hazarded ... [54]

Sensitivity to the strength of Protestantism did Denbigh credit. Disraeli for his part recognised that English Catholics demanded respect, not because they were strong but because they were not Irish. In the 1880 election Liberal accusations that he was anti-Catholic, and Home Rule claims that he was 'the mortal enemy of Ireland and the Irish,[55] were answered by a fine distinction:

> As regard the Catholic Anglo-Irish voters ... the careful avoidance of the subtle term Home Ruler throughout the whole of his manifesto and the reference alone to those 'who are attempting to sever the constitutional tie between Great Britain and Ireland,' a category from which the well-intentioned Irish are clearly excluded, places those classes outside Lord Beaconsfield's denunciation, and forms the distinction he wishes to draw.[56]

This was the best Disraeli could do by way of explicit courtship of Catholic votes: not much, but better than nothing. He knew the Irish vote was out of his reach, but also that many English Catholics considered it flattery enough not to be associated with Home Rulers. Too close a connection with the Irish was not to their taste. Bishop Vaughan's Toryism lost nothing for the gulf between himself and the 'poor Paddies';[57] Denbigh and Norfolk, not the Queen's favourite Parliamentarians, were at least better than their 'horrid Irish' brethren in another place.[58]

We end, therefore, acknowledging the one-sidedness of Catholic Toryism between 1874 and 1880; but there is a quixotic postlude. In the strange history of Disraeli's dealing with Catholics, there is no stranger feature than the belief that he himself died a Catholic. The death-bed scene is familiar to the point of parody – the slow decline, the anxious attendance, the last utterances, the final, wordless gesture.[59] Less known is a version which gained much currency in Liverpool in 1883. Lord Rowton, the former Montagu Corry, heard it from a distraught Disraelian:

> The subject I wish to refer to is as follows: one of our Liverpool Journals or newspapers a week ago in an article entitled 'Going over to Rome' makes reference to the late Earl of Beaconsfield & distinctly asserts therein that he 'on his deathbed received the last sacrament of the Roman Catholic Church' administered by a Father Clare & died a convert to the Roman Catholic religion. It also asserts that during the Earl's illness he frequently sent for ... Father Clare to visit him.... As I myself with very many others are very much pained by such an assertion let me hope that your Lordship will be able to give an explicit denial to such scandalous and cruel statements.[60]

The paper was *The Porcupine* ('A Journal of Current Events – Political, Social and Satirical') which had described, with elaborate detail, Disraeli's last days in the bosom of the Jesuits. Its tone, relentlessly gleeful, was established by a report of the rumoured conversions of the Duke and Duchess of Bedford:

> It is nearly half a century ago since *Punch* described Lord John Russell as the little Political Boy who wrote 'No Popery' on the walls and then ran away.... What revenge time works! Fancy the head of the ducal House of Bedford; the chief of the historic family of Russells; a Whig of Whigs; one of the wealthiest and most influential nobles in England, with his noble lady, 'going over to Rome!' ... If this be true, it will be the most remarkable conversion of modern times – except one.
>
> What was that notable exception? The late leader of the Tory Party![61]

Disraeli's relations with Fr. Clare were then explained: they had been 'old and intimate friends'; they had much in common – courtliness, learning, human insight, practical cunning; they had shared political interests – one eager for Catholic votes, the other capable of providing them. The friendship was almost Faustian:

> At Birkenhead during the Maelver-Williams election ... an inter-

view [took] place between Father Clare and Lord Beaconsfield, [during which] the leader of the Tory party *promised* that on condition of the Jesuit priest using his influence to obtain the Catholic vote for the Tories at the general election, he (Lord Beaconsfield) would guarantee that *the religious houses of the Roman Catholic body in England would in no sense be molested* ... At that time Father Clare was on the most intimate terms of friendship with the Tory leader, and there was no-one more welcome at Lord Beaconsfield's house and board.[62]

Little wonder that just before Disraeli's death, ' – in fact, when it was known that the great statesman's recovery was hopeless – *three confidential* messages were sent from the dying man to the Jesuit establishment at Farm Street, London, asking for the immediate attention at his bedside of Father Clare....'[63] It was thus that he completed the spiritual journey of his life: as it were, from Pentateuch through King James to Vulgate and beyond.

This farrago of circumstance and suggestion gave many Orangemen the fright of their lives, and their anguish long outlasted Rowton's denial of the death-bed rumours. As late as 1886 the belief was still current enough for William Johnston MP to record in his diary that Rowton had authorised him to deny 'the slander on Lord Beaconsfield that he had sent for a Jesuit priest dying'.[64] The longevity did tribute to the story's clever combination of vagueness and specificity. Protestants seemed not to notice that its rhetorical force was grounded on a singular contradiction:

Is Lord Rowton prepared to deny this? Will the truth-loving Lord Claude [Hamilton] ... assert with his usual placidity that such facts ... are without foundation?

The very next sentence unwittingly provided the answer:

The Jesuits were not likely to take the Orange Hamiltons and Corrys into their confidence, and no-one knew what took place between Father Clare and the Tory statesman but themselves.[65]

The episode is important both because it reveals the continuing power of anti-Catholicism – one Liverpool Tory wrote that the story, if uncontradicted, would 'certainly ... do a great deal of harm to the Conservative cause in this and other towns'[66] – and because it provides a snapshot of its complexion. Rowton's correspondents inhabited a world where Protestantism was less a creed than an all-purpose metaphor of political virtue:

> I have already seen your denial of the Radical slander that Lord Beaconsfield died a Roman Catholic. [I] admired him like numerous other patriots because he could wield the destinies of a great and mighty Empire, different to a medley Cabinet of Radical Incapables – admired him because of his unselfish devotion to his country and his queen.... Such slanders if uncontradicted become capital in the hands of the unscrupulous war waged by Radical nondescripts, who, living or dead, abused this noble man because they never had nor ever could produce his Radical Equal....[67]

Belief in Catholic 'progress', hope in the eventual re-conversion of England, were always overwhelmed by this Protestant fervour.

And yet for a while it seemed as if they had won a spectacular victory – Hebrew turned Orangeman turned Papist. Rowton's denials revealed the foolishness of the hope, and Liverpool's anger its futility. But the episode was symbolic of Catholic Toryism: hopes raised, triumphs dashed, even from beyond the grave.

6

Ripon: A Catholic in Government

INDIAN INTERLUDE

Ripon's career as an agent of Liberals and Catholics, an ageing radical and old-fashioned gradualist, flourished after 1880, the year he became Viceroy of India. Catholics were pleased by this appointment (disappointed only that his not being in the Cabinet was a 'terrible loss'[1] to their interests at home) and delighted that it was Gladstone who had made it. Years later, when passions might have been thought cooler, it still seemed 'a Liberal statesman's most perfect way of retracting his impeachment of Catholic loyalty',[2] and when Lord Kenmare was made Lord Chamberlain of the Household – an additional gesture – Catholic rehabilitation did indeed appear well advanced. To be Viceroy was to serve in an office 'than which none more honourable is open to the ambition of an Englishman', 'striking proof'[3] of Gladstone's high opinion of Ripon's talent. (No blame attached to Catholics for not knowing that he had been third choice, behind Kimberley and Goschen.)[4]

Historians have broadly agreed,[5] but contemporary criticism is not hard to find. The British Reformation Society was quick to inform Gladstone of its 'sincere regret and apprehension'[6] at the Ripon and Kenmare promotions; the *Glasgow News* preferred the sobriquet 'Pope's Viceroy'.[7] Such might have been predicted. Less prejudicially, the view of insiders was that the elevation was a surprise, perhaps a mistake. It puzzled Lord Esher who 'never for a moment'[8] thought that Ripon still aspired to office; and Gathorne Hardy was decidedly opposed:

> Ripon is not a good appointment: he is weak, pompous and mouthy. His personal appearance is unimpressive and ... he is much wanting in decision.[9]

As for Kenmare, the anxiety of the British Reformers was misplaced. Here was no deep-laid plot to further the papists, or, indeed, Kenmare himself. On the contrary, he was chosen in a moment of indifference. Granville, Gladstone's consultant in these matters, could 'see no objection to your plumping for Kenmare'.[10] There was no more to it than that.

Some Catholics denied that creed had played a part in Ripon's advancement. It was not religious tokenism, they claimed, but a recognition of merit. This was disingenuous. It suited them to depict 'incredulous amazement' at the choice 'not only [of] a Catholic but a convert',[11] the easier to demonstrate its folly: despite every prediction, they scoffed, Ripon had not required his entourage 'to attend morning prayers ... to make the sign of the cross ... to snuff out the candles after early Mass'.[12] And there was another conceit. Taking credit for Ripon's lack of zealotry, apologists nonetheless maintained that his successes could never have been achieved by a non-Catholic. Thus H. S. Jarrett in the *Month*:

> The fact that Lord Ripon is a Catholic ... certainly far from injured him in the eyes of the natives, the educated among whom hold Catholicism to be pre-eminently the only religion which believers in a revelation cannot successfully assail.[13]

Ripon's viceroyalty has been defined variously – as an application of Gladstonian principles to the problems of empire,[14] as reckless innovation,[15] as a well-intended flop,[16] even as the saving of India[17] – but hardly as a significant engagement of the great religions of East and West.

Nor indeed was it of much moment for English Catholicism. Ripon in India is beyond the scope of this study, but it had importance on the home front. Catholics may not have realised it, but Gladstone's had been a masterstroke of political balance: Ripon was still honorifically prominent in Liberal affairs, but away from the Cabinet he was unlikely to be a troublesome voice. His advice was still sought and given, but with the aim of keeping Catholics in their place. Lord Halifax, for instance, was a correspondent whose letters about the Pope's authority in Ireland,[18] or about education in India ('I hope that you will avoid raising any religious question & conscience clause: the Church has made a prodigious piece of work about a conscience clause')[19] signalled the government's desire for a quiet life. Ripon was happy to comply, India providing him with problems enough without his also having to contend with Catholic querulousness at home. And, as Newman noticed, with a leading patron oceans away, Catholic job-hunters would have to be patient.[20]

Besides, Ripon's viceroyalty won Catholic support without ever risking Catholic condemnation. Throughout all the controversies – the rows with the Anglo-Indians, the trouble over the Ilbert Bill, the resistance in the Cabinet even to modest change – they stood by him; an attack on him was an attack on them. Religion was the great all-explainer. Jarrett again: 'The fact that Lord Ripon is a Catholic has been in all probability the principal cause of the hostility of the *Times* to his policy.'[21] Likewise Newman: 'That you are doing great work in India, none of us doubts'.[22] If Gladstone thought to win himself Catholic support by promoting Ripon, there is evidence to show that he was successful.[23]

At home, the search for patronage went on much as before, even Ripon, for form's sake, pulling the occasional long-distance string.[24] Catholicism remained a card to be played, not last, when all else had failed, but often as the principal justification of otherwise outlandish hope. Typical was Hubert Jerningham, MP, who wrote thus to Gladstone:

> Being a strong supporter of yours, I left the diplomatic service for Parliament, believing that the presence of a member of an old Catholic family in the House of Commons would do much to stop the going over to the opposition of so many co-religionists who owe to the Liberal Party all they have, and show them that Liberalism in England is not, as it is abroad, synonymous of anti-clericalism.
>
> It occurred to me that should political reasons determine you to create any new Peers, I might without too much presumption ask to be remembered by you ...[25]

Gladstone's reaction is instructive. He forwarded the letter, significantly annotated, to Lord Richard Grosvenor:

> 1 Oct. 1884 Mr. H. Jerningham MP.
> 1. Intends leaving Parlt. on account of health.
> 2. For employment.
> 3. For consideration of claims to Peerage.
> (His claims to 3 would seem to be very slender. Moreover, those of another RC – Lord Herries – to a seat in the H. of Lds. are much stronger.)[26]

There are two points here. Catholicism *was* a card in the eyes of both claimants and benefactors: Catholic votes had to be won, and a peerage was one way of getting them. The same had been the case with Acton. But as with Acton, party managers had to play the numbers game.[27] Just as his elevation had been balanced by an honour likely to appeal to Nonconformists, so Jerningham's fell by a similar realisation that Catholic credit, in the shape of Herries, was for the moment used up. Such was the logic of tokenism.

It might also be added that Gladstone remained, despite his 'most perfect' gesture to Ripon, temperamentally suspicious of Catholics and their creed. The same month that Jerningham missed his peerage, Manning recorded 'somewhat sadly' that 'Gladstone never comes near to me now: he attacked my Church and I was bound to take notice of it – although Willy is my Godson'.[28] Even Harcourt – no ecumenist – noticed in him a disturbing obsessiveness. At the height of the international tension of May 1885, when war with Russia seemed an imminent possibility, the Prime Minister had other things on his mind:

> In the middle of the crisis yesterday H[ome] S[secretary] went into Gladstone's sitting room in Downing St. and found him lying on his sofa reading a French book on 'Chastity and Incontinence of Roman Catholic priests.'[29]

Against this, must be noticed that though Catholic slipperiness was his *idée fixe*, Gladstone could sometimes claim justification. Indeed, a case suggests itself immediately: Hubert Jerningham. Not only was he over-ambitious, he was unpredictable too. Deprived of the Lords, he suddenly re-discovered enthusiasm for the Commons:

> We [William Harcourt and son] went back to the H of C and I had a long talk with Hubert Jerningham, who is very angry with our whips for not having found a seat for him and he says that it is of the greatest importance to the Party that we should have him returned as a Catholic somewhere. He says that it could be very easily managed if Ld. Richard Grosvenor would write to some constituency to say that it would be a great assistance to Mr. Gladstone if he (Jerningham) were returned.[30]

Comment is hardly necessary, but a postscript is of interest. Understandably, Jerningham's schemes rebounded; once he had argued himself out of the Commons, he could not argue himself back.[31]

Thereafter, his career took on a familiar appearance: he ended up not in the Lords but, like a nuisance of an earlier generation, in the Colonial Service. In 1889 he succeeded John Pope Hennessy as governor of Mauritius.

CABINET AND ELECTION POLITICS, 1885

Ripon resigned the viceroyalty in December 1884 and returned to England in early January, disappointed that his plans for Indian local government reform had not been better supported by colleagues in the Cabinet. In his last months he had encountered strong opposition from Anglo-Indians abroad and Tories at home; and he thus re-entered English political life with a reputation for radicalism, if not for sense, much enhanced. His low standing was not simply the result of the blimpishness of opponents who detested Ripon's 'pompous platitudes ... and his love of applause', his 'miserable ... popularity hunting'[32] with the natives: his own colleagues also noticed, and were annoyed, that he had become, as he himself put it, 'more radical every day'.[33]

It is misleading for Professor Denholm to applaud this radicalism while ignoring its effect on colleagues; thus giving the impression that throughout 1885–6 Ripon could have been in a Liberal Cabinet for the asking. This is far from the case. His star had fallen since India, and efforts to resurrect it were forlorn. No-one wanted much to do with him. In the first leadership crisis of 1885, when Harcourt and Hartington met to draw up an alternative Cabinet in the event of Gladstone's expected retirement, Ripon was out of the reckoning. They came together on 4 January 'to consider the formation of a new Govt.,' and agreed among other things that 'Ripon is not to be offered a place'.[34] Later in the month his position had, if anything, worsened. Harcourt doubted if 'Ripon would be taken into this Govt., even if any of the present members of it resigned'.[35] A month later, things had improved slightly. 'Ld. Ripon might be taken in,' Loulou Harcourt recorded, 'but I don't think he would strengthen the Govt. in the country.'[36] In March, however, it was exclusion as usual:

[R]ipon is more radical than ever since he returned and it is obvious to me that he is very anxious to be in office again, though I do not think it is likely ...[37]

Thus hunger for office – 'very puzzling', Harcourt *fils* thought – became a received wisdom, and an embarrassment. Overwhelming ambition was never so unedifying (it was felt) as when combined with class betrayal:

> I know he is bidding for the radical support to force him into the next Cabinet but I did not think if likely that a large landowner would be willing all at once to adopt Chamberlain's programme ...[38]

Here is the clue. It was association with Chamberlain, who was not to be trusted, which rendered Ripon's claims so resistible. There were few easier ways in some circles of acquiring quick and lasting odium. That the radicalism may have been sincerely held was neither here nor there; sincerity did not erase an indelible reputation for deviousness. Ripon was thus ill-advised to force himself into the Cabinet via the door marked 'Chamberlain'; in more senses than one, a tradesman's entrance.

None of this decline in fortune is mentioned by Professor Denholm; nor even is the rumour, shortlived, that Gladstone intended making Ripon a Duke[39] – presumably (as circumstances required) part reward, part retirement, part buying off, part counter-weight to Norfolk.

The fall of Gladstone's ministry in June 1885 ended all the jockeying. With little sorrow, the Liberals left office; with little enthusiasm – but with the unexpected support of the Parnellites – the Tories assumed it. This *mésalliance*, whose history has been painfully reconstructed from scraps of hair and traces of fibre,[40] dominated political manoeuvre for the next six months. In that time, two things may be noticed: Catholic politics moved strongly in a Tory direction; and Ripon's star once again rose in the Liberal firmament.

The Tory-Nationalist alliance was originally conceived as an alternative to Liberal coercion, but it quickly developed, at least in Parnell's eyes, into a mechanism to test the respective amenability of both parties to the idea of Home Rule. Parnell's preference would have been for the Tories, the party more likely to bring the Lords to heel; but, *faute de mieux*, he would have settled for the Liberals if Gladstone could have been induced, in the summer and early autumn of 1885, to clarify his position in favour of Irish self-government. While Salisbury's Newport speech (October 1885) was carefully ambivalent on Home Rule – rejecting it if destructive of the empire, allowing it if not – Gladstone's utterances on the subject were entirely obscure. Where Salisbury merely promised 'prosperity, contentment and happiness' for Ireland, Gladstone argued that Ireland should vote first before he would commit himself to any policy. If after an election the 'vast majority' of Irish MPs demanded 'large local powers of self-government', then, provided the empire remained intact, such should be 'the first duty of Parliament'.[41]

Parnell saw at once the fatal flaw: there was nothing to stop the Lords rejecting any future Home Rule Bill on the grounds that it had not been properly put before the electorate. He therefore requested Gladstone to state his case more explicitly. Gladstone refused. Parnell accordingly instructed (21 November) the Irish in Britain to vote for Conservative candidates where this would prevent the election of either Liberals or Radicals.

This *coup de théâtre*, devastating to Liberal hopes, was accompanied by another equally fatal: Manning's famous instruction that supporters of 'free schools' – non-fee-paying undenominational board schools – should not be given Catholic votes. This was not a crude call to vote Tory; punctilious wording (Manning's *métier*) saw to that. Where a Liberal candidate's views on Catholic schools matched the hierarchy's – an unlikely contingency – Catholics were free to vote as conscience dictated. The effect, however, was to deliver yet more Catholic support to the Tories.

Whether Parnell shifted more votes than Manning, or vice versa is an open question.[42] What is beyond doubt is that both threw the Liberals into disarray. However, in doing so, they may have strengthened Ripon's hand; once again the party's best link with Catholics. Certainly, his advice was more eagerly sought in December 1885 than ever it had been in January; and as the year ended – as it had begun – with a round of Cabinet-making, first speculative, then actual, the general feeling was that 'Ld. Ripon must be taken in',[43] that 'of course' he should be given a major ministry.

This impressive return owed much to the sanity of Ripon's views. Loulou Harcourt spent a week-end with him in the middle of the election, and found his attitudes to Ireland, education and English Catholicism entirely to his taste. At last, he discovered, here was a Catholic who understood Liberal concerns about Ireland.[45] At last, one who endorsed Liberal education policy and was able to explain Catholic neuroses about it:

He is in favour of Free Education as long as the capitation grants are to be given to the denominational schools. He says the Catholics objected to it generally because they thought it would lead to State control of their schools and also because they are afraid of the tendency towards secular Education. They are also opposed to the disestablishment of the English Church because they think it will lead to Atheism and Infidelity.[46]

These last were not, of course, Ripon's views; he merely passed them on, making due apology for their unsubtlety.

In fact Harcourt needed few lessons in Catholic unsubtlety: he had discovered it first hand, having spent much of the election fleeing from the wrath of the mobs. Indeed, it is worth describing his experiences, if only to provide evidence for what one historian has called – a delightful euphemism – the Irish voters' 'traditional flair for political management'.[47] One meeting particularly shocked him, providing decisive proof of the 'ingratitude of Catholics in their desertion of the Liberal Party now they have got out of us all they want':[48]

Derby 20/11/85. We heard this morning the adventures of Alderman Sowter at the Catholic Schools last night.... Our men were at the school room door long before the time of meeting so as to fill the room as much as possible but the Priests, who hate us, seeing what was going to happen if we got our men in in force opened a back door and let all the Irish in first....

One of the Priests was heard to say yesterday morning to a stalwart Irishman, 'My man, you can fight?' and, on told 'Yes', he said, 'Then you go to the meeting to-night'.

We also hear that the majority of the disturbers at St. Andrew's schools on Wednesday evening were men and boys belonging to the choir, who were advised by the parson to attend our meetings. Verily the Church is putting its head in the Lions Mouth. I have always been in favour of disestablishment in theory and I am now so in practice and I expect I am not the only convert.[49]

However unpersuaded of the comic possibilities of a combination of Irish bruisers and Anglican choristers, Loulou recognised that its symbolic force boded ill for Liberalism. For this he blamed Manning more than Parnell, though the latter was no saint. The Irish he had encountered were more interested in schools than Home Rule. Manning was thus the villain, the one who had 'issued orders to all the priests to preach and practise Toryism', the instigator of this 'Irish attempt to break our heads'.[50]

In strict fact, the one thing Manning had *not* done was to preach Toryism; but Liberal anger at Catholic ingratitude was in no mood for fine exonerating distinctions. Still, there were some Catholic networks – Manning's included – which did have tangible connections with the Tories. One example is Wilfrid Scawen Blunt, a protégé of Lord Randolph Churchill and not the last quixotic Catholic to be so honoured.[51] After initial difficulty (an anti-papist on the selection panel), Blunt managed to have himself chosen as Tory candidate for Camberwell North. The Catholic connection then went into operation. Manning instructed the local parish priest to assist the candidacy:[52] later, after Blunt's defeat, he sympathised with him on a 'manly fight', fought 'with visor up as a Catholic – the first man who has [thus] faced a constituency in the metropolitan elections'.[53] Blunt's wife, the formidable Lady Anne, also had a plan of campaign:

> We drove to the monastery on Lower Park Road where we saw the handsome church and also Father Gabriel & the superior.... Father Gabriel gave me the names of several Catholic families in the division & also told me to call at ... Mr. Johnson's. This I did ... They are Catholics & are also working for the election & on our side of course....[54]

On election day, candidate and wife toured the constituency in an open carriage, along with such Catholic notables as Wilfrid Meynell, the Duke of Norfolk, and John Hungerford Pollen;[55] this last, by the way, Ripon's former secretary and one of the few people he had tried to fix up with a job when he was in India. Unsurprisingly, Catholicism also bulked large in explanations of defeat. Lady Anne blamed Liberal personation and Tory mismanagement, but Wilfrid saw the collective hand of the 5 per cent in any constituency who voted anti-Catholic, no matter what.[56] Perhaps he underestimated the effect of his own undoubted eccentricity; but as post-mortems go, his was reasonable.

Though they blamed Manning for their electoral troubles in 1886, Liberals also recognised that generalisation about Catholic desertion was hazardous. Local variations were too frequent, the

Priest/People/Party triangle too complex. Loulou Harcourt's breath-less punctuation suggests something of the confusion:

> 3/1/86. My father and I went out this afternoon and met Slagg of Manchester who said he was defeated entirely by the Irish vote and 5 minutes afterwards we met Lockwood who has just been returned for York and says that the Liberals there were carried by the Irish vote in consequence of Salisbury abusing Lockwood after the by-election last year for having bid for the Irish vote which made them furious and though the Priests were strong Tories they could not carry their flock with them.[57]

Using Manning as a scapegoat – and Ripon as an adviser – thus had the merit of creating order out of chaos. Moreover, it was easier for Liberals to make Manning a villain than to blame themselves for not having taken him more seriously in the past. After all, before he had moved decisively towards the Tories, he first thought of the Liberals:

> The General Election [Manning wrote to Dilke] is not far off and I am very anxious to talk with you about the point which will determine the Catholic vote. I seem to see a safe and open way. But no time is to be lost. The Liberalism of England is not yet the aggressive Liberalism of the Continent, but it may become so ...[58]

That was in May 1885; by November, the moment had been lost. Perhaps Manning, like Hubert Jerningham, could only be relied upon to do the opposite of what he had said.

CABINET AND ELECTION POLITICS, 1886

Ripon's reputation suffered no such injury. On the contrary, when Gladstone came to form his Home Rule ministry (February 1886), the question was which job he should be offered, not whether he should be offered one at all. The commonsense of his Catholicism guaranteed him a place; that, and a readiness to distance himself from Chamberlain. Of course, Catholicism also diminished his versatility. At one stage he was to be offered the Lord Presidency of the Council, until Harcourt pointed out that 'it would never do to put a Catholic at the head of Education'.[59] There was also talk of his being made Irish Viceroy, but, as special legislation would have been needed to allow a Catholic to hold the office, this came to nothing. Once again, it was Harcourt who opposed the idea; but this time for reasons which damaged two Catholic illusions.

The first of these illusions was the idea that prominent Catholics *wanted* appointment as, in some ways, representatives of religion. This was the piety from which the *Tablet*'s politics flowed. It hardly conforms to the facts. In Ripon's view, certainly in his wife's, one of the advantages of his being a Catholic was that he would *not* get certain jobs. Lady Ripon recognised the occasional value of anti-Catholicism:

> She had [she told Loulou Harcourt] heard the rumour about Ireland, which she said would be 'too cruel', but *comforted herself* with the idea that even if an 'enabling bill' was introduced it would certainly be thrown out by the House of Lords, who would not be likely, she thought, 'to look favourably on a Bill to make a Radical Roman Catholic Viceroy of Ireland'.[60]

Equally, it should not be thought that Harcourt opposed Ripon because he was a papist. Though true on other occasions, it was not on this. His reasons were purely personal, even trivial. Loulou Harcourt recorded them:

> It was first proposed that he should go as Viceroy to Ireland ... but my father, knowing how much Ldy. Ripon would dislike it, opposed it strongly and I hope successfully.[61]

He had no objection to the principle of the thing.

Ripon eventually went to the Admiralty, though he would have preferred the India Office.[62] Either way – and the irony hardly needs stressing – his fortunes were now firmly mortgaged to Gladstone's; persecutor turned patron. No other Liberal leader felt so warmly towards him, nor indeed did any have such a loyal lieutenant,[63] then or in succeeding years. As far as Home Rule was concerned, Ripon was Gladstonian to the hilt, an enthusiasm doubtless helped by his never having to win a constituency on it. Besides, he remained an important link with moderate Catholic opinion: a counterweight to the socially radical Manning on the one side, Norfolk on the other. Even his own priests thought that Manning's views on Ireland were extreme, and some looked to Ripon to dilute them. Equally, other Catholics despised Norfolk's Tory imperialism, and saw Ripon as an acceptable alternative. Both views depended for their force on the assumption that Ripon was 'sound': that his thoughts on Ireland were not anti-imperial, that his thoughts on the empire were not jingoist. Both, especially the second, were largely correct.

The party recognised this access to moderate Catholicism and sought to exploit it. So, of course, did Ripon. During the June 1886 election, in which he was 'very active'[64] and towards which he contributed £5,000, he worked hard both to maximise the Catholic Liberal vote and to take some of the shine from Norfolk's luminous reputation. Both endeavours were at once more and less difficult than they appeared. Norfolk he regarded as a political lightweight,[65] influential beyond his skill. What made Ripon's task easier was that others thought the same.[66] What made it harder is obvious: the metal may have been base, but the reputation still shone. Norfolk's dominance of Catholic life was considerable. This, indeed, *was* his skill: to make Catholic civic loyalty seem so similar to Toryism as to be hardly worth distinguishing. Even Catholic Liberals regarded Norfolk as a hero, especially those who endorsed his views on Home Rule.[67] Thus he posed formidable difficulties for anyone trying to prise votes from him.

In other respects, however, Catholic votes were offered to the Liberals with the same passion with which they had once been withheld. Ripon had problems coaxing support from English Catholics, but with the Irish his services were supernumerary. This was because of Gladstone's conversion to Home Rule. Where once there had been anger, now there was only sweetness and light. This was a relief to the Harcourts, who revisited the scene of their near lynching seven months before:

> June 29th. Chex and I then went to the Catholic Schools in Edward St., where we were unable to speak at the last election in consequence of the mob of raging Irishmen. This time we were met at some distance from the room by the Catholic brass band and conducted there in state. The room was crowded to suffocation and Canon MacKenna, who is *now* our fast friend, in the Chair. Ald. Sowter and F. Strutt spoke, as well as Chex ... Lily arrived in the middle of the proceedings, amid great enthusiasm.... On the whole, a great success.[68]

Yet other wounds – as Ripon himself had cause to know – took a long time to heal. Folk may indeed have been fickle, but parties often were not. Some Catholics rediscovered the Liberals, but the Liberals remained suspicious of them. Certain things, after all, had not changed: the same constituency pressures – as it were, Blunt's five per cent – made them dubious partners. One prospective candidate, once a Conservative Home Ruler, now a Gladstonian, discovered this to his cost. Seeking a seat in the Liberal interest, he thought it best, after much deliberation, to seek party advice. 'We have a good many Catholics on our lists,' he was told, 'but the constituencies say, 'Give us a Jew, if you like, but not a Catholic'.[69] His name was Wilfrid Scawen Blunt.

THE PARTY CATHOLIC

Ripon's position as a Catholic broker was thus necessarily ambiguous. Some votes he could not sway, others he had no need to protect, still others he had to hope could be won without too much complaint from the Protestant fraternity. Even Disraeli might have found this difficult; Ripon, better practised in the administrative than the electoral arts, found it insupportable. There were, it is true, occasions when he was the party's trump card. (The Isle of Wight election of 1891 was one: Loulou Harcourt thought that the Liberals stood to gain the Catholic vote because of the anti-Catholicism of the Tory, Sir Richard Webster. Ripon's role was clear: 'Before you speak I will send you some of Webster's speeches which you may find useful – especially one with an unprovoked attack on the Catholics ...'.)[70]

For the most part, he came into his own in less frantic moments – in the quiet, ordinary times of parliamentary tactics and political manoeuvre. Gladstone came to value his advice – always cautious, sensible, party-minded, never aggressive, counter-productive, imperative. As a spokesman for English Catholics, he never sought to disguise their weakness or their lack of numbers. Even his account of their parliamentary strength made depressing reading. Asked by Gladstone to suggest possible Catholics who might introduce a Religious Disabilities Relief Bill along the lines of the Ripon-Russell Bill,[71] his reply was not sanguine:

There is, I think, no English RC in the House of Commons who would be a good person to bring in the Bill. Charles Russell is ... out of the question, as being personally interested in the matter, &

T.P. O'Connor, though representing an English Constituency, counts as an Irishman. Mr. John Austin is a very good fellow and an excellent Liberal, but ... not ... equal as a speaker to introduce a Bill of that kind. De Lisle seems from his public proceedings (I do not know him personally) to be half cracked and that, with the exception of Matthews, exhausts the list ...[72]

Catholic disabilities, in short, were more than merely legal. Likewise, Ripon knew the boundaries of his own power. Self-knowledge was his great political virtue. As the anti-Norfolk voice in the Gladstone-Rosebery cabinet, he often spoke the language of apologetic impotence. Witness the attempt in 1894 to promote a politically acceptable bishop in the diocese of Cloyne:

> The priests ... of Cloyne have sent in to Rome the name of Canon Keller as *dignissimus* for the vacant appointment of Bishop. It is supposed that the Duke of Norfolk and his friends will oppose the selection of Canon Keller on account of his political opinions and I have been asked whether the Government could do anything at the Vatican to counteract this influence, failing that whether I would allow it to be said that I was in favour of Canon Keller. I now write to ask you what you would wish me to do about it. I do not believe that I have any influence at the Vatican, certainly none that would outweigh Norfolk's.[73]

This plea for guidance, let it be noted in passing, was addressed to the radical, free-thinking agnostic, John Morley: indication enough of Catholic bargaining-power within the Cabinet.

Perhaps it is apt that Ripon should have tried, however ineffectually, to give the Vatican lessons in radicalism. That, after all, was what he did most of the time in England. Indeed, it was his unceasing service to the party: to preach a sort of Catholic Nonconformity, especially but not exclusively in matters of education, which would not only weaken Catholics' Toryism, strengthen their Liberalism, but would also demonstrate that their loyalty to the Anglican Establishment was misguided not because it led *to* Toryism but because it followed *from* a flawed reading of their political interests and political strength. As late as 1903 he set this out clearly:

> We Roman Catholics are to be made to suffer for the privileged position of the Established Church. [He was writing of the Catholic

policy of alliance with the Anglicans to oppose sections of the Education Bill.] I, as an advocate of disestablishment, think this very hard. The RC case has, I am aware, been sadly mixed up with that of the Anglican Church. I have always protested against this suicidal policy, and I cannot be surprised that it has created a prejudice against RCs.... I am a nonConformist, and I therefore enter with many feelings of the nonConformists, but I do not think it just that the Church to which I belong should be confounded with a body in whose endowments and whose privileges she does not share.[74]

He was right to say that he had always protested against such a policy. With Manning, years before, he had been equally forthright. He regretted to inform the Cardinal that he differed 'very materially' with him on educational policy. Catholics, he told him, should never overestimate their capacity to influence governments or under-estimate their capacity to jeopardise concessions already made:

I'm convinced that the wise course for Catholics to pursue is to hold firmly to what they have got and not to risk that by seeking after more.[75]

He was referring to the Education Act of 1870, to which, he agreed, some administrative improvement might be made, but whose prin-ciples Catholics questioned at their peril. Indeed, he took ironic comfort on the matter: that anti-Catholicism would force them towards sense. If they forgot its power, they, not the Anglicans or the Noncomformists, would be the first victims of 'a storm which in a few years would sweep away not only the new arrangements [he was talking of the proposals of the Royal Commission of 1888] but most of, if not all of, the advantages which our schools now possess'.[76] This pessimistic view of things Ripon held with a fierce determination. For nearly forty years, if ever it seemed threatened, he insisted that Catholics 'should take their stand on the Act of 1870'.[77] As he once described their tactics on another occasion – they should 'sit still'.[78]

In 1906 he was still giving advice – not to Manning's successor, but to his successor's successor – as if the pressures of his political geology remained unaltered, unalterable. This time, the complaint was about the fourth clause of Birrell's Education Bill. Catholics were horrified by the 1906 Education Bill – a 'new Penal Law',[79] the *Tablet* called it – which they saw as an assault on their schools, their property, and on the whole principle of voluntaryism in education. Instead of religious education, there would be a bland undenominationalism tending towards secularism; instead of 'non-provided' or voluntary schools allowed by the 1902 Act, there would be a transfer of such schools to local education authorities (if the latter so desired) who would be responsible for maintenance and appointment of teachers. If the school were subject to charitable trusts, the owners were given the right to use the building when not required by the local authority. Instead of a religious 'test' for teachers, they were relieved of any obligation to give religious instruction, attend any place of worship, subscribe to any religious creed.

The Act repaid a debt. The Liberal majority in 1906 had been achieved with strong Nonconformist support, and Birrell's sweeping repudiation of 'Rome on the Rates' (the 1902 Act) acknowledged the fact. But Clause 4 of the 1906 Bill contained a measure designed to safeguard Catholic interests. This so-called 'extended facilities' clause allowed a local education authority to permit 'religious instruction of some special character' not permitted under Section 14 of the 1870 Act, so long as four-fifths of the parents of children attending the school desired it and provision was made for those children whose parents did not desire it. The clause required local education authorities to hold a public inquiry before granting such 'extended facilities'; enabled them to withdraw the facilities on six-months notice; and applied only to 'urban areas' – the county of London and boroughs with populations over 5,000.

Clause 4 annoyed the Nonconformists the Bill was supposed to please, and did little to soothe Catholics, who held that its guarantees were worthless.[80] A protest meeting at the Albert Hall (5 May 1906), addressed by Archbishop Bourne, attracted an overflow audience of 50,000.[81] Most of the Catholic establishment attended. Ripon did not. If he was embarrassed by membership of a Cabinet which had sponsored the Bill, he did not show it:

I am not insensible to the shortcomings of that clause but I cannot agree [that it is] of no value.... But ... if the Catholic body generally denounce [it] as valueless it will have little or no chance of passing the House of Commons – the Nonconformists dislike the clause, some of them vehemently; and if they are able to say that it is rejected by the Catholics, what probability is there that it will survive?[82]

It was the old refrain: 'What will the NonCons say?' Some might have replied, with justice, that they would have said what they had always said; which was all the more reason for making common cause with the Anglicans.[83] A simplification? Perhaps. Over-optimistic? Undoubtedly. But one observation seems fair: that Ripon seemed always anxious (when the Liberals were in, or when a Liberal solution was threatened) to stress the threatening strength of Nonconformity; and always anxious (when they were out) to scorn any Tory-tending alliance with Anglicanism.

The conclusions are plain as to who was the more immediate beneficiary of such a reading of the politics of religion.

THE CATHOLIC PARTY?

Ripon perfected an old technique (telling claimants not to expect too much simplified his world by complicating theirs), but he was right to imply that Liberal sympathy was never to be taken for granted. Occasions of tolerance, however genuine, too often had their antitheses, however trivial. During the debate on the 'Ripon-Russell' Relief Bill, which was opposed by the government as inexpedient, Asquith professed himself amazed by 'the procession of argumentative and rhetorical ghosts which ... stalked across the floor of the House in the broad daylight of [a] Wednesday afternoon in the last decade of the nineteenth century'.[84] But his own party believed in ghosts, too. When a prominent Catholic, Stuart Knill, became Lord Mayor of London in 1892, the *Tablet* noted with approval the end of 'those times of intolerance and bigotry which once discredited this country',[85] and even the *Times* felt moved to record 'a triumph of liberal and tolerant feelings'.[86] But others found it hard to see the Promised Land, as Loulou Harcourt recorded in his journal:

> Tonight is the Lord Mayor's dinner, to which neither Mr. G., Chex, Rosebery or J. Morley are going, which is much commented upon.
>   Ripon was at first to have replied for Ministers but it was thought this would give too Catholic a flavour to the affair ... [so] Kimberley does so instead.[87]

Likewise, any party which contained Harcourt remained open to strong Protestant pressure. At the end of the 1890s, when ritualism experienced a revival, Harcourt's postbag regularly contained matter which would have given a Catholic pause:

> Support Protestant measures – agitate till Roman Catholic convents are under Government inspection – why should they not be – agitate till the existing law is put in force against the residence and acquisition of property by the Jesuits – support Protestant Mayors and Protestant Churchwardens. Alas! that so many public offices should be filled by Roman Catholic[s].... what have we to do with Roman Catholic Home Secretaries or Roman Catholic Lord Mayors?[88]

Harcourt's view of Catholic Home Secretaries was surprisingly, even perversely favourable,[89] but that apart, he spoke for many. Pugnacious Protestantism was his political stock-in-trade. He was, in fact, classically Disraeli's 'Parliamentary Christian' – willing, by legislative enactment, to curb popish practices in the Established Church. Indeed, Erastianism was as much second nature to him as it was, in a different sense, to Ripon: both recognised in it a guarantee of their own distinct ecclesiologies, Harcourt being 'an old Whig and thoroughly consistent Protestant',[90] Ripon a Catholic prepared, indeed required, to tolerate others that he himself might be tolerated. If Harcourt seemed to get the better of the bargain, that was only because Ripon (as he often acknowledged) had less to offer.

This was never clearer than in Ripon's final public act. After the Colonial Office in the Gladstone-Rosebery ministry, Ripon became Lord Privy Seal and Leader of the Lords under Campbell-Bannerman – an 'Indian Summer' in Denholm's view, when he 'rejoiced in the approval of friend and foe alike'.[91] As Colonial Secretary he had continued to represent a channel between co-religionists and colleagues, always in a fashion calculated to protect the latter by sweetening the former; likewise as Privy Seal.

But Indian summers often end tempestuously; dull, overladen heat tending inexorably to thunder. So it was with Ripon. True, the warmth of approval was less general than Denholm claims,[92] the hold on power less assured;[93] but the final storm lacked nothing for drama.

In September 1908 a Eucharistic Congress was planned for London – a great triumphal coming together of Catholics from all parts of the globe, fitting end to an old and troubled century, fitting start to the new. Preparation was intense, excitement high. Too high, indeed, for the *Tablet*, which was reduced to impenetrable incoherence:

> The days of Interdicts are gone, and gone forever. The altar lights are relit all over the land; there is 'Faith found in London' ... The lights of the altars in the great Mother Church – the great Daughter Church – of the Capital of England ... and all the galaxy of Altar Lights set about it – these are the true lights of London – fires that fuse all Catholics in one indissoluble brotherhood; stars shining for those who sit in the shadow of darkness ... signals from the Rock of Peter to those buffeted by the waves; purging flames; the Lantern of Him who stands at the door and knocks. And so it will come to pass that there is no stranger within the Tabernacle Gate.[94]

Unfortunately, not everyone was of like mind, among them Asquith, Herbert Gladstone and (even the *Tablet* conceded) 'here and there a stray pedant'.[95] These last pointed out that the centrepiece of the Congress – a procession of the Blessed Sacrament through the streets of London – would have been illegal. This was true, but so also were many things long tolerated – the wearing of Catholic clerical dress in public, even the very presence in the country of Benedictines, Jesuits and Carmelites. However, the hope was that the spirit of Catholic Emancipation, not the letter, would win through.

It was a forlorn hope. As the *Tablet* went to press with news of 'almost universal goodwill'[96] towards the Congress, the government even then was becoming aware, prompted by its noisier supporters, that the event could not go ahead unaltered. That congeries of Protestant associations which Catholics (illumined no doubt by the lights of London) tended to dismiss as 'one or two comic colonels and a valiant Orangeman',[97] had become adamant that the papists were not to have their triumph. Riots in the streets, a London in ferment, were talked of darkly. Hitherto, the procession had been a purely administrative matter, the Home Office concerned only with the details of the route, happy to leave negotiations in the hands of the Archbishop of Westminster and the Chief Commissioner of Police. Now, however, a policy decision was required.

At this point it became clear that having a Catholic in the Cabinet was an advantage. Ripon was prevailed upon to use his good offices with the ecclesiastical authorities. Could they not see their way to accommodating the government? Was a procession really *so* necessary? With the greatest reluctance, he wrote.

> Under all the circumstances I feel it a great humiliation to have had to have made such a communication at the last moment. What [Archbishop Bourne] will do I cannot say. I have told him that it is my conviction that 'on grounds of public duty "the Procession" ought not to be proceeded with' – but he will be placed in a most painful position ...[98]

Ripon's position was painful too, in a way that needs only a little elaboration. His complaint was not that the procession had been disallowed, but that it had been botched:

> If the objection had been taken at first that the procession was contrary to the law, even an obsolete law, there would have been little or nothing to say ... I would have been quite prepared to defend either the prohibition of the Procession on the ground of [illegality] ... or its permission in accordance with ... precedent.[99]

It was the appearance of having bowed to pressure which annoyed him. Pressure from whom? He began to see a villain, or, rather, two villains:

> It is clear that Gladstone paid no attention to the matter until he was stirred by the King ...[100]

Part of this is certainly true. Gladstone emerges with very little credit from the episode: ignorant, indecisive, insouciant.[101] The King's role is a little more unsure. He probably suffered a recurrence of the old family trouble – acute intermittent inflamed Coronation Oath. Whatever his motives, he thought himself (a little absurdly, it must be said) the victim of a Catholic conspiracy; 'deceived by the Roman Catholic authorities, who kept him in the dark as to the real character of the procession ... they have behaved very badly'.[102]

Asquith, once the chronicler of rhetorical ghosts, now became their servant. He allowed the procession to be cancelled. For Ripon, it was the final indignity. After a lifetime's trimming, resignation for once appeared the only honourable course. Yet even now, in the manner of his going, he somehow captured the character of a career:

> I am *very* sorry to send you this enclosed letter. But I cannot see that I have any other course open to me. I cannot totally desert my own people ...[103]

Nor, indeed, could they totally desert him. Still they clung to the myth of his influence. 'He is being severely pressed by his Prelates,' Walter Runciman noticed sourly, 'who mean mischief.'[104] (A reasonable inference: Bourne's reaction to the snub was truculent and threatening.)[105] But Ripon meant only what he had said: that if he had no power left, at least he had some pride.

Procrastination robbed him even of that. Asquith, the great political analgesic, tried to soothe the pain; hesitated about accepting the resignation; fudged the issue. In the end, Ripon's last defiant gesture, lachrymose as it was, turned out to be more like conventional retirement:

I have quite determined, as you request, to rest my retirement from the Government upon my great age and increasing infirmities ... better, I think, for us all [that] I rest my retirement upon the personal and not the political ground.[106]

Thus exhausted, he left office for the last time, mustering what good grace remained to him ('I do not blame you ... but I do blame Gladstone'),[107] taking comfort from the thought that longevity alone had given him lustre; 'in the midst of meteors, the fixed star of the political heavens'.[108]

There was about Ripon's career a fearful symmetry: he was twice driven out of politics, on both occasions by a Gladstone. Between times, like Abbé Sieyès, he survived; discretion personified, tenacity triumphant. Courtenay Ilbert got it about right when he described him as having a big heart and a less big head, a sort of 'Gladstone with water'.[109] Yet dull decency does not wholly account for him: behind the pieties lay a sharp operator, a consummate 'fixer'. Very few Catholics saw this side of him, but one who did – Wilfrid Scawen Blunt – made a better political obituarist than most. He thought that Ripon had been 'corrupted' by 'association with his Whig friends in office',[110] which was certainly true, and not just in the trivial sense, much favoured by Catholic Manichees,[111] that *all* politics was a form of corruption, a departure from Eden. He was a party man, happy to make the world safe for Gladstones, Harcourts, Asquiths, even Morleys; he could swallow more things in the name of 'realism'; he could tell Catholic lobbyist after Catholic lobbyist that their best policy was 'to sit still';[112] in short, he could appear for all the world like a Fabian who failed, a gradualist who had come to a full stop.

Yet this is unfair. He realised better than most that to enjoin

Catholics to know their place, to tell them to sit still, was less to treat them as children as it was to call them to a kind of political adulthood; to make them not passive, but pluralist. Perhaps that made him not much different from the Nonconformists whose power he so frequently called forth; less Gladstone with water than Bright with interest. If so, he cared little. Catholics needed most what he was most able to provide – a strong bromide. Like many compounds, the effect may have been sedative but the chemistry was highly intricate.

7

The Duke of Norfolk, Catholics and Toryism 1880–1900

THE CATHOLIC TORY WORLD

If Ripon's later contribution to Catholic politics had a plaintive quality, it was because his was an increasingly lone voice. During the 1880s and into the 1890s, Catholics lost faith with the Liberals and renewed it with Tories; a matter not merely of shared interest in denominational schooling, or even of Manning's instruction of November 1885, but of broad cultural convergence. There were many avenues to Catholic Toryism, all prosperous. Consider the Primrose League, which Catholics joined in droves, to which the *Tablet* devoted hundreds of inches every year, whose Grand Council contained the Duke of Norfolk and Henry Matthews, and whose Vice-Chancellor in 1889 was George Lane-Fox, squire, huntsman, and convert to Catholicism since his days at Oxford. One attraction, apart from theatricality, was the League's apparent religious toler-ance; another, its respectability; a third, and not the least, the opportunity it afforded those many English Catholics wishing to differentiate themselves from their Irish brethren.[1] The marriage, naturally, was never of equals. The League boasted of 'earnest and consistent'[2] efforts to recruit Catholics, but in neither respect was this the case. Early debates on Catholic membership – highly muddled affairs – might have given pause: where there was not hostility there was certainly much ignorance. Some Grand Councillors, clear evidence to the contrary notwithstanding, insisted that Catholics were forbidden to join by express command of the Pope. Others, knowing better, merely wished that they were.[3] Still, many Catholics felt at home in the League, and it proved an important channel of their votes.

Consider also the Catholic Conservative Association, a flower which bloomed and quickly died but whose roots were in the rich soil of instinctive popular Toryism. Its agenda was unexceptional (to unite 'the Catholic vote along Conservative lines, [and to wean] the Irish from Radicalism')[4] but it deserves attention for a unique contribution to political iconography. Its letterhead was a configuration of Bible, crown and triple tiara of the Pope: powerful proof of a desire to graft Disraelian Imperialism onto English Catholicism. The operation was not wholly a success, for two reasons – Catholic zealotry and Tory embarrassment. The Association's founders, seeking party approval, lapsed into hyperbole ('The importance of the Catholic vote to the Conservatives cannot be over-rated ... no ministry can sit in Downing St. without it');[5] and the party, mindful of other constituencies, stopped short of enthusiasm. Here, for instance, is Lord Carnarvon, when asked to be a patron:

> It seems to me desirable that the names of such as myself should be kept rather in the background than brought forward: any belief that the Soc[iety] was established at our instance wd. be likely to do mischief.[6]

This was prudent, also astute: Carnarvon recognised in his suitors an ardour which even contradiction could not jeopardise. Home truths could do no harm, possibly much good.

What the League and the Association had in common was an over-eager patriotism. Many Catholics developed their own form of imperialism, and proclaimed it without a tremor of self-doubt. Thus T. W. Allies in 1892:

> Why do I give my vote at the coming election as a Unionist? How do I as an Englishman look upon Home Rule? ... I look upon it as a rapier thrust at the heart of England.... [And] how do I feel as a Catholic? As a Catholic my abhorrence is scarcely inferior to what I feel as an Englishman.[7]

Allies' rhetoric was typical: when John Dillon sneered at the 'mock heroics of English Catholic snobs'[8] he might almost have been referring to him. In fact, Dillon was speaking a while before the Duke of Norfolk went on a mission to the Vatican in the winter of 1887–8. As polemic, Dillon's phrase was good; as prophecy, it was even better. Thirteen years after his Roman excursion, Norfolk resigned from Salisbury's government to enlist against the Boers, furious that the Vatican, by not wholeheartedly supporting the ministry, had left English Catholics open to the charge of disloyalty. He was fifty years old. Before he left for South Africa (whence he quickly returned, having seen little action) he had his regimental sword blessed by

Cardinal Vaughan. This was an *imprimatur* which proved useless against the scorn of Catholic Liberals. They reviled his indifference towards the 'moral murders' of the concentration camps, the 'terrible loss of ... children and women', the 'sorrow ... and shame'[9] with which decent Catholics viewed the war.

Indifferent or not, Norfolk had participated in an episode symbolic as well as bizarre. The gesture was less empty than it seemed. For one thing, it demonstrated yet again the ineffectiveness of Catholic Liberal protest. Even Ripon, long an anti-jingoist, conceded that there would be no point in trying to organise a pro-Boer voice among Catholics.[10] It would be too feeble to be audible. The affair also captured Vaughan's political partisanship. Unlike Manning, whose election intervention in 1885 was highly conditional and whose imperialism waned as the Eastern question became a memory and Home Rule a serious possibility,[11] Vaughan was a Tory pure and simple. Socially conservative where Manning was radical, hostile to the Irish where Manning was sympathetic, opposed to Home Rule where Manning was in favour, sleek, even, where Manning was lean, Vaughan seems the very antithesis of his predecessor. In fact, they shared at least one enthusiasm: political fixing. Whenever he did business with Salisbury, Vaughan regarded himself as a party colleague, not a sectional supplicant. Thus his contempt for the 'deplorable' Irish clergy and hierarchy:[12] thus, too, his advice that the Irish bishops should be blackmailed into loyalty by a measure on Catholic education – 'compelled to choose', was his phrase, between nationalism 'and what they must consider to be the interests of religion'.[13] Away from Ireland, he proved himself an eager partisan. As electoral tactician, for example, he sounded indistinguishable from other party leaders:

> There is one subject, and one only ... that will pull the Catholic vote together and bring back defaulters, and that is Education. The radicals are employing a forward movement against the Voluntary system. Many Catholics believe that the Conservative leaders are less than half-hearted on this subject and they need to be strongly re-assured.[14]

Catholic politics, at least at the top, had turned Tory: only three years before, Manning had also been promising the votes of his flock; not, on that occasion to Robert Cecil, but to Sidney Webb.[15] Nor was Vaughan the only partisan prelate. Bishop Clifford of Clifton was an unapologetic Unionist. So was Bishop Virtue of Portsmouth. 'I never have and I hope I never shall give a vote for any but a Conservative candidate,' he wrote to Norfolk in 1891, 'and I have always done all in my power to promote Conservative interests.' 'The majority of the English bishops', he added, acted likewise. This was foolishly fulsome. The more the hierarchy protested its Toryism, the more the party could feel safe in its Orangeism. Virtue's letter is a case in point. It was less an endorsement of Salisbury than a complaint about him:

> I wish it could be brought home to Lord Salisbury that he is doing a serious injury to Conservative interests by his extremely injudicious speeches.... I have felt not a little indignant of late at several of the Prime Minister's allusions to Catholic matters.[16]

There was reason for indignation – the Prime Minister had recently urged the need for electoral reform and described the illiterate vote 'as a contrivance to enable the Catholic priest to terrorize his flock'[17] – but the anger was impotent. By the bishop's own admission, Catholics voted Tory because they had nowhere else to go.

But to return to Norfolk. It is with him that most interest lies. Quixotic as his South African jaunt may have been, he was the central figure of this powerful Catholic Toryism. Most Catholics looked to him for leadership: an all-purpose writer of letters, chairman of committees, leader of delegations, patron of good causes. Seen from a distance, Norfolk appears to be the lobbyist's lobbyist – discreet, well-connected, indefatigably busy with Catholic matters. He certainly worked far harder than Ripon on behalf of his Church. He was also the best guarantee of the respectability of its case. There was no arguing with the Earl Marshal and Premier Duke of England. (That indeed was sometimes the problem: Norfolk was occasionally too imperative for his own good.)[18] Most politicians found him a man with whom they could do business. 'Clear and forcible' was Gathorne Hardy's verdict, and few disagreed.[19]

There was another reason for the efficiency of the relationship. Tories themselves realised that Catholic votes were theirs for the taking. The evidence of Primrose League and Catholic Conservative Associations was not to be denied. Salisbury, for example, hoped to cultivate Catholics as much as possible on matters of probable agreement in order to cancel matters of probable disagreement. 'I should strongly counsel acting with [Manning] heartily,' he urged

Richard Cross – 'upon a subject on which we and the Roman Catholics can co-operate with complete sincerity.'[20] The subject was voluntary schools, and the distinction well-made: often with Salisbury, mutual convenience was the most that could be hoped from a political alliance.[21] Here, however, was the prospect of genuine co-operation.

Salisbury also knew the value of flattery, the less risky the better. In 1887 he congratulated the Primrose League for its religious tolerance, for being as he put it, 'Catholic in the highest sense'.[22] The phrase, apparently anodyne, concealed consummate political artistry. Salisbury's reference was to Bishop Bagshawe of Nottingham, a Home Ruler, who had warned Catholics that membership of the League was not compatible with their religion.[23] The ensuing row, a considerable embarrassment to the *Tablet* and other engines of Catholic Toryism, was only resolved when the errant bishop was publicly rebuked by Manning. There were no grounds, he said, for such an utterance. Nor indeed, added Salisbury, were there any for thinking that the League was cool towards Catholics. On the contrary, it was Catholic in the highest sense.

It was a clever intervention, for hidden in the welcome was a warning: the League was for Wesleyans, Methodists and Baptists too. More than that, Salisbury had condemned a Catholic bishop while at the same time courting his flock. Protestants therefore had something to cheer, Catholics something to ponder. In ways hardly realised, Catholics had been both welcomed to the fold and put in their place.

Too much may be made of this convergence of Catholic enthusiasm and Tory amenability. Not every slender gesture towards Catholics can carry the weight of interpretation which some dispose. It is not true, for example (as some were inclined to believe), that Henry Matthews was appointed to the Home Secretaryship to 'please his co-religionists'.[24] Rather, it was the whim of Randolph Churchill,[25] the reluctant connivance of Joseph Chamberlain (who squared things in East Birmingham, Matthews' seat)[26] and the laconic indifference of the Prime Minister, which foisted on the political world a promotion bemusing where it was not bewildering. Catholics thought much would come of it; but Matthews proved a poor investment for their capital. With qualifications so nugatory and charms so evanescent, he found the Commons harder to conquer than the provincial bar. What passed for learning on the Oxford circuit struck the House as so much pedantry. Worse, his oratorical dignity did not survive the discovery that, in moments of high passion, he knocked his knees together.[27] Even Catholics realised the error of their hopes. Matthews eventually became for them the embarrassment he had long been for his colleagues. When Balfour discussed Cabinet changes, a vacancy at the Home Office was his first assumption;[28] when Gathorne Hardy examined the health of the government, the decrepitude of the Home Secretary was his readiest target;[29] when Loulou Harcourt attended the great annual rally of the Primrose League in 1893, it was a speech by Matthews which crowned the tedium;[30] when the Queen complained of her ministers, Matthews ('certainly not fit for the Home Office')[31] was villain-in-chief; when Salisbury pondered tactics ('The difficulty is to get Mr. Matthews out'),[32] one problem remained constant – '[Matthews'] unpopularity is quite phenomenal'.[33]

Egregiousness of such a high order may even have helped Catholics. Matthews was so clearly *sui generis* they could disown him in all good conscience. That, in effect, was what they did. Newspapers which regretted his 'lack of Catholic chivalry'[34] merely anticipated obituarists who conceded he should never have been appointed.[35] He quarrelled with Manning,[36] refused to vote for the Ripon-Russell Relief Bill, and left office unmourned by all. Catholics believed they had found in him a new leader; instead, they got a man who hanged Jews,[37] fought the police,[38] and failed to catch Jack the Ripper.[39]

PARTISAN POLITICS

It was Norfolk, then, not Matthews, who was the central figure of Catholic Tory politics. 'Who has been your Roman adviser?' Salisbury once asked Balfour; 'I should prefer Norfolk.'[40] Roman advice was indeed Norfolk's *métier*, his best effort on behalf of political friends. According to opponents (Ripon included), he was the ultimate Vatican fixer. They were right in a negative sense: other Tories had played papal politics with far less effect. (Even Matthews tried his hand, having a notably unfortunate encounter with Leo XIII in 1893.)[41] No-one else could equal his pedigree, his celebrity in the country, his standing in the party. After he had been captured by Disraeli, Norfolk became Tory nabob *par excellence*: Primrose League Grand Councillor, President of the Yorkshire and Midland divisions of the National Union of Conservative Associations, Chairman of the

Party Conference – the list could be extended. Gathorne Hardy was right to notice that Norfolk was 'keen for work'.[42] Too keen, in fact: what to do when he wanted to translate essentially ceremonial duties into positions of substantial authority? On the one hand, no-one wanted the embarrassment of Grandee as Office Boy:

> I ... spoke [to Salisbury] of his training someone at the F.O. and he was pleased at the idea & thought he might so dispose of the D. of Norfolk who is keen for work even as an Under Secy., which seems hardly consonant with the Earl Marshall's high place.[43]

On the other hand, he was hardly Cabinet material: youth, inexperience and religion all told against him.

A solution soon came to hand: he was sent to the Vatican as head of an undercover diplomatic mission to secure Papal condemnation of Irish violence and the 'Plan of Campaign', the latest in a long line of tenant protection schemes to force landlords to accept reduced rents and limit evictions. Honour and utility alike satisfied, Norfolk could claim to be serving his country and his colleagues; a supporter neatly dispatched, Salisbury could also hope for substantial benefit in Ireland.

Norfolk's activities in Rome in the winter of 1887–8 must be seen in the context of continuing efforts by the British government to influence Papal policy on Ireland. In June 1887 Archbishop Ignazio Persico was sent by Pope Leo XIII on a special mission to Ireland to investigate the state of the Church and to urge clerical moderation in politics. During his six months there, both sides – nationalist and unionist – tried to persuade him of their cause. Oddly, both believed they had succeeded. Archbishop Walsh, for example, felt 'very confident' that Persico's views were 'favourable' to his own.[44] Lord Emly, on the other hand, met the Monsignor and pronounced their talk 'most successful'. 'He sees through here with the same eyes as we do,' he told Norfolk, '[and] no amount of misrepresentation will throw dust in his eyes. The Pope's eyes will be opened by him.'[45]

It was the government's intention that the Pope's eyes be opened by Norfolk also. The Duke went first to Rome in December 1887 as a Special Envoy of the Queen to thank the Pope for his congratulations on the occasion of her Golden Jubilee. He then returned in January 1888 as head of a pilgrimage of Catholics to congratulate him on his own Golden Jubilee – fifty years in the priesthood. When that pilgrimage left, Norfolk stayed on to begin his 'weary exile',[46] which did not end until early April. He was assisted in his endeavours by Captain John Ross of Bladensburg and Lords Denbigh and Selborne.

Norfolk's presence in Rome was ostensibly neutral; he was merely a prominent Catholic attempting to persuade the Pope of a course in Ireland. That he happened to be a unionist was neither here nor there; the fiction had to be preserved that he acted as a Catholic first, a Tory second. Perhaps he even believed as much himself, but without conviction. As diplomat, he aspired only to ventriloquism: 'I have written to Cardinal Howard in the sense you wish',[47] he assured Salisbury in 1886, the sense being that Irish bishops should be warned of the need for loyalty. A year later, his dependence was even clearer. 'I think it would be a most important thing,' he wrote to Balfour from Rome, 'if you would furnish me with the names of such priests as you would wish to see nominated as Bishops.'[48] This assumed that he was a figure of authority. Other communications, however, suggested one who needed guidance:

> Supposing the Pope were preparing some letter or manifesto on Irish questions, dealing specifically with the moral aspects, can you give us any points that would be of practical importance to be noticed by him.... Such as
>
> 1.   Plan of Campaign
> 2.   Debtors ...
> 3.   Boycotting
> 4.   Boycotting at School (corruption of youth)[49]

In other words, as a Vatican expert Norfolk was self-effacing to the point of muteness.[50] It may be countered that initiative and self-promotion are no part of the diplomat's armoury, but this does not diminish the general charge. What made Norfolk a good diplomat made him also a good party man: an overwhelming desire to please. He was not without opinions of his own, but these reflected above all irritation that Irish clerical radicalism prevented him from converting or winning the respect of upper-class England. Witness his thoughts on certain Irish bishops:

> Let me urge that the more Dr. Walsh repudiates all gifts from the British Government the more clear it is that he and the party he has espoused dread the result of such gifts being accepted. He and his friends have got this grievance [a Catholic University] and it suits

their purpose very well, but I am assured that *many* of the Bishops would gladly welcome a measure which, sanctioned from Rome, they could accept as an opportunity for thrusting off the yoke of Dr. Walsh and his nationalist allies ...

A full and generous settlement of this question would undermine the position now taken up by the Irish Bishops, would bring to our side the sympathy and support of the Holy See in our struggle with the Irish, and would bring to their senses the numbers of English Catholics who are shaky about the Union.[51]

Such could easily have come from Clarendon, Derby or Granville. Even from Norfolk, the *aperçu* is unsurprising. Leading English Catholics had always treated Ireland as a place apart. Norfolk, if anything, was tolerant enough to advocate 'full and generous' measures to break the hierarchy. Others were less patient. Lord Petre thought the Irish priest a 'surpliced ruffian',[52] and Lord Denbigh (whom Balfour admired as the sanest of the lot)[53] urged a smear campaign against the hierarchy as the best means of restoring order.[54] Norfolk, too, understood the uses of black propaganda,[55] but it was not his only solution to the Irish problem.

Norfolk did his job in Rome remarkably well, far better than Irish nationalists had feared. The aim had been to dash Dr Walsh, whom he loathed, and he succeeded to an extent that amounted to humiliation for the Archbishop. In February 1888 Walsh had an audience with the Pope in which he was asked to prepare an account of the Irish land question. Thus informed, the Pope could consider the legitimacy of the Plan of Campaign. Walsh was happy to comply. Working under pressure he produced a substantial historical treatise: over 300 pages in six weeks, fully setting out the nature of Irish land tenure. When the work was still in the hands of the printers, the Pope having seen not a word of it, Walsh opened his *Times* of 19 April to discover that the Plan of Campaign and boycotting had been officially condemned. This was an extraordinary snub. Walsh and the other nationalist bishops tried to put a favourable gloss on the decision, but without success.[56] Norfolk had undoubtedly won the round.[57]

The qualities displayed in Rome were also evident at home. Norfolk handled the politics of English Catholicism with devotion less to his people than to his party. Entrusted by Catholics with the arguing of their case, he was interested mainly in the securing of their votes. Consider his priorities in the matter of voluntary schools:

Nothing [he wrote to Salisbury] tends to shake Catholic loyalty to our party more than any sign of weakness on this great question. I am bound to say a feeling is growing ... that the Government are much more indifferent and flabby on this question than one would have thought possible ...

There are many Catholics who only support the Conservative Party on account of this question of Education and there are plenty who do not support us who will make ruinous capital out of [it]. but putting aside all questions of party danger, I do hope as a Christian Englishman that the Government will not destroy us ... [58]

This was not an isolated case of election nerves. It was a constant political preoccupation. Catholics, in Norfolk's book, were temperamental, scrupulous about their dignity, and always in need of flattery. Deprived of attention, they could turn nasty: 'I fear ... that at the last General Election,' he wrote of one shaming episode when they all backed the Radical, 'the English Catholic vote at Preston went wrong.'[59] It was his task to ensure that it went right.

Tories had some reasons to expect Catholic votes, but none to take them for granted.[60] Liberals, for all their refusal to make Home Rule a priority in the 1890s, remained nonetheless an attractive option for some Irish Catholics in England; who, quite apart from the question of a Parliament in Dublin, had good cause to dislike Tory landlordism. Norfolk, however, attempted to convince Salisbury that Catholic support would not be hard to win: all the more reason to ensure that it not be stupidly lost. In this he was correct, but the implications were more subtle than he allowed. Shared interest in voluntary schools, for instance, did guarantee Catholic sympathy for the Conservatives, but it was precisely this which made the relationship with the party so fraught. Catholics liked to be relied on, but not taken for granted. They naturally resisted the conclusion that they needed the Tories more than the Tories needed them. It would therefore have been politic of the party to play along with the polite fiction that they were equal partners.

Norfolk's dilemma was a variation of this. He was annoyed that he constantly had to chivvy the party into making the right noises:

In many important places, such as Leeds, etc., the Catholic vote will be hard to keep if belief is lost in the Government's soundness on ... Education ...

> Accept the apathy of [your] immediate followers as a guide for
> ... conduct, [and] the game is up.
>
> It is the appearance of the Government not thinking the whole
> question one not worthwhile making a fuss about that so disgusts
> me ... [61]

The disgust was purely political. Norfolk was interested in voluntary schools only insofar as they were vote-winners. Why otherwise
tell Salisbury of 'Catholics ... turning in our direction through educational sympathies'[62] as if referring to a body separate from himself?
He was, of course, in favour of denominational schooling, as all
Catholics were.[63] His urgency, however, was of a different order:
politics, not piety, was the first consideration.

Delivering the vote was easier for Norfolk than Ripon, but
Catholics still required, as well as constant assurance on schools, the
tangible flattery of patronage. Jobs remained the surest token of
political esteem, and Norfolk was anxious that they be distributed
intelligently. This involved two things: ensuring that the right
people were rewarded, and denying the Liberals any opportunity of
Catholic favouritism.[64] The election of Alderman Stuart Knill as Lord
Mayor of London is a case in point. Knill was a Conservative and as
a matter of course should have become Lord Mayor in 1892. However, in his own party there was disquiet that a Catholic should be
thus honoured. Norfolk was much concerned by the matter, but only
from the point of view of the party's 'image':

> Catholic conservatives will be very indignant if in this affair his
> party do not give him such countenance as may be proper and
> legitimate. It most unfortunately happens that ... the Conservative
> element in the City is ... against him and that our opponents are
> supporting him. If it could be known [he wrote to Salisbury] that
> you would regret [such opposition] ... it would prevent it being
> supposed that if he [is] not elected it was owing to the bigotry of
> the Conservatives as a Party. If he is not elected, I know Catholics
> will be 'up' about it ... [65]

... with, it would appear, every justification.[66] Knill promised to
appoint an Anglican clergyman to say grace at official banquets and
the row petered out.

Patronage was Norfolk's constant refrain. During the ministry-making of 1895, for example, he urged the case for a token Catholic, in however lowly a position:

> Catholics in England have worked for years exceedingly hard. If Matthews does not come back to the Cabinet, do you think it would be possible to offer an undersecretaryship to Denbigh?[67]

In fact, it was Norfolk himself who carried the flag, becoming Postmaster General from 1895 until his dramatic resignation in 1900. In that capacity, when himself the dispenser of government patronage, he was faced from time to time with a cruel logic:

> There is a strong feeling often impressed upon me by my loyal Irish Catholics ... that when patronage in Ireland is in Tory hands, no Catholic need apply.... I own it would be intensely painful to me if as a Catholic minister I did anything to lend colour to the belief. But I cannot find an Irish Catholic I can appoint ... [68]

Sympathy is difficult. Norfolk seemed to resist the obvious: Matthews had shown the dangers of tokenism, Knill the precariousness of Protestant sympathy, Denbigh's hoped-for under-secretaryship the littleness of Catholic claims, his own appointment as Postmaster General the almost insane anti-popery of certain Tories.[69] Thus each time he lectured Salisbury on the need to disprove 'the bigotry of the Conservatives' he only confirmed the conviction that it remained a potent force.

THE DUKE USED AND ABUSED

What, then, was Norfolk's real position in the party? Like Ripon, there was little he would not do to make life easy for his colleagues; also like Ripon he was often given scant reward for his pains. It is true that his efforts in Rome were appreciated, but much of the diplomacy of Papal intervention in Ireland was an exercise in cynicism of which he was unaware. In 1889, for instance, when Norfolk's aim was to secure the Pope's approval of Salisbury's Irish policy, Salisbury himself viewed the Duke's efforts a little differently.[70] Norfolk's role was to get the Pope to speak out, but for Salisbury it was more important that the Pope get Norfolk to keep quiet. The Duke, he reasoned, would be less able to make trouble over Catholic schools if it could be shown that he had exaggerated his influence at the Vatican. These were the considerations of real politics. Salisbury acted not duplicitously but with a delicate sense of the possibilities of the situation. Clearly he did not expect much trouble from Norfolk.

It must be confessed that the party never treated Norfolk as an equal. When he was not humoured, he was humiliated. The tragedy was that he realised as much himself. In 1891, when the Tories opposed the 'Ripon-Russell' Relief Bill, the Catholic Union, of which Norfolk was President, passed a resolution expressing 'deep pain' at the slur thereby cast upon their patriotism and loyalty. The deepest pain Norfolk felt was at another betrayal by his friends. 'What have I done to this Government,' he begged of Salisbury, 'that they should force me into [this] humiliation?!!!'[71] What he had done, though he seemed not to realise it, was to have assured them so often of Catholic support that reciprocation became redundant.[72]

The theme recurred in March 1893 when Norfolk was due to chair a Sheffield public meeting on Home Rule with Colonel Saunderson as speaker. A few days before, the Colonel made a characteristic speech in Liverpool, in which he rounded on 'Rome Rule' in Ireland and the baneful influence of 'Popish priests'. The embarrassment to Norfolk was obvious:

> You make it extremely difficult for us to fight at your side. During the elections I had to go to Salisbury to make a speech to undo the effect on the Catholic voters there of a speech you delivered shortly before, and now in face of the fact that we shall be on the same platform at Sheffield it is impossible for me to let what you said ... pass unnoticed.[73]

A correspondence ensued, later published, in which (by Norfolk's admission), Saunderson evaded the question.[74] Yet, honour apparently satisfied, the Duke felt able to chair the meeting, indeed to welcome the Colonel as 'one of the hardest hitters in the House of Commons'.[75] It cannot have been an unmixed pleasure.[76]

Salisbury in time became used to this spectacle of a lion roaring, then apologising. Doubtless he came also to understand what is signified. At the heart of things, Norfolk's concern was a personal one: less to keep Catholics Tory or even, as it were, to keep Tories Catholic, but to ensure that he was not rendered foolish in the eyes of people whose respect he desired. He went to great lengths to protect his good name, suggesting perhaps how little he deserved it. One episode captured the priorities of an entire career. In September 1895 Rome celebrated the twenty-fifth anniversary of its liberation. The festivities, organised for the most part by the Freemasons, were predictably anti-Catholic in tone. Less predictably, the British Embassy in the city was decorated for the occasion. Considerably aggrieved, English Catholics pressed for an apology. Norfolk thought the matter trivial, but was able none the less to save the day. On instruction from the Foreign Office, he assured a meeting of the Catholic Union that other embassies had also flown their flags. The explanation seemed to satisfy, but within an hour of giving it he was informed by Salisbury that his information had been wrong:

> An hour after the meeting ... I got your letter and I am in a fix! I was very happy to find an excuse for taking no notice but as that excuse has gone I feel equally strongly that we cannot let the matter pass in silence. Would you object to my writing you a few lines expressing the pain the incident has given us to which you would send me a reply saying that ... in the absence of the Ambassador an unavoidable misapprehension had arisen. Or something which would meet the point. This correspondence I would send to the *Times* and I think that would quiet people ... [77]

Such were the troubles and such the responses of the hapless Earl Marshal.

FIN DE SIÈCLE

When Ripon left office in 1908 it was because his Party had abandoned his Church; with Norfolk in 1900, it was the other way around. On that occasion, the quarrel was with the apparently pro-Boer Pope, not the Prime Minister. The contrast is instructive, for although both seemed to perform analogous services for their respective friends, Ripon and Norfolk came from different moulds. One was a competent professional, albeit of the second rank, the other merely an eager amateur of no notable gifts except perhaps elasticity of conscience. Norfolk had much pride but little shame. Besides, his role was different from Ripon's. The Liberals had to win Catholic votes, the Tories only to preserve them. In that respect, Ripon did a hard job well, Norfolk an easy one badly. Of course, he got little help from his colleagues, but that was partly his own fault: if Catholics were as reliable, compliant, and tolerant as he said they were, courting their votes would have been an act of supererogation.

Yet we should not be too quick to condemn. His difficulty, after all, was genuine: Catholics *were* keen to vote Tory, *were* anxious to make common cause with a party 'naturally [regarded] as the champion of Religious Education'.[78] Perhaps Norfolk's fault was not to have represented Catholics badly but too well. No-one captured better in his own person their contrarieties: querulous but at heart quiescent, cantankerous but ultimately conformist. One of his obituarists likened him to Sir Thomas More, 'that great uncompromising Chancellor'.[79] It might be thought, given Norfolk's career of compliance, that no comparison could be more inept. Yet maybe not: he tried hard to be a man of the world, even affected the language of cynical detachment, but in the end he remained as innocent as the people for whom he ambiguously spoke.

Conclusion

This study rightly ends with Norfolk, the leading English Catholic and the most characteristic spokesman-supplicant of that small but notable group. But how well had that group fared? With the end of the century approaching, Catholic pamphleteers had opportunity to assess progress. An era had ended 'glorious beyond compare',[1] when Catholics were at last able to 'breathe and walk without fear, and to speak freely';[2] a hidden people had emerged from 'the gloom and shadow' of one age into the 'brighter ... religious peace and sunshine' of another;[3] a church had triumphed over falsehoods from all sides, 'from the advanced Anglican to the most extreme Protestant'.[4]

This was the official anthem to which only a few took exception. One was Thomas Murphy, who wrote a prize essay in 1891 called *The Position of the Catholic Church in England and Wales During the last Two Centuries: Retrospect and Forecast*. Murphy's characterisation of the half-century to 1900 was unusually cautious: progress, certainly, he argued, but of a modest, patchy, often impermanent sort. Against 'specific and visible'[5] success in some areas had to be weighed equally visible failure in others: many churches remained unconsecrated because they were massively burdened with debt; many towns, some of 'considerable size', had no regular Mass, even on a Sunday;[6] many seminaries were proposed, some even founded, for the education of perhaps no more than three or four priests; many Catholics were narrow and selfish, lacking a 'missionary spirit';[7] many were blind to the extremes of wealth and poverty among them; many thousands of pounds were frequently spent on one elaborate church which would have been better devoted to the building of several smaller chapels; many Catholic estates had changed hands, causing a loss of Catholic identity among the tenantry; many Catholics had left the country altogether, emigrating 'in great numbers' to the United States, where, though they remained Catholic, they represented nevertheless 'a direct loss to the Church in England'.[8] The indictment was considerable and the conclusion gloomy:

The Anglican [i.e. Oxford] movement was one affecting the learned and the rich. What is desired is that it be extended to the middle classes, and the toilers. In the rural districts of England particularly the knowledge of Catholic doctrines is utterly unknown.... It is useless to wait for miracles ...[9]

Murphy was not alone in his assessment. When his essay was published in 1892, its preface was supplied by Lord Braye, whose account was even more despondent than the book it introduced. 'The twentieth century,' he observed, 'will not dawn on a Catholic England.' And for this there was good reason:

The fountain and origin of our present disaster is the over-abounding hopefulness of our predecessors.... Their work was noble, but the fruit of it was much marred by the prevailing notion that England was ready to accept the Faith.... they imagined anti-Catholicism about to die, and behold it lives, for the punishment of their successors.[10]

According to Braye, the 'great and far-reaching calamity'[11] which had befallen English Catholicism could be explained in a word: over-confidence. Everything flowed from that first error: the building of churches where chapels would have done; the creation of dioceses where before there had not even been parishes; the establishment of several seminaries where one or two would have been enough; the concentration of resources on certain urban areas when some priests in the country were over-worked on a Sunday and under-worked for the rest of the week; the funding of a Catholic university college (almost to spite the Oxbridge Protestants) when not even the schools were adequate. The list of failed dreams seems almost endless.

Braye's analysis was sound, also versatile: it may be applied with equal force to Catholic endeavour in politics. Here Catholics consistently failed to read the signs. They were neither as powerful as they thought nor as sought after by statesmen. Rather, they placed trust in leaders who seemed destined only to betray it. The Whigs under Russell denounced them, the Tories under Derby derided them, the Liberals under Gladstone despaired of them, the Conservatives under Disraeli and Salisbury disarmed them. As Braye concluded, in the eyes of their fellow-countrymen they were only one of many different competing sects and even then not the most favoured. 'We are counted a small, insignificant, harmless thing.'[12]

If Catholics were indeed only one of many, it is important to ask how the others fared. Did the Nonconformists, the Jews or the extreme Protestants do any better than the Papists? On the face of it the obvious comparison is with organised Nonconformity. They too required their political leaders to be moral heroes, and in Gladstone they seemed to find the perfect type. But dissenters made the mistake of thinking that because Gladstone professed a mission he must therefore have been one of them. This was far from the case. There was a whiff of sharp calculation in his appeal to conscience politics, in 1874 certainly and, especially, in 1876 when one of the motives behind the Bulgarian atrocities agitation was the wooing of the 'conscience-stricken Nonconformist vote away from confessional politics back to the generalized, highly moralistic Liberalism with which he had everlastingly beguiled them'.[13] As a purely confessional interest, dissent was prone to the same solipsism as popery and thus open to the same criticisms. Gladstone once scorned the Nonconformists' 'Brobdignagian estimates of their Lilliputian proceedings',[14] and the phrase could equally apply to the Catholics.

Recent fashion seems to agree with the Grand Old Man. Nineteenth-century political Nonconformity is now disparaged, a frustrated and important movement 'with an exaggerated opinion of its own significance', tactically inept and poorly led, easily silenced by 'small but timely concessions',[15] above all blind to working-class dislike of that dreary, pleasure-denying moralism which merely reinforced the community of interest of Tory brewer and proletarian bibber. These arguments are persuasive, but need to be given context. That there were tensions within Nonconformity, particularly within the Liberation Society, Nonconformity's major lobby, is clear. There were geographic divisions, too: between London (the headquarters of Liberationism) and East Anglia, the Midlands and the North (its popular base); between Confessional militants and secular reformers, the latter opposing the Establishment less from religious indignation than social pique; above all, between the politics of the past and of the future – Liberationism's greatest appeal in the 1850s lay in county constituencies and small market towns, whereas after 1867 and 1885 the political geography of Britain was based much more on large urban electorates and large rural ones.

Such fissiparousness considerably facilitated the politics of appeasement, the art at which Disraeli and Gladstone were past masters. Often, Dissent was allowed to congratulate itself on political triumphs which were, in fact, nothing of the sort. The 1867–8 Parliament did away with the Indemnity Acts and Church Rates, both repeals giving much pleasure to the Nonconformists. But the joy was misplaced. In both cases they had been pushing against doors palpably open. The Indemnity Acts were the deadest of dead letters, and Church Rates had lost its savour as a political crusade in town and shire alike. (In fact, abolition had less to do with Nonconformist pressure than with Broad Church and evangelical Anglicans on one side and Gladstonian Voluntarism on the other.) Likewise, Irish Disestablishment was not the Dissenting victory which some claimed. It was hardly Nonconformist power, but simple political talent on his own part, which enabled Gladstone to persuade Catholics to accept disendowment rather than concurrent endowment.

This inventory of apparent yet insubstantial triumph might be continued; here it is enough to notice the distance between the rhetoric of Dissent and its achievement. But it is also important to retain perspective. Nonconformists may have been less important than they imagined, but they had an influence far outreaching any which Catholics might boast. Consider, as only one example, the statistics of the Liberal victory of 1892: thirty Methodists, twenty-seven Congregationalists, twenty Unitarians, eleven Baptists, ten Quakers, ten Presbyterians, and a solitary Swedenborgian all took their seats behind Gladstone. Dissenters did not hold the Liberal Party in thrall, but they could never be discounted. Witness Ripon: 'What will the NonCons say?'; 'all kinds of Protestants ... can make a much greater noise than we poor Catholics'; 'English RCs are not an influential body'. Ripon had his reasons for stressing the abiding strength of Nonconformity, muzzling the Catholics being one. Dissenters may not have troubled the politicians too much, but they could still scare the Papists.

The most telling comparison is not, in fact, with the Non-conformists but with the Jews. Here was a group whose experience closely matched that of the Catholics, and contemporaries had long been alive to the similarities. Just as Catholic Emancipation had revived interest in the emancipation of the Jews, so the very tactics of the Catholics seemed to anticipate those of Anglo-Jewry. Thus Lord George Bentinck to John Wilson Croker:

The city of London having elected Lionel Rothschild one of her representatives, it is such a pronunciation [*sic*] of public opinion that I do not think that the [Conservative] party, as a party, would do themselves any good by taking up the question against the Jews.

It is like Clare electing O'Connell, Yorkshire Wilberforce. Clare settled the Catholic question, Yorkshire the slave trade, and now the city of London has settled the Jew question.[16]

Nor did the parallels end there. In the 1850s, Jewish and Catholic interest in parliamentary oaths ran closely in tandem: to concede one, the obscurantists held, would be to admit the case of the other; better, then, to deny both. And here was another connection: Jews, like Catholics, looked to the Liberals as the best protectors of their interests. This was natural: repeated rejection by the Lords of Oaths Bills which had passed through the Commons encouraged in Jews the conventional Liberal demand for restriction of the Upper House's power of veto. In 1855 the *Jewish Chronicle* argued for such a measure in terms indistinguishable from any likely to be used by a Liberal. And in 1857 the General Election revealed the striking links between Liberalism and Jewry.

When emancipation eventually came, Jews were thus expected to feel a debt of gratitude to the party which had done most to bring it about. Yet, as was to happen with the Catholics, the Liberal party got a poor return on its investment. Jews, it was discovered, had minds of their own. Certainly, Emancipation was in its early days a Liberal measure, but in its final form it commanded support from both sides. Tories – Bentinck is a good example – realised that nothing was to be gained from opposition to a measure which could be delayed but not defeated. Besides, even when the Liberal courtship of the Jews was at its most ardent, the bonds between Anglo-Jewry and Toryism remained stronger than some imagined. Constituency evidence – patchy, anecdotal, but altogether persuasive – points to a Jewish Toryism entirely unmoved by Liberal appeals to gratitude. In 1865 a ' Consistent Jewish Conservative' from Southampton informed the *Jewish Chronicle* that Jews had voted Conservative there and had 'for upwards of thirty years' supported the Conservatives in Portsmouth and Salisbury. Likewise there was heavy Jewish support for the Conservatives in Newcastle in 1868 and 1874. Baron Henry de Worms contested Sandwich for the Tories as early as 1868, scarcely ten years after the passage of emancipation.[17]

Debt incurred, then ignored: the pattern is a familiar one. The history of Catholic relations with the Liberal Party could be cast in similar terms. The Liberals, it appeared, had emancipated the Jews not badly but too well: they not only failed to feel grateful, they also began to develop the argument that true political freedom lay in a refusal to be bound to any particular party. 'There is nothing whatever in the faith of a Jew,' announced one writer, 'that need, of itself, influence his political proclivities.'[18]

Such choosiness was not political neutrality: it was embryonic Toryism. Jews so feared typification as a mere sectional lobby that they over-compensated in a way that led straight to Disraeli:

The ethics of Judaism [editorialised the *Jewish Chronicle*] constitute a kind of moral guarantee that the Jewish vote will ever be given to uphold the Monarchy, to disseminate morality and education, to advance social and sanitary reforms, and to preserve peace ... the political and social status of the Jew has so far altered since his enfranchisement that he is now in a position to give a free and independent expression to the opinions he holds.[19]

Freedom of choice could often be chimerical, a new form of slavery: released from one political restraint, Jews found themselves in thrall to another – the need to demonstrate respectability by voting Tory.

Such was also the Catholic experience. And there is another point of comparison. If one man can be said to have made Catholics into Tories, it could just as well be said of him that he did the same for Jews. That man was Gladstone. Jews never forgave him his altogether excessive opposition to the Bulgarian atrocities in 1876. Like English Catholics (who had had an appetiser of the same in 1874), they found Gladstonian populism personally affronting and politically unbalanced. Where, they wondered, in all his bluster, was any trace of sympathy for the Balkan Jews? Where any appreciation that the Turks had been far more tolerant of Jews than most orthodox Christians? Where any realisation that English Jews had invested heavily in Turkey and stood to lose much by Russian expansion? Gladstone, it appeared, was a militant Christian first, a Liberal statesman second, a Jewish sympathiser very much last.

The contrast with Disraeli could not have been more telling. Almost without exception, English Jews found Gladstone's reaction repellent and Disraeli's laudable. For some, it strengthened a Toryism already lively; for others, it wrought conversion to a party hitherto ignored, even derided. Consider the Rothschilds – whose example influenced many – when they abandoned the Liberals: in September 1876 they were 'practically in open revolt' and by October they had 'gone Tory altogether'.[20] Singular in so many things, they were not singular in this. Between 1876 and 1880 the same pattern is evident: Jewish electors from Liverpool to Sheffield and elsewhere supported Tory candidates explicitly on grounds of foreign affairs.

Disraeli's policy (and his origins) had something to do with this, but mostly it was the Liberals, and especially their leader, who pushed Jews into the Tory camp. Abandoning any historic claim upon Jewish support, some of them did not baulk at appeals to simple anti-semitism. If not the worst offender then certainly the most prominent was Gladstone himself. Intolerant of contradiction whether from Jew or Catholic, no-one was more capable of indignant response. Compare two counter-blasts against his opponents. First, a letter to Leopold Gluckstein, author of *The Eastern Question and the Jews*:

> I deeply deplore the manner in which, what I may call Judaic sympathies, beyond as well as within the circle of professed Judaism, are now acting on the question of the East.[21]

His anger at the Catholic line had been equally self-righteous:

> The Turk has two special allies, the Pope and the English Government ... [the Pope's] wretchedly false position [is the work of the Curia, which has] betrayed him and with him the Roman Church ...[22]

He seemed dead to the resentment he had caused and the damage he had done: the bee in his bonnet, in stinging others, also stung himself.

Jews and Catholics thus became anti-Gladstonian Tories almost by accident, but in a way which strengthened already existing and self-conscious ties of interest. Each group, the Catholics particularly, saw in the other an image of itself. Whenever Ripon was appointed to office, the *Tablet* often welcomed the fact that his career was not falling behind his counterpart's, Baron Henry de Worms. There were even trivial connections between the two. If Henry Matthews had any distinctive qualification for the Home Office it was perhaps the fact that he could speak Yiddish: a talent, however, which failed to save Israel Lipski from the gallows. Bizarrerie aside, Catholics and

Jews could generally be relied upon to mimic the 'received pronunciation' of Tory imperialism – another sign (they liked to think) of political maturity. Jews made good jingoes. 'The Government of our Queen,' Hermann Adler, son of the Chief Rabbi, told the North London Synagogue at the outbreak of the Boer War, 'had no alternative but to resort to the fierce arbitrament of war, with the view of restoring just and righteous Government to the Transvaal and to vindicate the honour of England.'[23] The words might almost have been spoken by the Duke of Norfolk.

By the end of the century, we must conclude, Jewish Liberalism was a declining force. Those Jews who had tried – as Ripon had tried with Catholics – to argue the case against Toryism, were left to reflect on the thanklessness of their task. As Bertram Straus, losing candidate at St George's in the 1900 election, remarked:

> Having got all they want, namely their freedom and the franchise, from the Liberals ... [Jews] now belong to the party who had opposed them tooth and nail. [24]

A caricature of the truth, but not a significant distortion.

The political culture of Anglo-Jewry reflected a social division strikingly similar to the fissure within English Catholicism. Just as many English Catholics were at pains to distinguish themselves from the migrant Irish, so also was there a sharp cleavage between wealthy Jewish industrialists and financiers, and their co-religionists in the sweated trades of the East End. There was a world of difference between the Levy-Lawsons and the people who made their suits. Toryism served much the same function for Hebrew as for Papist: it made them into Englishmen. Whether it made the English any less anti-semitic or anti-Catholic is doubtful.

Finally, extreme Protestants. Were they taken any more seriously than Catholics? In an obvious way, they were. Most English politicians were better at playing Orange cards than waving Green flags. Even so, aptitude does not require affection. Good at winning Protestant votes, statesmen were better still at deriding the donors. The last letter Disraeli ever wrote to Salisbury was about Orangemen and their treachery. In time, Salisbury himself came to despair of these 'troublesome and unreliable allies', knowing full well that he was stuck with them. Black was not the only colour in the white man's burden.

Tories regarded sectarian politics much as actors regard signing autographs: a wearisome chore, but necessary to keep the fans happy. Theatrical metaphors, certainly, are as apt as any: for Stanley in 1852, wooing the Protestants by means of anti-popery was a justifiable case of 'playing to the pit'; twenty years later, he was still advising Disraeli that a 'slap in the face' for the Ultramontanes was 'exactly what the public wants'. Disraeli's acting was notable for its panache, Salisbury's for its restraint. Others, unfortunately, were mere hams – Newdegate, Saunderson and Randolph Churchill, for example. And occasionally, by way of diversion, a member of the audience would somehow wander by mistake onto the stage, knocking over props, embarrassing the professionals, ruining the cues, but in the end winning the cheers of the pit because it was whence he had come. The inimitable Colonel Sandys, member for 'brutal' Bootle and implacable foe of all things Popish, was surely one such.

The play itself was neither tragedy nor farce, but somewhere between the two. The story of English Catholics and politics is one of misplaced hopes and disappointed enthusiasms. Such is hardly a surprise: it is in the nature of things for enthusiasm to be discounted; statesmen ask of their followers merely votes, not ardour. Thomas Murphy's end-of-century report was apt: over-confidence was a fearful condition. It had been the cause of some notable reverses: Pope Hennessy's banishment to ludicrous Labuan, Ryley's dismissal by Disraeli as a Jesuit to be kept 'at arm's length', Gladstone's implacable tract-writing of 1874, Derby's unrepentant playing to the pit, Salisbury's refusal to take seriously the bluster of the Duke of Norfolk. The one Catholic who did not ground all his hopes on theodician politics was the only one to be taken at all seriously. Ripon's reading of Catholic affairs was characteristically pessimistic: the vast armies of a Hennessy or a Ryley were, for him, phantoms; the showy deputation-leading of Norfolk, an embarrassment; the political interventions of bishops, exercises in inanity. Politics, he recognised, was the art of being properly humble in the face of complexity: the silly simplicities of most Catholics held for him no charm. Thus his political longevity. If co-religionists had cared to attend to his career, there was a lesson in it for them all.

Notes

CHAPTER ONE

1. Gladstone–G. J. Goschen (1875), quoted P. Colson (ed.), *Lord Goschen and His Friends* (London, n.d.), p. 62.
2. Cf. M. V. Sweeney, 'Diocesan Organisation and Administration' in G. Beck (ed.), *The English Catholics 1850–1950* (London, 1951), pp. 116–23.
3. Cf. Lynn H. Lees, *Exiles of Erin* (Manchester, 1979); J. Hickey, *Urban Catholics: Urban Catholicism in England and Wales from 1829 to the Present Day* (London, 1967).
4. Some married clergymen who converted were reduced to penury or schoolmastering. See P. Adams, 'Catholic Converts in England 1830–1970', unpublished Oxford B.Litt. thesis, 1977.
5. Cf. L. Strachey and R. Fulford (eds), *The Greville Memoirs 1814–1860* (London, 1938), vi, pp. 258–62.
6. J. M. Capes, *To Rome and Back* (London, 1873), p. 229, quoted J. Altholz, *The Liberal Catholic Movement in England 1848–1864* (London, 1962), the most useful source for this topic.
7. 'Catholic Policy' in *The Rambler*, n.s., v (May 1861).
8. Ibid.
9. 'Shams and Realities' in *The Rambler*, n.s., i, p. 224.
10. 'How to Convert Protestants' in *The Rambler*, n.s., i, p. 1.
11. 'The State's Best Policy' in *The Rambler*, n.s., vi (June 1854), p. 495.
12. Ibid., p. 500. ('Tax them moderately ... throw them a stray lord or so ... to go to their meetings and tolerate their unctuous adulation').
13. Ibid.
14. Capes believed that Catholicism was merely probably and not absolutely true; Simpson held erroneous views on original sin.
15. *The Rambler*, October 1856, p. 316.
16. *Dublin Review*, December 1856, p. 465.
17. *The Rambler*, January 1859, p. 17.
18. Wiseman, quoted Altholz, op. cit., p. 95.
19. Ibid., p. 109.
20. Ibid., p. 111.
21. Acton–Mary Gladstone 3/6/81 in H. Paul (ed.), *Letters of Lord Acton to Mary Gladstone* (New York, 1904), pp. 208–9.
22. Acton–Simpson 16/2/58 in Cardinal F. A. Gasquet, *Lord Acton and His Circle* (London, 1906), p. 4.
23. Granville–Canning 10/3/57 quoted Lord E. Fitzmaurice, *The Life of Granville George Leveson Gower, 2nd Earl Granville*, (London, 1905), vol. I, p. 227.

24. Wiseman–Acton 27/11/57, quoted in J. Auchmuty, 'Acton's Election as an Irish Member of Parliament', *English Historical Review*, lxi, p. 395.
25. Auchmuty, op. cit.
26. For a useful summary of the politics of the Italian revolution, see Philip Hughes, 'The Coming Century' in G. A. Beck (ed.), *The English Catholics (1850–1950)* (London, 1950), pp. 17–19.
27. L. Strachey and R. Fulford (eds), *The Greville Memoirs* (London, 1936), vol. vii, p. 418.
28. Auchmuty, op. cit.
29. Quoted Altholz, op. cit. p. 39.
30. Simpson, 'The Theory of Party', *The Rambler*, September 1859, p. 347.
31. Ibid. Acton did not differ with Simpson on the point. 'The separation of religion from politics can do no harm to the Catholic mission in England.'
32. Altholz, op. cit., pp. 132–5.
33. *Carlow Post* quoted in J. Auchmuty, 'Acton as a Member of the House of Commons' in *Bulletin of the Faculty of Arts*, Farouk I University, vol. v (1949) (hereafter *Acton as MP*).
34. Cf. Altholz, pp. 188 sqq.
35. Acton–Gladstone 28/2/63, Add. MS. 44093 ff. 20–1; also ff. pp. 28–31.
36. 'The Conservative Reaction', *Home and Foreign Review*, i, July 1862.
37. Acton–Gladstone 28/2/63, Add. MS. 44093 f. 21.
38. Cf. Auchmuty, *Acton as MP*.
39. Ibid., p. 8.
40. Döllinger had argued, as President of a Congress of Catholic scholars at Munich in 1863, that historical and scientific theology, because they had a capacity for self-correction, must be allowed complete freedom. The 'Brief' (5 March 1864) condemned this as an assault on the *magisterium*. See Altholz, op. cit., pp. 220–3.
41. D. McElrath, *The Syllabus of Pius IX: Some Reactions in England* (Louvain, 1964).
42. See, for example, *Punch*, 7/1/65.
43. Wm. Monsell–Newman 10/1/65 in C. T. Dessain (ed.), *Letters and Diaries of John H. Newman*, xxi, p. 383.
44. Ibid., p. 70.
45. G. Shaw Lefevre, quoted *Daily News*, 7/2/65, p. 2.
46. *Daily News*, 16/2/65, p. 6.
47. Ibid. Witness G. Shaw Lefevre on the Tories and Church schools:

> Even in this country there were people who thought that the government should use its powers to enforce a particular form of religion, and, on the other hand should use the ministers of religion as a means of governing. On this subject we had had recently something like an encyclical from Mr. Disraeli.

48. See, for example, Milner Gibson at Ashton-under-Lyne, *Daily News*, 26/1/65, p. 3:

> But why was the liberal party to lose the support of so many of their

old friends, the Catholics of Ireland? It was a combination of the extreme Catholic party and Lord Derby's Conservative party.... That was not a combination – a combination between the Ultramontane Catholics of Ireland and the high Conservatives of this country – which either could or ought to govern this country, or that could ever promote the cause of civil and religious liberty (*Cheers*).... But the liberal party in this country had no cause for despair ... if [Roman Catholics] valued their religious liberty ... the great bulk of the liberal Catholics of Ireland would rejoin their natural allies.

49. *Weekly Register*, 29/7/65.
50. *Daily News*, 18/7/65, p. 3.
51. Quoted ibid., p. 3.
52. Quoted Altholz, op. cit., p. 234.
53. Newman–Ambrose Phillipe de Lisle, 18/3/66, in C. T. Dessain (ed.), *The Letters and Diaries of John H. Newman*, vol. xxii (1972) p. 192.
54. Clarendon–Gladstone, 16/1/70, Ms. Clar. c. 501, ff. 127–9: 'like Frankenstein [the Pope has] run away from the monster of his own creation'.
55. H. C. G. Matthew, 'Gladstone, Vaticanism and the Question of the East' in K. D. Baker (ed.), *Studies in Church History*, xv (1978).
56. Ibid.
57. Cf. J. D. Clayton, 'Mr. Gladstone's Leadership of the Parliamentary Liberal Party 1868–1874', Oxford: unpublished D.Phil. thesis, 1961. For a summary of the strength and disposition of denominational groups in Parliament at the beginning of the ministry, see G.I.T. Machin, *Politics and the Churches in Great Britain, 1869–1921* (Oxford, 1987), pp. 19–22. For the continuing importance of Whiggery in Liberal politics, see J. P. Parry, *Democracy and Religion: Gladstone and the Liberal Party, 1867–1874* (Cambridge, 1986).
58. Noticed by H.C.G. Matthew, op. cit.
59. A Gladstonian weekly, founded in 1867 by Thomas Wetherell. It lasted only a year.
60. Clarendon–Odo Russell, 17/12/68, Ms. Clar. c. 475, ff. 200–1.
61. Russell–Clarendon, 16/12/68, Ms. Clar. c. 487, ff. 1–5.
62. Clarendon–Russell, 25/1/69, Ms. Clar. c. 475, f. 211.
63. Clarendon presumed that such was the purpose of Lord Cairns' visit to Rome, Ms. Clar. c. 475, f. 208.
64. Clarendon–Russell, 25/1/69, Ms. Clar. c. 475, f. 211.
65. Ibid.
66. Ibid., f. 212.
67. Russell–Clarendon, 13/1/69, Ms. Clar. C. 487, f. 15.
68. Russell–Clarendon, 27/1/69, Ms. Clar. c. 487, f. 18.
69. Ibid.
70. Russell–Clarendon, 21/4/69, Ms. Clar. c. 497, f. 41.
71. Clarendon–Russell, 17/5/69, Ms. Clar. c. 475, f. 239.
72. Russell–Clarendon, 19/5/69, Ms. Clar. c. 487, f. 51.
73. Russell–Clarendon, 10/2/69, Ms. Clar. c. 487, f. 24; Clarendon–Russell, 17/5/69, Ms. Clar. c. 475, f. 239.

74. Clarendon–Russell, 22/2/69, Ms. Clar. c. 475, f. 220; Clarendon–Russell, 17/5/69 as note 1.
75. Quoted Russell–Clarendon, 16/6/69, Ms. Clar. c. 487, ff. 66 sqq.
76. Russell–Clarendon, 10/6/69, Ms. Clar. c. 487, f. 70.
77. Clarendon–Russell, 28/6/69, Ms. Clar. c. 475, f. 253 sqq.
78. Ibid.
79. 'The Govt. would willingly help the Catholic clergy in a way agreeable to themselves but the Scotch and nonconformist members [of the House of Commons, "Where real bigotry and intolerance reside"] won't hear of it and we cannot break up the majority.' Clarendon–Russell, ibid.
80. Russell–Clarendon, 30/6/69, Ms. Clar. c. 487, f. 75.
81. Clarendon–Gladstone, 20/8/69, Ms. Clar. c. 501, ff. 21–4.
82. Ibid.
83. Russell–Clarendon, 21/4/69, Ms. Clar. c. 487, f. 41.
84. Gladstone–Clarendon, 26/8/69, Ms. Clar. c. 498, f. 34.
85. Clarendon–Gladstone, 25/8/69, Ms. Clar. c. 501, f. 30; f. 34.
86. Clarendon–Gladstone, 9/9/69, Ms. Clar. c. 501, f. 46.
87. Clarendon–Gladstone, 11/9/69, Ms. Clar. c. 501, f. 52.
88. The *Tablet* recorded his defeat without comment. Earlier (14/11/68, p. 38) it had reported: 'All Catholics will learn, with great satisfaction, that Lord Edward Howard is considered safe at Preston. Sir John Acton, it is said, is sure to be returned for Bridport (*sic*), and Sir John Simeon for the Isle of Wight.' This was scarcely an enthusiastic endorsement of the latter two. All three lost.
89. See D. A. Quinn, 'English Roman Catholics and Politics in the Second Half of the Nineteenth Century', Oxford: unpublished D.Phil., 1985, p. 47.
90. 'Poor Hartington-Bruce-Gibson-Mill-Acton–now the list of killed and wounded mask the triumph.' Simpson–Acton 21/11/68 in J. Altholz and D. McElrath (eds), *The Correspondence of Lord Acton and Richard Simpson* (hereafter *Correspondence*) (London, 1975) vol. iii, p. 260.
91. Ibid.
92. See John Kenyon, *Time Literary Supplement*, 6/1/1973, p. 3, for whom Acton's peerage is 'still largely unexplained'. J. D. Holmes in *More Roman than Rome: English Catholicism in the Nineteenth Century* (London, 1978), p. 250, adduces Acton's peerage as another proof of how Catholics 'were increasingly treated with respect'.
93. Holmes, op. cit., is typical of the Catholic 'progress' school.
94. O. Chadwick, *Acton and Gladstone* (London, 1976), p. 14.
95. Gladstone–C.S.P. Fortescue, Carlingford Mss. CP1/57; Add. Ms. 44121, f. 147.
96. Gladstone–Bright, 4/8/69, Add. Ms. 43385, f. 38.
97. Queen–Granville, 22/8/69, quoted Clayton, op. cit., p. 246.
98. Granville–Queen 23/8/69, in Fitzmaurice, *The Life of Granville*, op. cit. ii, p. 17.
99. Granville–Gladstone 25/8/69, in A. Ramm, *Camden Third Series*, lxxxi (hereafter *Ramm*), p. 48.
100. Acton–Gladstone, 24/11/69, Ms. Clar. c. 498, f. 185.
101. Ibid.

102. Clarendon–Russell, 13/12/69, Ms. Clar. c. 475, ff. 262–4.
103. Manning–Gladstone, 19/5/68, Add. Ms. 44249 f. 56.
104. 'Not ... a leap in the dark, but a step onward into the light ... ' Manning–Gladstone, 28/3/68, Add. Ms. 44249 f. 33.
105. Manning–Gladstone, 20/11/67, Add. Ms. 44249 ff. 14–15.
106. Manning–Gladstone, 2/6/69, Add. Ms. 44249 f. 76. This referred to the Scotch Schools Bill and the Endowed Schools Bill, both potentially harmful to separate Catholic religious teaching. 10/4/69 Add. Ms. 44249 f. 74.
107. Manning–Gladstone, 13/7/69, Add Ms. 44249 f. 84.
108. Ibid.
109. Manning–Gladstone, 7/4/70, Add. Ms. 44249 f. 150.
110. Manning–Gladstone, 11/11/70, Add. Ms. 44249 f. 238.
111. Gladstone–Manning, 12/11/70, Add. Ms. 44249 f. 239.
112. Gladstone–Clarendon, 5/3/70, Ms. Clar. c. 498 f. 276.
113. Gladstone–Granville, 23/11/70, G/D 19/58 *Ramm* I, p. 167. Gladstone had been sent a memorial by Edward Dease, MP for Queen's County, on behalf of his constituents, urging diplomatic intervention to 'secure to the Pope the continuance of ... Temporal Sovereignty, together with an adequate income'. Gladstone replied, in a letter published in *The Times* (8/12/70, p. 10), that the government had not interfered and would not interfere 'with the Civil Government of the City of Rome or of the surrounding countryside'; that the Pope's 'personal freedom and independence in the discharge of his spiritual functions' was a legitimate matter for the government's attention; and that he was satisfied that the Italian government had pledged itself 'in the most explicit manner' to respect that freedom.
114. Gladstone–Granville, 10/12/70, G/D 29/58 *Ramm* I, p. 183. The paper attacked Catholic support for Temporal Sovereignty as indignation on the cheap.

> Why should Rome be ill-governed in order that Roman Catholics in well-governed countries may have a Sovereign as their spiritual head? Surely the Romans are themselves better judges of ... Temporal Sovereignty ... than those who look at it through the enchantment of theoretic sympathy and practical distance. (*Daily News*, 10/12/70, p. 5).

115. Clarendon–Russell, 2/5/70, Ms. Clar. c. 475 f. 291.
116. Kimberley Journal, 30/6/70, ed. E. Drus, *Camden Third Series* XCI, p. 16.
117. *Hansard's Parliamentary Debates* (House of Lords, 22/5/70) 3rd Series CCI, p. 1471.
118. *Tablet*, 2/7/70s, p. 2. See also Ch. 4, p. 000.
119. See G. I. T. Machin, *Politics and the Churches in Great Britain 1869–1921* (Oxford, 1987), pp. 33–5.
120. *Tablet*, 30/7/70, p. 130.
121. Cf. Gladstone-Manning, 2/8/70, Add. Ms. 44249 f. 170.
122. This is controversial. McCormack (op. cit., p. 279) argues that Vaughan was not anti-Irish. Perhaps so; admittedly, references to 'poor

Paddies', 'a queer people', 'bravado and folly of some of our poor Irish ... beyond words' (*The Correspondence of Herbert, Cardinal Vaughan and Lady Herbert of Lea*, ed. Shane Leslie (London, 1942): (hereafter *Letters*), pp. 256, 330, 347, as well as p. 86) suggest confusion more than contempt. McCormack's later argument (p. 216), that Vaughan opposed Home Rule to keep some Catholic MPs at Westminster, is not really to the point. His letters to Lady Herbert reveal an inhabitant of a paternalist, slightly fearful world: on in which, 'if the people are going to rule, or to stir up rebellion, equally it is vital that we should not be strangers to them or bear a hostile name' (*Letters*, p. 39, October 1867).

123. Vaughan–Lady Herbert, 11/2/71, *Letters*, p. 188.
124. A frequent theme of Vaughan's *Tablet*, and correspondents to it.
125. Newman–Fred G. Lee, 5/5/72, *Letters and Diaries*, xxci, p. 55.
126. All the more so because the massive haemorrhage of support from the government, as shown in by-elections between 1870 and 1874, was partly due to Nonconformist dislike of the Education Act. See Machin, op. cit., p. 40.
127. Granville–Gladstone, 4/12/71, G/D 29/60 *Ramm*, II, p. 289.
128. Granville–Gladstone, 25,8,73, Add. Ms. 44169 f. 250.
129. Gladstone–Granville, 21/8/72, G/D 29/61 *Ramm*, II. p. 341.
130. Cf. E. R. Norman, op. cit.
131. *Tablet*, 22/3/73, p. 358.
132. Newman–Alfred Plummer, 21/2/73, *Letters and Diaries*, xvvi, p. 259.
133. Monsell–Newman, 7/9/73, *Letters and Diaries*, XXVI, p. 362.
134. *Tablet*, 22/11/73, p. 643.
135. Ibid.
136. *Tablet*, 31/1/74, p. 133.
137. Ibid.
138. Quoted *Tablet*, 7/2/74, p. 184. A minor query: did Catholic rhetoric about education always correspond to Catholic educational practice? See, for instance, Simpson-Acton, 17/5/69 in *Correspondence*, III, p. 271. 'Renouf came across a nun teacher last week who not liking to teach her infants A for Ass had changed her alphabetical lore to A for Donkey.'
139. Vaughan-Lady Herbert, 11/2/74, *Letters*, p. 243.
140. See Machin, op. cit., pp. 63–5.
141. *Tablet*, 14/2/74, p. 198.
142. Quoted Machin, op. cit., p. 64.
143. Gladstone-Granville, 25/11/74, G/D 29/29a, *Ramm* II, p. 459.

CHAPTER TWO

1. Cited, *Letters*, IX.
2. R. A. J. Walling (ed.), *The Diary of John Bright* (London, 1930), p. 361.
3. 'Catholicism a Conservative Principle' in *Dublin Review*, December 1850, 416 sqq.

4. *Tablet*, 25/7/74.
5. *Some First Lines of Catholic Politics* (1880), p. 12.
6. *Letters*, August 1867, p. 18.
7. *Tablet*, 12/9/74, p. 339.
8. Quoted J. Vincent (ed.), *Disraeli, Derby and the Conservative Party: The Political Journals of Lord Stanley 1849–1869* (London, 1978), p. 167 (18/2/61).
9. Ibid., p. 228, 17/2/65.
10. Ibid., p. 173, 5/7/61.
11. Ibid., p. 40, 16/7/51.
12. Ibid., p. 178, 17/11/61.
13. Gladstone to Bp. Samuel Wilberforce, 2/10/62, quoted Machin, *Politics and the Churches in Great Britain 1832–1868* (Oxford, 1977), p. 301.
14. Quoted A. Hawkins, *Parliament, Party and the Art of Politics in Britain, 1855–59* (Stanford University Press, 1987), p. 18. This paragraph follows Hawkins' excellent summary of Church politics.
15. Quoted ibid.
16. Quoted ibid.
17. *Trelawny Journal* (hereafter TJ), 18/6/62, Ms. Eng. Hist. d. 413 f.167 (Bodleian Library).
18. *TJ*, 8/8/60, Ms. Eng. Hist. d. 412 f.77.
19. Ibid.
20. *TJ*, 4/7/61, Ms. Eng. Hist. d. 413 ff.83–4.
21. *TJ*, 16/8/60, Ms. Eng. Hist. d. 412 f.84.
22. *TJ*, 24/6/64, Ms. Eng. Hist. d. 415 f.74.
23. *TJ*, 23/3/65, Ms. Eng. Hist. d. 416 f.37.
24. Trelawny fancied himself an expert in the politics of pronunciation. Cf. *TJ*, 26/3/63, Ms. Eng. Hist. d. 414 f.35.
25. An important point. Trelawny thought the Irish only revealed themselves when drunk. This allowed him to maintain that they were both hypocritical and in the pocket of the Pope. Witness *TJ*, 26/5/61, Ms. Eng. Hist. d. 413 f.28.
26. *TJ*, 2/6/63, Ms. Eng. Hist. d. 414 g.91. ('Maynooth. The usual dull speeches from Whalley and Newdegate.')
27. *TJ*, 29/5/62, Ms. Eng. Hist. d. 413 f.151.
28. *TJ*, 7/5/63, Ms. Eng. Hist. d. 414 f.75.
29. *TJ*, 4/3/63, Ms. Eng. Hist. d. 414 f.2.
30. *TJ*, 3/3/65, Ms. Eng. Hist. d. 416 f.16.
31. *TJ*, 31/3/65, Ms. Eng. Hist. d. 416 f.48.
32. *TJ*, 4/5/70, Ms. Eng. Hist. d. 417 f.116.
33. *TJ*, 3/3/65, Ms. Eng. Hist. d. 416 f.16.
34. *TJ*, 9/7/63, Ms. Eng. Hist. d. 414 f.127.
35. Vincent, op. cit., xii.
36. Ibid., xvi.
37. Ibid., p. 40, 16/12/51.
38. Disraeli–Viscount Barrington, 11/9/78, Add. Ms. 58210 f. 60 (Supplementary Disraeli Papers).
39. Derby–Disraeli, 15/11/50, *DP*, B/XX/S/19.

His 'indignation' did not rise to a great height till he found how strong was the feeling among his own Low-Church and Protestant supporters....

40. Stanley–Disraeli, 19/7/52, *DP*, B/XX/S/554. Stanley's last point was faulty. What made the election problematic for Tories was that the religiously 'unreasonable' were *not* behind them as usual. Although the proclamation (June 1852) against the wearing of Catholic vestments in public appealed to ultra Protestants, the effect was diminished by reluctance to repeal the Maynooth Grant, and the Liberals' appeal to Protestantism on the basis of the Ecclesiastical Titles Act. See Machin, op. cit., pp. 229 sqq.
41. Derby-Disraeli, 26/2/53, *DP*, B/XX/S/113. See also, K. T. Hoppen, *Elections, Politics and Society in Ireland 1832–1885* (Oxford, 1948), p. 243.
42. Stanley–Disraeli, 28/11/53, *DP*, B/XX/S/601.

I have been doing little here, except opening a Mechanics' Institute, and founding a public library, but feel in good fighting order – like the Turks. 'Allah be' is a better cry than 'No Popery'.

43. *Hansard*, CXXXIII 967 (25/5/54). The Bill was defeated on Second Reading by 251 to 247.
44. Stanley–Disraeli, 19/20/54, *DP*, B/XX/S/611.
45. Vincent, op. cit., p. 41.
46. Ibid., 30/11/61, p. 179.
47. Stanley–Disraeli, 24/10/54, *DP*, B/XX/S/612.
48. Derby–Disraeli, 5/2/52, *DP*, B/XX/S/671.
49. Stanley–Disraeli, 10/1/59, *DP*, B/XX/S/671.
50. Acton–Simpson, 21/5/59, in *Correspondence I* (ed. Altholz *et. al.*), p. 182; two years later his reputation had plummeted: cf., 7/4/61.
51. Ms. Brit. Emp. S. 409 Box 1/1, f. 23 (Rhodes House Library, Oxford).
52. Stanley–Disraeli, 5/9/59, *DP*, B/XX/S/692.
53. Arundell–Disraeli, 13/2/61, *DP*, B/XXI/A/213.
54. *Life of Benjamin Disraeli, Earl of Beaconsfield* (1916), IV, pp. 349, 80.
55. One example of their oddity: 'Aspinall ... tells me that the Catholic families of Lancashire, such as the Gerards, De Traffords, etc., make it a rule to give their chief entertainments on Sundays, as a practical protest against the Puritan theory.' This may well have endeared them to Disraeli more than Arundell's contrived metaphysics ever could.
56. See, for example, Edward Ryley-Col. Taylor, 7/10/68, *DP*, B/XXI/R/364:

The Whigs disperse their patronage freely amongst the Catholic gentry, professional men and impoverished families, and thus raise their social status, whilst your friends exclude those classes.... Years and years ago Monsell said to me "My dear R., you don't understand this question of Whig and Tory in Ireland – it is a question of 'daily life' – when the Whigs are in we breathe and eat."

Lord Naas, likewise, acknowledged that the Whigs had beaten the

Tories at the patronage game, even though the effects were deleterious:

> We all feel that it would be most advisable to make a few Catholic appts., but the difficulty is how to do it.... Our policy has been to appoint competent men to every office – Ten years of Whig Rule has crammed every department with Catholic incapables, appointed solely on account of their religion – we cannot follow that example. It is both dishonest and *impolitic*. (Naas–Disraeli, 17/5/59, *DP*, B/XX/Bo/10)

57. Eglinton–Derby, 30/5/59, *DP*, B/XX/S/227.
58. Vincent, op. cit., p. 173.
59. Earle–Disraeli, 22/8/61, *DP*, B/XX/E/233, citing Stanley.
60. Derby–Disraeli, 27/9/66, *DP*, B/XX/S/366.
61. Ibid.
62. Derby–Disraeli, 4/8/65, *DP*, B/XX/S/335.
63. *Tablet*, 29/7/65, p. 473.
64. Ryley–Disraeli, 17/2/66, *DP*, B/XX/R/352. The reference was to the Oaths Bill as originally proposed by Monsell, which Ryley thought too ready to concede that Catholics had something to apologise for.
65. The exception to this rule is that Pope Hennessy is of interest to historians of the British Empire. Cf., G.G. Endacott, *A History of Hong Kong* (Oxford, 1958, revised 1973), chs XVI–II for his remarkable governorship; for his colonial career generally, see the excellent James Pope Hennessy, *Verandah: Some Episodes in the Crown Colonies 1867–1889* (London, 1964).
66. Where he was a controversial governor in the late 1880s.
67. *Times*, 15/4/96, p. 10.
68. Vincent, op. cit., 17/4/50, p. 15.
69. Ryley-Colonel Taylor, 11/8/63, *DP*, B/XX/T/36.
70. Ibid.
71. *Hansard*, 3rd Series, Vol. CLXXX, 52 sqq. (12/6/65).
72. Ryley-Disraeli, 23/6/65, *DP*, B/XXI/R/351.
73. I, A.B., do swear that I will faithfully bear true allegiance to Her Majesty, Queen Victoria, and defend her to the best of my power against all conspiracies whatever which may be made against her power, crown or dignity.
74. Stanley Journal, 15/3/66, in Vincent, op. cit., p. 247.
75. Vincent, op. cit., p. 247 (15/3/66). The Bill's passage through the Lords was fairly uncontentious. Derby thought that the Oath, in whatever form it was cast, ought to recognise the Protestant Succession and the supremacy of the Crown; but he did not object to the main force of the Bill. In Committee an amendment to exclude Jews from Parliament was defeated. Lord Chelmsford moved that the Supremacy of the Crown should not be impaired by the repeal of any of the Acts in the Schedule. The Catholic peer, Lord Camoys, did not demur, though along with Earl Grey he thought it redundant. Russell thought that it would have no effect in practice, but he did not oppose it. It was thus adopted.

76. Francis Wegg-Prosser–Disraeli, 25/2/66, *DP*, B/XXI/P/449.
77. Ibid. 'The English Catholics would take the oath of allegiance as a graceful recognition of their respect and affection towards their sovereign,... and the Irish ... as a real safeguard against Fenian opinion.'
78. Ryley–Disraeli, 28/2/66, *DP*, B/XXI/R/356.
79. *Tablet*, 29/7/65, p. 473.
80. Ryley–Disraeli, 10/3/66, *DP*, B/XXI/R/335.
81. Earle–Disraeli, 2/7/66, *DP*, B/XX/E/386.
82. Ryley–Disraeli, 23/6/66, *DP*, B/XXI/R/361.
83. Disraeli–Corry, 16/.10/66, *DP*, B/XX/D/22.
84. Disraeli–Corry, 17/10/66, *DP*, B/XX/Co/23.
85. Ryley–Disraeli, 16/10/66, *DP*, B/XXI/R/362.
86. Not only youth, but clerical pressure told against him. His Toryism was too much for the local clergy. But, as K. T. Hoppen has shown, Church influence on elections was never straightforward and could often be counter-productive. See K. T. Hoppen, *Elections, Politics and Society in Ireland 1832–1885* (Oxford, 1984), pp. 245–53.
87. Edmund Yates, *Broken to Harness* (London, 1864), II, Ch. IX, p. 178. See also Charles Gavan Duffy, *My Life in Two Hemispheres* (Athlone: Irish University Press reprint, 1969), Vol. II, p. 257, for the early and impressive impact Pope Hennessy made on the London political world.
88. Pope-Hennessy–his father, 30/10/55, Ms. Brit. Emp. S. 409, 2/1 f.9.
89. Pope-Hennessy–his father, 20/4/57, Ms. Brit. Emp. S. 409 2/1, f. 25.
90. Pope-Hennessy–his father, 25/10/55, Ms. Brit. Emp. S. 409 2/1, f. 5.
91. Pope-Hennessy–his mother, 8/8/58, Ms. Brit. Emp. S. 409 2/1, f. 11.
92. Pope-Hennessy–his mother, 3/1/57, Ms. Brit. Emp. S. 409 2/1, f. 23.
93. Ryley–Disraeli, 23/6/65, *DP*, B/XX/R/351.
94. Pope-Hennessy–his father, 2/4/59, Ms. Brit. Emp. s. 409 4/2, f. 44.
95. Quoted *Verandah*, p. 35.
96. Justin McCarthy, *Reminiscences* (London, 1899), II, P. 149.
97. Pope-Hennessy–his father, 2/12/60, Ms. Brit. Emp. S. 409 2/2, f. 1.
98. Quoted *Verandah*, p. 41.
99. *Hansard*, 3rd Series CLXXX 431 (20/4/63).
100. Pope-Hennessy–Colonial Office (confidential dispatch, 23/11/75, answering complaints that, as a Roman Catholic governor of the Gambia, he was working against Anglican missionaries there). Ms. Brit. Emp. S. 409 6/2 f. 32.
101. Ryley–Colonel Taylor (forwarded to Disraeli), 7/10/68, *DP*, B/XXI/R/364.
102. Pope-Hennessy–Disraeli, 1/8/65, *DP*, B/XIII/193. 'It was worth my while to be defeated if only to get such a letter as yours...'.
103. Pope-Hennessy–Disraeli, 25/4/67, *DP*, B/XXI/H/491.
104. Pope-Hennessy–Disraeli, 26/4/67, *DP*, B/XXI/H/492. The Stafford Club in London was a social centre for recusants, clerical and lay.
105. Pope-Hennessy–Disraeli, 17/8/67, *DP*, B/XXI/H/493.
106. Disraeli–Corry, 17/10/66, *DP*, B/XX/D/23.
107. Disraeli–Corry, 19/10/66, *DP*, B/XX/D/24.

108. One word, in fact, came regularly to mind when Catholic claimants overreached themselves. Compare Disraeli–Corry, 16/10/66, B/XX/S/22 and Derby–Disraeli, 11/6/73, B/XX/S/890:

> I enclose a letter from Hennessy. I shan't answer it, nor do I wish you to notice it, but I thought as you had some knowledge of his proceedings, you shd. be kept *au fait*. Take care of his letter and keep it in the archives, as he is a slippery customer.

The Derby communication was not specifically about Hennessy, but it struck the same note of impatient suspicion:

> The enclosed reached me last night [untraced]. Pray read it and tell me if you know the man, if you think him honest, and capable, or neither. Is he a priest? I have an idea that I have seen his name connected with Catholic journalism. *By his disclaimer of influence, he evidently thinks he has some.* His friends are a slippery lot, and I am not disposed to have much to say to them, beyond what civility requires. [My italics].

This is important because the quality of slipperiness seems to have been an explicitly Catholic attribute. Other interest-groups could be tiresome, but were rarely seen as duplicitous. Note also the contempt for the ill-imagined 'influence'.

109. Pope-Hennessy–Disraeli, 19/10/68, *DP*, B/XXI/H/497.
110. *Tablet*, 29/2/68, p. 136.
111. Ibid.

> We have spoken hitherto of Lord Derby's claims upon the goodwill of all Catholics, without regard to their peculiar political opinions. Let us not forget a special claim upon one class of Catholics – we mean the Catholic Conservatives. They are particularly his debtors ... [he] enabled them to feel for the first time that they could follow their own inclinations without violating their religion or their political principles. That was no slight service ... we feel confident that it will not be departed from by his immediate successor.

112. Manning–Disraeli, 13/4/67, *DP*, B/XXI/M/160.
113. Manning–Disraeli, 5/4/67, *DP*, B/XXI/M/161.
114. Manning–Disraeli, 21/5/67, *DP*, B/XXI/M/163.
115. R. Blake, Disraeli (London, 1966), p. 497.
116. Hoey–Mayo, 19/5/70, *DP*, B/XX/Bo/90a.
117. Here, for instance, is Montagu Corry (now Lord Rowton) to Alfred Austin in 1881. He is referring to their mutual friend, John Pope Hennessy:

> I feel small doubt that if all Catholics and Irishmen had been as Pope-Hennessy, Ireland and things would now be different. But they were not so; and, to quote my old chief's words, he was 'stabbed in the back' in 1868 ... (Ms. Brit. Emp. S. 409 2/1 f.84.

To be still current thirteen years after its first use was to bear impressive witness to the strength of feeling which it expressed.
118. *Tablet*, 21/3/68, p. 184.
119. Taylor–Disraeli, 19/4/68, *DP*, B/XX/T/112.
120. Derby–Disraeli, 3/3/68, *DP*, B/XX/S/483.
121. Corry–Disraeli, 14/4/68, *DP*, B/XX/Co/37.
122. J. C. Colquhan–Disraeli, 9/4/68, *DP*, C/III/A/45.
123. W. F. Dick–Disraeli, 1868, *DP*, B/XXI/D/253.
124. *Hansard*, 3rd Series, CXCI, 924 (3/4/68).
125. *Tablet*, 8/8/68, p. 504.
126. Denbigh–Disraeli, 1868, *DP*, B/XXI/D/106.
127. *Tablet*, 24/10/68, p. 680.
128. *Tablet*, 17/10/68, p. 664.

CHAPTER THREE

1. See above, Ch. II.
2. Bowyer–Disraeli, 25//11/68, *DP*, B/XXI/B/718.
3. Bowyer–Disraeli, 1/12/68, *DP*, B/XXI/B/718.
4. Ibid.
5. For Hardy's generally tolerant religious views, his 'real and deep faith', see N. E. Johnson (ed.), *The Diary of Gathorne-Hardy, later Lord Cranbrook* (Oxford, 1981).
6. Hardy Diary, 16/7/70, p. 119.
7. Ibid., 17/6/71, p. 138.
8. Corry–Disraeli, 9/10/66, *DP*, B/XX/Co/17; see also the language of Disraeli–Corry, 29/1/81, *DP*, B/XX/D/315 and Disraeli–Corry, 2/4/70, *DP*, B/XX/Co/58.
9. Badenoch–Disraeli, 22/2/71, *DP*, B/XXI/B/2.
10. Ms. Clar. c. 475 f. 208.
11. Bowyer–Disraeli, Jan. 1869, *DP*, B/XXI/B/721–4.
12. Ibid., *DP*, B/XXI/B/724.
13. Bowyer–Granville, 15/9/70, *DP*, B/XXI/B/729.
14. See their strange correspondence of March 1876, *DP*, B/XXI/M/459c; also Ch. 4, p. 000.
15. Hardy Diary, p. 270; see also p. 35 for his 'folly' and p. 240 for his wrongmindedness.
16. Montagu–Disraeli, *DP*, B/XXI/M/454 sqq.
17. Ibid.
18. See *Disraeli Papers*, Box 234.
19. See the sneering reference of Corry–Disraeli, 26/11/70, *DP*, B/XX/Co/68.
20. See R. Blake, *Disraeli*, p. 520.
21. Bishop of Gloucester and Bristol-Disraeli, 10/6/70, *DP*, E/VI/S/13.
22. Arthur Helps was more intelligently critical than most:

It is very brilliant as everything that proceeds from you is sure to be.... But I am very cross with you (forgive me for daring to say so) for some of the political views. Why should you have made a determined enemy of the Catholic party? Now I know what you will say: 'My dear Philosopher, don't you see that I could not make that party behave better or worse to me than they have done?' No: I do not: political parties have very short memories, and states of feeling which are wonderfully transitional – that is, unless you write something which can always be brought up against you.... (Helps–Disraeli, 29/5/70, *DP*, E/VI/S/7).

23. See, for instance, James Kennedy–Disraeli, 9/5/70, *DP*, E/VI/S/43: 'Your *Lothair* is a wonder ... quite a foundation stone for a Protestant ministry of which I hope you may be the Head.'
24. Leiding(?)–Disraeli, 16/6/70, *DP*, E/VI/S/20.
25. Bowyer–Disraeli, 16/9/70, *DP*, B/XXI/B/729.
26. Austin–Disraeli, 8/4/71, *DP*, B/XXI/A/249.
27. Montagu–Disraeli, *DP*, B/XXI/M/454 sqq.
28. Ibid. (The audience took place on 5 April 1871. Pius IX listened 'with attention and in unbroken silence'; perhaps speechless.)
29. Montagu–Disraeli, *DP*, B/XXI/M/454.
30. Corry–Disraeli, 21,4/70, *DP*, B/XX/Co/59.
31. Montagu–Disraeli, *DP*, B/XXI/M/454.
32. For example, Gladstone's Irish Church policy.
33. Kenelm Digby–Pope Hennessy, 18/9/78, Ms. Brit. Emp. S. 409, Box 4/3.

     As the friend of your great friends Mr. Marley and Mr. Cashill (*sic*) Hoey, I venture to take the liberty which I should not otherwise have done of writing to you on behalf of Mr. Adams, a most worthy man and meritorious Constable Officer ... and a most deserving Catholic ...

34. Lord Arundell of Wardour–Pope Hennessy, 19/2/79, Ms. Brit. Emp. S. 409 Box 4/3 f. 80–1.
35. Wallis–Pope Hennessy, 10/10/75, Ms. Brit. Emp. S. 409 Box 4/2 f. 147.
36. Ripon–Newman (1883) in C. S. Dessain (ed.), *The Letters and Diaries of John Henry Newman* (London, 1970–7) XXX, p. 168.
37. Quoted K. T. Hoppen, *Elections, Politics and Society in Ireland 1832–1885* (Oxford, 1984), p. 246.
38. His health collapsed and a continental sojourn failed to restore it. He attacked his valet, then cut his own throat, on 30 September 1878.
39. Derby–Disraeli, 11/7/72, *DP*, B/XX/S/684.
40. Lord Claude Hamilton–Disraeli, 12/6/72, B/XXI/H/55.
41. For the episode, see E. R. Norman, *The Church in Ireland in the Age of Revolution* (London, 1965), pp. 422–7.
42. G. Buckley Mathew–Disraeli, 23/10/73, *DP*, B/XXI/M/252.
43. J. M. Hols–Disraeli, 15/1/74, *DP*, B/XXI/H/610.
44. Notice J. E. Gorst–Disraeli, 16/12/74:

     The High Church Party has always seemed to me to occupy on our side a position somewhat analogous to the ultra-dissenters on the other: it has an electoral importance beyond what is due to its mere numbers, and holds opinions to which party interests are subordinated ... [There is] a good deal of sore feeling.... If the Archbishop of Canterbury pursues his career of Ecclesiastical Legislation, there seems to me great danger of our Government being broken up by the High Church Party as Gladstone's was by the Dissenters. (*DP*, B/XXI/F/81a).

45.   See G. I. T. Machin, *Politics and the Churches in Great Britain 1869–1921* (Oxford, 1987), pp. 70 ff.
46.   Derby–Disraeli, March 1874, *DP*, B/XXI/F/34.
47.   See for example Reverend Reginald Barnes–Disraeli, 18/12/74, *DP*, A/VII/D/2 and John Silvester–Disraeli, 4/9/79, *DP*, A/VII/D/15.
48.   Hardy Diary, 29/6/73, p. 184.
49.   Bowyer–Disraeli, 5/3/73, *DP*, B/XXI/B/731.
50.   *The Liberal Party and the Catholics* (1874). See Ms. Brit. Emp. S. 409 Box 1/1.
52.   Denbigh–Disraeli, Ash Wednesday 1874, *DP*, B/XXI/D/100.
53.   Manners–Pope Hennessy, 17/4/74, Ms. Brit. Emp. S. 409 Box 2/6 f. 8–9. (Notice that this is at virtually the same time as Derby's letter, note 46.)
54.   Manners–Pope Hennessy, 13/1/75, Ms. Brit. Emp. S. 409 Box 2/6 f. 10.
55.   *Tablet*, 14/2/74, p. 198.
56.   Derby–Disraeli, 28/2/75, *DP*, B/XX/S/1106.
57.   Henry Ponsonby–Disraeli, 22/2/74, *DP*, B/XIX/B/16.
58.   Bowyer–Disraeli, 27/7/74, *DP*, B/XXI/B/737. This was not disillusion on Bowyer's part; just another opportunity to give Disraeli free advice.
59.   General Grey–Disraeli, 3/2/68, *DP*, B/XIX/D/37.

CHAPTER FOUR

1.   Quoted, *Tablet*, 26/9/74.
2.   Ibid.
3.   See V. McClelland, *English Roman Catholics and Higher Education 1830–1903* (Oxford, 1973). Some Catholics ignored the hierarchy's condemnation of Anglican Oxbridge as a threat to their faith, arguing that attendance at the universities was an entitlement of citizenship.
4.   *Downside Review*, April 1886, p. 136.
5.   Bodley Papers, 13/10/74, Ms. Eng. Misc. e. 459 f. 20 (Bodleian Library).
6.   H.C.G. Matthew (ed.), *The Gladstone Diaries* (London, 1978–82), viii, p. 520 (20/8/74).
7.   Helps–Disraeli, *DP*, B/XXI/H/462.
8.   Granville–Ripon, 27/8/74, in *Ripon Papers* (hereinafter *RP*), Add. Ms. 43521 f. 125.
9.   Kimberley–Ripon, 22/8/74, *RP*, Add. Ms. 43522 f. 251.
10.   Aberdare–Ripon, 23/8/74, *RP*, Add. Ms. 43535 f. 96.

11. Granville–Ripon, 27/8/74, *RP*, Add. Ms. 42521 f. 125.
12. Halifax–Ripon, 23/8/74, *RP*, Add. Ms. 43529 f. 100.
13. Lady B. Balfour (ed.), *Personal and Literary Letters of the Earl of Lytton* (London, 1906), vol. i, p. 315.
14. Lucien Wolf, *The Life of the First Marquess of Ripon* (London, 1921). Anthony Denholm, *Lord Ripon 1827–1909* (London, 1982). Also interesting are W. S. Blunt, *Ripon in India: A Private Diary* (London, 1909) not least because Blunt himself was a Catholic of sorts; and S. Gopal, *The Viceroyalty of Lord Ripon 1880–1884* (Oxford, 1953).
15. *Times*, 5/9/74, p. 9.
16. Ripon–Gladstone, 1/10/74, Add. Ms. 44286 f. 197.
17. Gladstone–Ripon, 4/10/74, Add. Ms. 44286 f. 200.
18. Ripon–Gladstone, 14/10/74, Add. Ms. 44286 ff. 206–14.
19. Acton–Simpson, 4/11/74, in Gasquet (ed.), *Lord Acton and his Circle*, p. 358.
20. Ambrose de Lisle–Gladstone, 8/7/74, in E. S. Purcell, *The Life of Ambrose Phillipps de Lisle* (London, 1900), p. 87.
21. De Lisle–Herbert Vaughan, 1875, in op. cit., ii, p. 69.
22. Gladstone–Ripon, 17/10/74, Add. Ms. 44286, ff. 215–16.
23. Gladstone–Granville, 2/11/74, in *Ramm*, I, G.D.29/25a.
24. Granville–Gladstone, 10/11/74, Add. Ms. 44170 f. 99.
25. Ibid.
26. Gladstone–Granville, 25/11/74, in *Ramm* I G.D. 29/29a.
27. Ibid.
28. Gladstone–Granville, 2/11/74, in *Ramm* I G.D. 29/25a.
29. Gladstone–Granville, 25/11/74, in *Ramm* I G.D. 29/29a.
30. Ibid.
31. Granville–Gladstone, 14/12/74, Add. Ms. 44170 f. 109.
32. *A Letter Addressed to the Duke of Norfolk* (London, 1875).
33. Ambrose de Lisle–Newman, 13/2/75, in *Ambrose de Lisle* (op. cit.) ii, p. 59.
34. Frederick Rogers–Dean Church, 24/4/75, in G. E. Marindin (ed.), *Letters of Frederick Rogers, Lord Blachford* (London, 1896), p. 362.
35. Denbigh–Ripon, 8/9/74, *RP*, Add. Ms. 43625 f. 176.
36. *Tablet*, 12/9/74, p. 325.
37. Ibid., p. 321.
38. Lady Anabel Ker–Ripon, 6/8/74, *RP*, Add. Ms. 43625 f. 116.
39. Lady Anabel Ker–Ripon, 26/12/74, *RP*, Add. Ms. 43625 f. 230.
40. Much of this section depends on Denholm, in structure if not always interpretation.
41. There is uncertainty here. Denholm opts for 2258, but other sources (e.g., F.W.S. Craig, *British Parliamentary Election Results 1832–85* (London, 1977), p. 169) give Goderich 2242 votes. It makes little difference.
42. Denholm, op. cit., pp. 19–22.
43. Ibid., p. 43.
44. Ibid., p. 45.
45. Ibid., p. 83.
46. Ibid., p. 84.

47. Ibid., p. 98.
48. *Tablet*, 12/9/74, p. 321.
49. *Tablet*, 10/2/66, p. 81.
50. Vaughan–Lady Herbert of Lea, 20/3/74, in *Leslie*, op. cit., p. 247.
51. Vaughan–Lady Herbert of Lea, 11/2/74, ibid., p. 243.
52. Letter to the *Tablet*, 10/10/74, p. 463.
53. Granville–Gladstone, 9/8/73, Add. Ms. 44169 f. 227.
54. Granville–Gladstone, 13/8/73, Add. Ms. 44169 f. 31.
55. As he described himself in a letter to his sister, quoted A. G. Gardiner, *The Life of Sir William Harcourt* (London, 1923), i, p. 63.
56. Thomas J. Collins MP–Harcourt, 8/2/74, Ms. Harcourt dep. 205 f. 346.
57. Rev. Carr John Glynn–Harcourt, 1/8/74, Ms. Harcourt dep. 205 f. 78.
58. Wm. Johnston MP–Harcourt, 4/8/74, Ms. Harcourt dep. 205, f. 74.
59. Denholm, op. cit., p. 121.
60. Ibid.
61. Ripon Diary, 8/12/78, *RP*, Add. Ms. 43641 f. 12.
62. Ripon Diary, 11/12/78, *RP*, Add. Ms. 43641 f. 14.
63. Denbigh–Ripon, 29/1/76, *RP*, Add. Ms. 43626 f. 3.
64. For which, cf. John P. Rossi, 'Catholic Opinion on the Eastern Question, 1876–1878' in *Church History*, vol. 51 (1982), pp. 54–70. See also G. I. T. Machin, *Politics and the Churches in Great Britain 1869–1921* (Oxford, 1987), pp. 104ff.
65. Quoted, ibid., p. 56.
66. Ibid., pp. 55–6.
67. Gladstone–Ambrose de Lisle, 3/9/76 in *Ambrose de Lisle*, op. cit., ii, p. 155.
68. Manning–Ambrose de Lisle, 8/9/76, in ibid., p. 156.
69. Rossi, op. cit., p. 55.
70. Ibid., p. 70.
71. Salisbury, writing to Lord Randolph Churchill, reported with relief that the Queen accepted Matthews 'without a word'. The appointment owed far more to Churchill's unexpected enthusiasm for Matthews than to Catholicism. What would have happened to the process if the Queen *had* said a word? Salisbury–Churchill, 29/7/86, *RCHL*, vol. 13, n. 1591a (Randolph Churchill papers, housed in Churchill College, Cambridge).
72. Ripon–Denbigh, 1/1/77, *RP*, Add. Ms. 43626 f. 5.
73. Ripon–Denbigh, 2/1/77, *RP*, Add. Ms. 43626 f. 7.
74. Cf. Rossi, op. cit., p. 61.
75. Ibid., note 29.
76. In 1876, for instance, tired of being passed over for office, he tried to blackmail Disraeli. Claiming that he had 'documentary evidence' which would do him 'great injury', and asserting that the only reason for withholding it was a desire not to harm the Catholic church which the Prime Minister had 'professed always to serve', he extracted from Disraeli a classic response: 'Mr. D has only to observe that he is in the habit of receiving threatening letters, but .. this is the first one he has received from a member of the H of C and he will keep it as a curiosity'. Disraeli–Montagu, 18/3/76, *DP*, B/XII/M/459b.

77. Denholm, op. cit., p. 121.
78. Ripon–Manning, 14/6/76, *RP*, Add. Ms. 43545 ff. 4–6. Montagu's attitude to the Bill was curious. He began by thinking it 'a most excellent measure' (*Hansard*, CCXXIX, 959 (H. of C. 18/5/76)) On the Second Reading he argued that no Irish Roman Catholic could possibly vote for it (*Hansard*, CCXXIX, 1942, 15/6/76). His fear – an exaggerated one – was that in poor districts Catholic children might be compelled to attend Anglican schools. He abstained on Second Reading but supported the Bill in committee.
79. For a definitive expression of which view, see his speech to the House of Lords on Second Reading, *Hansard*, CCXXXI, 798–802 (8/8/76).
80. Ripon–Manning 14/6/76, *RP*, Add. Ms. 43545 ff. 4–6.
81. Ibid.
82. Ibid.
83. Ripon–Petre, 9/3/77, *RP*, Add. Ms. 43626 f. 20.
84. Ibid.
85. Gladstone–Granville, 10/12/70, G/D, 29/58, *Ramm* I, p. 183. See also above, Ch. 1, p. 00.
86. Ripon–Petre, 9/3/77, *RP*, Add. Ms. 43626, f. 20.
87. As a corrective, notice Ripon Diary, 19/4/80, Add. Ms. 43643 f. 7:

    > Gladstone will not take any office but that of Prime Minister; but he would take that – he is said to have told Wolverton that if he had not had office, he would not be muzzled – this is too bad – it is impossible not to feel he is behaving very ill to Hartington – who on the other hand appears to be behaving very well indeed.

88. Quoted Denholm, op. cit., p. 127.
89. Ripon Diary, 7/12/78, *RP*, Add. Ms. 42641 f. 11.
90. Denholm, op. cit., p. 125.
91. Ibid., p. 131. The Bill proposed the establishment of a new university (the University of St Patrick) with affiliated colleges along the lines of the existing Queen's University. The initial endowment – about £1.5 millions – would, it was assumed, come from the Irish Church surplus. There was strong Nonconformist opposition to this scheme, which seemed to endow sectarian colleges from a fund explicitly intended for non-sectarian purposes. Thus the dilemma of the Liberal leadership. The embarrassment was in some measure resolved by the government's proposing an Irish University Bill of its own (30 June 1879), an altogether weaker measure by which the Queen's University would be abolished, a new university established, but this latter merely an examining body, with power to award degrees to candidates from various institutions but with no professorships of its own. This was far from the Catholic university long dreamed of by the Irish hierarchy. The Bill received the Royal Assent on 15 August 1879.
92. Ripon Diary, 20/5/79, *RP*, Add. Ms. 43641 f. 65.
93. Ripon Diary, 25/5/79, *RP*, Add. Ms. 43642 f. 2.
94. Ripon Diary, 23/6/79, *RP*, Add. Ms. 43642 f.37.
95. Ripon Diary, 20/5/79, *RP*, Add. Ms. 43641 f. 65.

96.   Ripon Diary, 8/7/79, *RP*, Add. Ms. 43642 f. 16.
97.   Notice, for instance, the warmth of Ripon–Harcourt, 19/11/79, Ms. Harcourt Dep. 89 f. 32.
98.   P. Gordon (ed.), 'The Red Earl: The Papers of the Fifth Earl Spencer', vol. i, p. 6, in *The Northamptonshire Record Society*, 1981.
99.   See J. Evans and J.H. Whitehouse (eds), *The Diaries of John Ruskin* (Oxford, 1959), iii, p. 843 (2/5/75).
100. Gladstone–Bury, 7/4/80, Ms. Eng. lett. b. 4 f. 139 (Bodleian Library).
101. Bury–Gladstone, 8/4/80, Ms. Eng. lett. b. 4 f. 141.
102. Ripon Diary, 11/4/80, *RP*, Add. Ms. 43634 f. 4.
103. Ripon Diary, 15/3/80, Add. Ms. 43643 f. 3.
104. *Tablet*, 20/3/80, p. 367.
105. *Tablet*, 27/3/80, p. 393.
106. Fisher–Ripon, 18/3/80, *RP*, Add. Ms. 43642 ff. 52–3.
107. As quoted by Ripon to Rathbone, 20/3/80, Add. Ms. 43626 f. 54.
108. Ibid.
109. Ripon–Rathbone, 21/3/80, Add. Ms. 43626 f. 56.
110. Ibid.
111. Ripon–Risher, 21/3/80, Add. Ms. 43626 f. 57.
112. Ripon–Rathbone, 20/3/80, Add. Ms. 43626 f. 54.
113. Ripon–Fisher, 21/3/80, Add. Ms. 43626 f. 57.
114. Ibid.
115. Fisher–Ripon, 22/3/80, *RP*, Add. Ms. 43626 f. 63.
116. Ibid.
117. Ibid.
118. Ibid., f. 64.
119. Ibid.
120. Fisher–Ripon, 23/3/80, *RP*, Add. Ms. 43626 f. 65.
121. Hon. Francis Stonor–Ripon, 23/3/80, *RP*, Add. Ms. 43626 f. 67.
122. Ripon–Wm Rathnone, 25/3/80, *RP*, Add. Ms. 43626 f. 75.
123. Ripon–Primrose, 13/6/86, Add. Ms. 44287 ff. 56–7 (My italics).
124. J.E.C. Bodley–Manning, 17/6/87, Ms. Eng. lett. c. 188 f. 129. Bodley, not himself a Catholic, was, through his association with Manning, familiar with the higher spheres of the Catholic world.
125. Hon. Francis Stonor–Ripon, 23/3/80, *RP*, Add. Ms. 43626 f. 67.
126. Aberdare–Ripon, 23/3/80, *RP*, Add. Ms. 43535 f. 135.
127. Aberdare–Ripon, 30/3/80, *RP*, Add. Ms. 43535 f. 137.
128. Ripon–Dilke, 27/3/80, Dilke Papers, Add. Ms. 43894 f. 2.
129. Ibid.
130. Fisher–Ripon, 4/4/80, *RP*, Add. Ms. 43626 f. 79.
131. Fisher–Ripon, 10/4/80, *RP*, Add. Ms. 43626 f. 84.
132. Ibid.
133. Ibid.
134. Braye–Ripon, 6/4/80, *RP*, Add. Ms. 43626 f. 81.
135. Ibid.
136. Fisher–Ripon, 29/3/80, *RP*, Add. Ms. 43626 f. 77.
137. Ripon–Primrose, 13/6/86, *RP*, Add. Ms. 44287 f. 56.
138. Harcourt–Ripon, 7/2/92, *RP*, Add. Ms. 43532 f. 71.

CHAPTER FIVE

1. Pope Hennessy–Carnarvon, 8/3/74, Ms. Brit. Emp. S. 409 Box 7/1 fol. 21.
2. Pope Hennessy–Disraeli, 8/9/74, Ms. Brit. Emp. S. 409 Box 7/2 fol. 2.
3. Pope Hennessy–Disraeli, 12/11/74, *DP*, B/XXI/H/505.
4. Wallis–Pope Hennessy, 10/10/75, Ms. Brit. Emp. S. 409 Box 4/2 f. 147. A. M. Sullivan (1830–84): journalist, politician, and barrister; sole editor and proprietor of *The Nation* 1858–77; Constitutional Home Ruler and anti-Fenian. MP for Co. Louth 1874–80, Meath 1880–1. His moderation is shown by his request that £400 raised as a national testimonial to him – he had spent three months in prison after protesting the execution of the Manchester Martyrs – be used for the erection of a statue to Henry Grattan.
5. Derby–Disraeli, 18/8/75, *DP*, B/XX/S/1092.
6. Derby–Disraeli, 28/11/74, *DP*, B/XX/S/968.
7. Henry Ponsonby–Disraeli, 22/2/74, *DP*, B/XIX/B/16.
8. Queen–Disraeli, 28/1/75, *DP*, B/XIX/B/200.
9. See for instance Derby–Disraeli, 12/4/75, *DP*, B/SS/S/1111:

   I had an important communication from Pope Hennessy today – if true. He comes from Manning to tell me that the Pope is taking steps to be reconciled to Italy, and that Italy will meet him half-way. I shall hear more. If the fact is so, it is a blow to Bismarck, and may explain his recent rage.

   Three days later the correspondence continued (Derby–Disraeli, 15/4/75, *DP*, B/XX/S/1112): 'Here is Pope Hennessy's letter and one from the Cardinal enclosed. He has pared down his concessions till they come to very little: still, they indicate a change of feeling.'
10. Queen–Disraeli, 4/4/75, *DP*, B/XIX/B/245.
11. Queen–Disraeli, 15/4/75, *DP*, B/XIX/B/251.
12. Pope Hennessy–Aubrey de Vere, 17/2/75, Ms. Brit. Emp. S. 409 Box 1/1 ff. 234–5.
13. Derby–Disraeli, 19/8/74, *DP*, B/XX/S/922.
14. For which, see R. Carr, *Spain 1808–1939* (Oxford, 1956), pp. 345–59.
15. Derby–Disraeli, 21/2/75, *DP*, B/XX/S/1104.
16. Derby–Disraeli, 14/9/74, *DP*, B/XX/S/933.
17. Derby–Disraeli, 28/2/75, *DP*, B/XX/S/1106.
18. Norfolk–Disraeli, 13/11/79, *DP*, B/XXI/N/161.
19. Disraeli–Queen, 15/11/79, *DP*, B/XIX/B/1585.
20. Queen–Disraeli, 14/11/79 (9:50 a.m.), *DP*, B/XIX/B/1584.
21. Queen–Disraeli, 15/11/79, *DP*, B/XIX/B/1586.
22. Disraeli–Queen, 16/11/79, *DP*, B/XIX/C/234.
23. Quoted J. M. Robinson, *The Dukes of Norfolk: A Quincentennial History* (London, 1983), p. 220.
24. Charles Hastings (created Baron Donington 1880) – Disraeli, 31/3/79, *DP*, B/XXI/D/281.

25. Norfolk–Disraeli, 12/3/78, *DP*, B/XXI/N/157.
26. Disraeli–Queen, 15/3/78, *DP*, B/XIX/C/505.
27. Norfolk–Disraeli, 10,12/79, *DP*, B/XXI/N/162.
28. Disraeli–Rowton, 12/12/79, *DP*, B/XX/D/299.
29. Bowyer–Disraeli undated (1880?) *DP*, B/XXI/B/789.
30. Ibid.
31. Ibid.
32. Ibid.
33. Ibid.
34. Bowyer–Disraeli, 10/3/?80, *DP*, B/XXI/B/782.
35. Disraeli–Queen, 10/4/80, *DP*, B/XIX/C/274.
36. Queen–Disraeli, 13/4/80, *DP*, B/XIX/B/1661.
37. Disraeli–Queen, 7/10/79, *DP*, B/XIX/C/221. The Queen's inflexibility gave him little room for manoeuvre, which made all the more exasperating the criticism he had taken on her account:

   > Your Majesty is aware of the great hostility excited against himself by carrying the Public Worship's Bill 'in obedience to Yr. Majesty's commands.' The extreme High Church party ... have always taken advantage of this feeling against Lord Beaconsfield.... Of late, the justly great influence of several members of the present ministry, notably Ld. Salisbury, Sir Stafford Northcote, Ld. Cranbrook & others ... have counteracted and mitigated this hostility, & the great body of the clergy have ... become more placable. Ld. Alwyn Compton is the individual who has, to a great degree, brought this about.... Tho' a high Churchman [he] is ... moderate and patriotic. A recognition of his character and services would, at this moment, be beneficial.

38. Manning–Disraeli, 7/4/77, *DP*, B/XXI/M/175.
39. Manning–Disraeli, 29/1/79, *DP*, B/XXI/M/176.
40. Manning–Disraeli, 6/2/79, *DP*, B/XXI/M/177.
41. Manning–Disraeli, 1/4/79, *DP*, B/XXI/M/178.
42. Manning–Disraeli, 4/6/79, *DP*, B/XXI/M/179.
43. *Memorandum respecting the Latin Rite in the Island of Cyprus*: Manning–Disraeli, 7/7/79, *DP*, B/XXI/M/183a.
44. Manning–Disraeli, 30/12/79, *DP*, B/XXI/M/185.
45. Ibid.
46. Ibid.
47. Cf. Newman–Alfred Plummer, 17/4/80, in Dessain (ed.), *Letters and Diaries*, XXIX, p. 261: 'For myself, at the risk of differing from you, I must confess to an extreme joy that Disraeli is gone I hope never to return.'
48. Letter to *Tablet*, 27/3/80, p. 393.
49. Manning–Disraeli, 14/2/80, *DP*, B/XXI/M/188.
50. Letter to *Tablet*, 27/3/80, p. 393.
51. Denbigh–Disraeli, 22/6/79, *DP*, B/XXI/D/101.
52. For which, see Ch. 4, p. 000.
53. Denbigh–Disraeli, 22/6/79, *DP*, B/XXI/D/101.
54. Ibid.

55. Quoted W. F. Monypenny and G. E. Buckle, *Life of Benjamin Disraeli Earl of Beaconsfield*, (in 6 vols, London, 1910–20) vol. VI. p. 516.
56. Algernon Turner (pp. Disraeli) – W. P. Talbot, 16/3/80, *DP*, B/XXI/T/48a.
57. S. Leslie (ed.), *Letters of Herbert Vaughan to Lady Herbert of Lea*, p. 256.
58. Queen–Disraeli, 12/2/80, *DP*, B/XIX/C/266.
59. See Buckle, op. cit., VI, pp. 616–17.
60. Geo. H. Ryan–Rowton, 5/2/83, *DP*, A/IX/D/24.
61. *The Porcupine*, 27/1/83, cutting of at *DP*, A/IX/D/24.
62. *Porcupine*, 17/3/83, *DP*, A/IX/D/17a.
63. Ibid.
64. Johnston Diary, 20/5/86, *Public Records Office of Northern Ireland*, D880/2/38. I am indebted to Mr T. A. Jackson, Nuffield College, Oxford, for this reference.
65. *Porcupine*, 17/3/83, *DP*, A/IX/D/17a.
66. George Smith–Rowton, 29/1/83, *DP*, A/IX/D/23.
67. J. H. Crellin–Rowton, 17/3/83, *DP*, A/IX/D/17.

CHAPTER SIX

1. *Tablet*, 1/5/80, p. 546.
2. 'Lord Ripon' in F. C. Burnand (ed.) *The Catholic Who's Who and Year Book 1908* (London, 1908).
3. See Note 1.
4. Cf. S. Gopal, *British Policy in India 1858–1905* (Cambridge, 1965), p. 129. The belief that Goschen was offered the viceroyalty has a long pedigree. Morley mentions it in his *Life of Gladstone* (II, p. 629); but in conversation with the author, Dr H. C. G. Matthew has pointed out that no letters between Gladstone and Goschen seem to exist which would confirm it. It must therefore be treated with caution.
5. Cf., for instance, W. O. Chadwick, *The Victorian Church* (London, 1970) II, p. 406.
6. *The Times*, 14/5/80.
7. *Glasgow News*, 25/5/80. Worse still, they would even have preferred Charles Bradlaugh. Cf. W. L. Arnstein, *The Bradlaugh Case* (Oxford, 1965), p. 58.
8. M. V. Brett (ed.), *The Letters and Journals of Reginald Viscount Esher* (London, 1934) 17/1/80, I, p. 67.
9. N. E. Johnson, *The Diary of Gathorne Hardy, later Lord Cranbrook* (Oxford, 1981), 28/4/80, p. 448.
10. Granville–Gladstone, 29/4/80, Add. Ms. 44172 f. 29.
11. H. S. Jarrett, 'Lord Ripon's Indian Administration' in *The Month* (January 1885), p. 1.
12. Ibid., p. 4.
13. Ibid., p. 15.
14. A standard view, one which Professor Denholm (*Ripon*, p. 139) is keen to attack.

15.   The Tory view, well exemplified in the Gathorne Hardy diary.
16.   The view of W. S. Blunt: cf. his *India Under Ripon* (London, 1909), esp.
      p. 229.
17.   A view which Randolph Churchill, of all people, was prepared to
      express in private: cf. the journal of Lewis Harcourt (herafter *HJ*),
      10/4/85, Ms. Harcourt dep. 366 f. 79 (Bodleian Library).
18.   Halifax–Ripon, 1/6/83, *RP*, Add. Ms. 43531 f. 9.
19.   Halifax–Ripon, 6/7/83, *RP*, Add. Ms. 43531 f. 25. A reference to the
      Hunter Commission, whose main recommendation – the desirability
      of making primary education more appropriate to Indian custom –
      worried Anglicans and Catholics alike.
20.   Newman–Ripon, 1883 in *Letters and Diaries* (ed. Dessain), XXX, p. 168.
21.   Ibid., p. 15.
22.   Newman–Ripon, 1883, op. cit., loc. cit.
23.   Herbert Vaughan was typical: (to Lady Herbert, 10/12/80), 'Perhaps
      [Gladstone] has not forgiven me my opposition of some time back:
      though his nominations of Ripon and now of Herries led me to feel
      that [he is now more amenable to us]'.
24.   For instance, Ripon–Gladstone, 28/2/81, *RP*, Add. Ms. 44286 ff. 234–6
      on behalf of John Hungerford Pollen.
25.   H. Jerningham–Gladstone, 11/10/84, Add. Ms. 44487 f. 246.
26.   Gladstone–Grosvenor, 11/10/84, Add. Ms. 44487 f. 248.
27.   See below Chapter 1, pp. 21 ff.
28.   As recorded by J. E. C. Bodley in his diary, 31/10/84, Ms. Eng. Misc. d.
      498 (Bodleian Library).
29.   *HJ*, 15/4/85, Ms. Harcourt dep. 366 f. 25.
30.   *HJ*, 8/7/85, Ms. Harcourt dep. 371 f. 1.
31.   He even tried to enlist the Duke of Norfolk's tacit support as a Liberal
      candidate for Sheffield ('we differ in politics but we don't in religion'),
      and was predictably rebuffed. Cf. Jerningham–Norfolk, 17/7/85,
      Norfolk–Jerningham, 10/8/85. C. 765 (Arundel archives).
32.   *Hardy Diaries*, op. cit., pp. 540, 549. See also pp. 515, 523, 535, 551, 802
      for an incomparable catalogue of obliquity.
33.   Quoted Denholm, op. cit., p. 161.
34.   *HJ*, 4/1/85, Ms. Harcourt dep. 363 ff. 9–12. Users of A. B. Cooke and
      J. R. Vincent, *The Governing Passion: Cabinet Government and Party
      Politics in Britain 1865–86* (London, 1974), should note that this
      sentence, among others, is omitted without indication when this
      passage is quoted p. 28. Not a good omen of accuracy.
35.   *HJ*, 25/1/85, Ms. Harcourt, dep. 363 f. 92.
36.   *HJ*, 28/2/85, Ms. Harcourt, dep. 365 f. 63.
37.   *HJ*, 11/3/85, Ms. Harcourt, dep. 365 f. 96.
38.   *HJ*, 21/3/85, Ms. Harcourt, dep. 366 f. 27.
39.   *HJ*, 11/3/85, Ms. Harcourt, dep. 365 f. 96: 'I hear no more talk of his
      being made a Duke so I suppose Gladstone has decided not to do
      so ... '.
40.   The best account is F. S. L. Lyons, *Charles Stewart Parnell* (London,
      1977), pp. 282 ff.
41.   Quoted, ibid., p. 301.

42. The point is discussed in C. H. D. Howard, 'The Parnell Manifesto of 21 November 1885 and the Schools Question', in *English Historical Review*, XXIX (January 1947). See appendix for a close analysis of Catholic voting strength in key constituencies.
43. *HJ*, 22/10/85, Ms. Harcourt dep. 370 f. 61.
44. *RJ*, 3/2/86, Ms. Harcourt dep. 377 f. 98.
45. *HJ*, 12/12/85, Ms. Harcourt dep. 374 f. 86. 'Ld. Ripon is strongly in favour of Home Rule but is frightened of the possibility of the Irish imposing protective duties on our manufactures, which he justly says would never be tolerated by our people in Lancashire and the Western Ports'.
46. Ibid.
47. C. H. D. Howard, op. cit., loc. cit., p. 42.
48. *HJ*, 12/12/85, Ms. Harcourt dep. 374 f. 86.
49. *HJ*, 20/11/85, Ms. Harcourt dep. 373 f. 64.
50. Ibid.
51. The other was, of course, Henry Matthews.
52. Cf. E. Longford, *A Pilgrimage of Passion: The Life of Wilfrid Scawen Blunt* (London, 1979), p. 219.
53. Quoted, ibid., p. 222.
54. Lady Anne Blunt, diary, 12/9/85, Add. Ms. 53954. (Unfoliated)
55. Cf. Longford, op. cit., p. 221. The same Hungerford Pollen whom Ripon had recommended to Gladstone for a job as 'a thorough gentleman' who had 'stuck to the Liberal Party under circumstances of some difficulty'. Catholic ingratitude (if such it was) was as evident in small matters as in large.
56. Ibid., p. 222.
57. *HJ*, 3/1/86, Ms. Harcourt, dep. 375 f. 98.
58. Manning–Dilke, 17/5/85, Add. Ms. 43896 f. 83.
59. *HJ*, 2/2/86, Ms. Harcourt dep. 377 f. 93.
60. *HJ*, 2/2/86, Ms. Harcourt dep. 377 f. 91.
61. *HJ*, 27/1/86, Ms. Harcourt dep. 377 f. 32.
62. *HJ*, 2/2/86, Ms. Harcourt dep. 377 f. 91.
63. Denholm's phrase.
64. Granville–Gladstone, 1/7/86, Add. Ms. 44772 f. 168.
65. Witness his spoonfeeding advice. Two good examples are Ripon–Norfolk, 9/10/92, Add. Ms. 43636 f. 220 (on how best to lobby the government on behalf of endangered Catholic missionaries in Uganda), and Ripon–Norfolk, 6/12/02, Add. Ms. 43638 ff. 123–32 (on Catholic education). The first of these is worth quoting as a demonstration of Ripon's skill in stemming potentially embarrassing Catholic pressure:

    > My advice would be get up the facts as accurately as you can, sift them as much as possible and then, but not before, ask Rosebery to see you and one or two others if you like.... But don't go with a deputation which would get into the papers, as you will have counter Deputations from ... all kinds of Protestants who can make a much greater noise than we poor Catholics.

66. One of the clearest assumptions of the correspondence of Manning

and J. E. C. Bodley was Norfolk's absurd but dangerous meddle-someness, particularly as a Tory envoy to the Vatican in 1887. Manning, unwisely, refused to take seriously this 'Envoy Extra-ordinary', and was 'not sorry to know that his influence was not potent'. (Manning–Bodley, 20/6/87, Ms. Eng. lett. c. 188 f. 83). Bodley was of like mind, and thought that the mission could be understood in two ways – as a sop to Norfolk's vanity after his failure to be appointed to the Cabinet, and (a purely secondary consideration) as a very long shot from which some good might derive:

> Not even the Tory Government can have expected any result; but I fancy they thought they might combine solacing this unaccredited envoy for their non-recognition of his electioneering services with what in vulgar parlance is termed 'trying it on'. (Bodley-Manning, 17/6/87, Ms. Eng. lett. c. 188 f. 129.

See below Ch. 7, p. 167ff.

67. F. Von Hugel–Newman, 15/7/86, *Letters and Diaries*, XXXI, p. 155.

> I hope it is not impertinent if I [say] how warmly I admire, how proud I feel, of the Duke of Norfolk's attitude and conduct during this anxious and sad political crisis. The sight of the union of love of Church and love of Country ought to be common, but it is not: it is doubly refreshing to see it in the social head and leader of English Catholics ... and this I may perhaps without presumption trace back to Edgbaston and [Newman].

68. *HJ*, 29/6/86, Ms. Harcourt dep. 379 f. 5. 'Chex' (Chancellor of the Exchequer) was Harcourt junior's nickname for his father. Previously he had been 'HS' (1880–5). Loulou's greatest regret was, of course, that he never became 'PM'.

69. Quoted E. Finch, *Winfrid Scawen Blunt* (London, 1938), p. 212.

70. L. Harcourt–Ripon, 13/10/91, Add. Ms. 43636 f. 197 [Richard Webster, later 1st Viscount Alverstone: Attorney General 1885, 1886–92, 1895–1900. M P Launceston, July-November 1885, Isle of Wight, November 1885–May 1900].

71. Gladstone had introduced in February 1891 a Religious Disqualifica-tions Removal Bill (popularly, the 'Ripon-Russell' Bill) which would have permitted Roman Catholics to hold the offices of Viceroy of Ireland and Lord Chancellor. The conventional wisdom was that its purpose was to enable Ripon and Sir Charles Russell respectively to be appointed to those offices. The Bill failed to get a second reading by 256 votes to 223. Gladstone received some Tory support, for example Lord Cranborne (Salisbury's son-in-law) who represented Darwen (Lancs.), a constituency with a substantial Catholic population. Henry Matthews abstained. See below p. 165–6.

72. Ripon–Gladstone, 28/12/91, Add. Ms. 44287 f. 87.
73. Ripon–Morley, 22/1/94, Add. Ms. 43541 f. 66.
74. Ripon–Anderton, 20/12/03, Add. Ms. 43638 f. 166.
74. Ripon–Manning, 18/11/88, Add. Ms. 43545 f. 52.

76. Ibid.
77. Ripon–Bishop of Leeds, 31/12/84, Add. Ms. 43635 f. 36.
78. Ripon–Mgr. Fisher, 22/3/80, Add. Ms. 43626 f. 60.
79. *Tablet*, 14/4/06, p. 561.
80. The clause did not apply to many schools in rural areas; it need not apply if the objecting one-fifth of non-Catholics attending a school could not be accommodated elsewhere; granting of 'extended facilities' still lay entirely with local authorities, who could be unfriendly; permission was still needed for Catholic religious instruction; teachers who were non-Catholic, even anti-Catholic, could still be appointed; Catholics had no right of appeal to the Board of Education.
81. At least some profit may have come from the crisis. Archbishop Bourne made a gramophone record of his speech which retailed at five shillings.
82. Ripon–Archbishop Bourne, 18/4/06, Add. Ms. 43545 f. 54.
83. It was thus that the Bill was defeated. The Lords mercilessly amended it and the Bill fell when Campbell-Bannerman successfully moved the rejection *en bloc* of the amendments. The Lords, by insisting on their amendments, forced the government to withdraw the measure. The *Tablet* was luridly euphoric: 'Dead! ... the Education Bill is dead. Today it lies with its jaws tied up for the burial, and tomorrow it shall be hurried away and safely rammed down under the stones' 22/10/06, p. 961.
84. *Hansard*, 4/2/91, CCCXLIX 1775.
85. *Tablet*, 12/11/92, p. 770, quoting Lord Chief Justice Coleridge.
86. *The Times*, 10/11/92, p. 6.
87. *HJ*, 9/11/92, Ms. Harcourt dep 387 f. 60.
88. *The Battle: On Which Side?*, by E. A. Bouet (London, 1897). Many of Harcourt's letters were from disillusioned Tories, resentful that their party was 'tied hand and foot to Sacerdotalism', or worse still, to 'the Paddies'. The addresses – Ealing and Clapham seem to predominate – suggest perhaps less Colonel Blimp than Mr Pooter.
89. Cf. Harcourt–E. Ruggles-Brise, 25/8/87, Ms. Harcourt dep. 729 f. 193, praising his handling of the Lipski case.
90. Quoted A. G. Gardiner, *The Life of Sir William Harcourt*, II, p. 481.
91. *Ripon*, p. 241.
92. Cf., for instance, Herbert Gladstone–James Bryce, 19/3/07, Ms. U.B. 32 (Bodleian).
93. Asquith was unsure whether to include him in his Cabinet in the first place. Ms. Asquith 11 f. 3. (Bodleian).
94. *Tablet*, 12/9/08, p. 402.
95. Ibid.
96. Ibid.
97. *Tablet*, 19/9/08, p. 441.
98. Ripon-Asquith, 9/9/08, Ms. Asquith 20 f. 107.
99. Ibid.
100. Ripon-Asquith, 10/9/08, Ms. Asquith 20 f. 122.
101. 'You will find H[is] M[ajesty] very bitter about Herbert, and longing to get rid of him.' (Crewe–Asquith, 16/9/08, Ms. Asquith 20 f. 167).

102. We should not forget the element of farce.

     The King has taken this d—d procession greatly to heart, and asked
     me to say he was 'greatly cut up about it' – rather a curious phrase ... he
     has received dozens of letters from enraged Protestants, who compare
     him disadvantageously with his revered Mother, now with God, and
     hint that his ultimate destination may be directed elsewhere.
       He is also annoyed with Ripon, Norfolk and co. for not having told
     their foreign friends that something of a storm would be raised ... and
     with us for not having definitely forbidden or sanctioned the
     procession ... on distinct grounds. (Crewe–Asquith, 12/9/08, Ms.
     Asquith 20 f. 154.)

103. Ripon–Asquith, 14/9/08, Ms. Asquith 20 f. 163.
104. Runciman–Asquith, 25/9/08, Ms Asquith 20 f. 31.
105. 'At the general election, and many a time since I might easily have
     armed a very formidable opposition to your political party; I have
     refrained from doing so ... ' (Bourne–Runciman, 24/9/08, Ms. Asquith
     20 f. 33.)
106. Ripon–Asquith, 20/9/08, Ms. Asquith 20 f. 171.
107. Ripon–Asquith, 14/9/08, Ms. Asquith 20 f. 163.
108. *Tablet*, 13/10/08, p. 6. Colleagues thought differently. Note Haldane's
     implied attitude to 'single-issue' politics: '[Ripon's] loss will not now
     be felt. Not only was he becoming very deaf, but he was getting more
     and more absorbed in the affairs of his Church ... ' (Haldane–Asquith,
     7/10/08, Ms. Asquith 11 f. 207.)
109. Ilbert–James Bryce, Ms. Bryce 13 f. 53.
110. Quoted, E. Finch (op. cit.), p. 118.
111. For example, *Some First Lines of Catholic Politics* (London, 1881).
112. Ripon–Fisher, 22/3/80, Add. Ms. 43626 f. 60.

CHAPTER SEVEN

1. For instance, Wm. Geary–Norfolk, 17/9/86, C766 (Arundel archives).

   The question of the admission of Catholics to the League is one of
   the highest moment.... [It] would give confidence to the whole
   Catholic-Conservative community and impose a lasting obligation
   upon the constitutional party.

2. *Primrose League Gazette*, 6/4/89, p. 7.
3. Grand Council Minutes, 3/6/87, p. 207 (Bodleian Library). Apart from
   occasional anti-Catholicism, the League was conventionally anti-Irish.
   In Chevening, Kent, knights and dames regularly staged *The Three Ps
   or The Pig, the Paddy, and the Patriot MP: A Hibernian Hyperbole*, written
   (to maintain the symmetry) by a Mr. A. S. Pratt (*Primrose League Gazette*,
   28/1/88).
4. J. Prest, Secretary of the Catholic Conservative Association-Lord
   Carnarvon, 16/11/82. Add. Ms. 60875, 6th letter (Carnarvon Papers).

5. Ibid.
6. Ibid. (Draft reply written on back of original letter).
7. T. W. Allies, 'Why I shall vote for the Unionists', in *The Nineteenth Century*, 32, July 1892, p. 172.
8. Commons Debates, 21/9/86, *Hansard*, 3rd Series, CCCIX 1225.
9. John G. Kenyon–Ripon, 30/10/01, Add. Ms. 43638 f. 55.
10. Ripon–Kenyon, 1/11/01, Add. Ms. 43638 f. 59.
11. I have always told my friends that I am a Radical after the manner of Moses, God and the people. Among my upper-ten-thousand friends I stand alone. they think me past praying for, because I would not denounce Parnell, & I would defend Archbishop Walsh. I believe I can say that, laying aside our old grudge of the Temporal Power, I am in politics what you have ever known me: and I have watched your policy, not foreign, but domestic and Irish, with large assent. (Manning–Gladstone, 25/9/87, Add. Ms. 44250 f. 253.)
12. Vaughan–Salisbury, 14/3/89, Salisbury Papers (hereinafter *SP*).
13. Vaughan-Salisbury, 14/1/88, *SP*.
14. Vaughan-Salisbury, 13/10/93, *SP*.
15. This morning I saw Cardinal Manning.... He thought at first that I wanted help for my own candidature and offered to do various things for me. But I managed to explain what I wanted, namely that he should stir up the Irish to vote, and he said he would. (Sidney Webb to Beatrice Potter, 28/9/91, in N. MacKenzie (ed.), *Letters of Sidney and Beatrice Webb* (London, 1978), p. 312.)
16. Bishop John Virtue–Norfolk, 20/7/91, C721 (Arundel archives).
17. *Tablet*, 18/7/91, p. 86.
18. One example of several.

The whole question [of Catholic schools] is of such extreme importance and at the present moment appears to be so critical that we should feel forced to strenuously oppose ... any measure which failed to contain provisions which we deem to be absolutely essential to a fair settlement. (Norfolk-Salisbury, 9/12/01, Add. Ms. 49691 f. 146.)

Salisbury, forwarding the letter to Balfour, could not have been more laconic. 'I suppose you have received an ultimatum of this kind. But I send it in case of accidents.' (10/12/01, Add. Ms. 49691 f. 150.)

19. *The Diary of Gathorne Hardy, Lord Cranbrook* (ed. N. Johnson), 6/6/86, p. 606.
20. Salisbury–R. A. Cross, 3/7/83, *SP*.
21. Salisbury generally reserved his deepest scorn for his most ardent supporters. 'I am afraid I am not competent to quell the Irish Orangemen,' he once wrote to Churchill. 'They are troublesome and unreliable allies. I remember the last letter I ever had from Beaconsfield he denounced them for having "sold the pass" about the Irish land legislation.' (Salisbury–Churchill, 16/11/85, *SP*.)
22. *Primrose League Gazette*, 19/5/86.

23. See J. H. Robb, *The Primrose League* (New York, 1968), p. 198. For Bagshawe, the League comprised 'heretics, Freemasons and Orangemen'. Bishop Clifford of Clifton was more relaxed. Catholics could join as long as it was 'not opposed to religion or morality'. Manning exonerated the League by refusing to take it seriously – 'a League of Innocents', he called it.
24. Hardy Diary, op. cit., 31/7/86, p. 616.
25. Churchill had been delighted by his destruction of Sir Charles Dilke in the Crawford case.
26. The relevant correspondence is in the Churchill Archive, Churchill College, Cambridge. Matthews emerges as capable but innocent, quite unaware of the strings being pulled on his behalf. (Matthews–Churchill, 12/8/86, *RCHL*, vol. 14, no. 1662.) Chamberlain's initial co-operativeness soon gave way to petulance. Matthews' career, evidently, was ill-omened from the very start. 'My dear Churchill, You have got us into a devil of a hole over this Matthews business. Whatever the ultimate result, I shall certainly lose friends and influence over it.' (Chamberlain–Churchill, 8/8/86, *RCHL*, vol. 14, no. 1664.)
27. Lord George Hamilton, *Parliamentary Reminiscences and Reflections 1868–85*, (London, 1916), p. 260.
28. Balfour–Salisbury, 23/11/88, Add. Ms. 49689 ff. 38–43. 'It is important ... to keep the possibility of coalition [with the Liberal Unionists] at least in view when we are considering possible vacancies in the Cabinet – say, in the Home Office.'
29. Hardy Diary, 15/3/88 (p. 697), 18/11/88 (p. 719), 3/8/89 (p. 744), 12/8/89 (p. 745). Also recorded is dinner with the Prince of Wales. 'He was hot against Matthews & said he was enough to ruin any Government!' (16/6/90, p. 770.)
30. Harcourt Journal, 19/4/93, Ms. Harcourt dep. 393 f. 52.
31. Queen's Journal, 17/11/88, in G. E. Buckle (ed.) *Letters of Queen Victoria, 3rd Series, 1886–90* (London, 1931) I, p. 450.
32. Salisbury–Queen, 31/11/88, ibid., p. 445.
33. Salisbury–Queen, 20/7/90, ibid., p. 623.
34. *Catholic Household*, 9/7/87, p. 8.
35. *Tablet*, 12/4/1913, p. 587.
36. 'Henry Matthews, Lord Llandaff' in *Dublin Review*, March 1921, vol. 168, p. 14. Manning, wishing to preserve his own dominance of the English Church, asked him to stop any plans to establish a Papal nunciature in England. Matthews, who cordially disliked the Cardinal and who saw in his unchecked power an obstacle to the defeat of the Irish bishops, refused.
37. Israel Lipski: Matthews was unfortunate in his cases. W. T. Stead hounded him viciously over Lipski, the public was reluctant to forgive his lack of lenience with Mrs Maybrick the poisoner, and it was bad luck that Miss Cass, the most genteel of seamstresses, was falsely arrested for importuning by an over-zealous constable.
38. Cf. W. W. Williams, *Life of General Sir Charles Warren* (Oxford, 1941), p.

219; 'Mr. Matthews and Sir Charles Warren' in the *Saturday Review*, 29/10/87, p. 576.

39. Much to the annoyance of the Queen, who, in her capacity as amateur sleuth, sent him detailed instructions on how to capture the Ripper (13/11/90).

40. Salisbury–Balfour, 16/11/89, Add. Ms. 49689 f. 45.

41. 'Henry Matthews, Lord Llandaff' in *Dublin Review*, op. cit., p. 7.

42. Hardy Diary, 9/2/87, p. 651.

43. Ibid. Salisbury's offer, declined because of his wife's illness, was couched characteristically. 'It has been whispered to me that ... you might possibly ... accept the Under Secretaryship for the Colonies.... I feel in all a cold perspiration with horror at my own boldness in making such a suggestion to the Earl Marshal' (Salisbury–Norfolk, 11/2/87, C. 767, Arundel archives).

44. Walsh–Manning, 4/10/87, quoted P. J. Walsh, *William J. Walsh, Archbishop of Dublin* (Dublin, 1928), p. 299.

45. Emly–Norfolk, 2/8/87, C767 (Arundel archives).

46. Norfolk–Salisbury, 16/3/88, quoted D. L. Fenech, 'Britain's Relations with the Vatican 1880–1922', Oxford: unpublished D. Phil. thesis, 1977, p. 91.

47. Norfolk–Salisbury, 9/1/86, *SP*.

48. Norfolk–Balfour, 25/12/87, Add. Ms. 49821 f. 89.

49. Norfolk–Balfour, 12/2/88, Add. Ms. 49821 f. 93.

50. Why was Norfolk so keen to see the Plan of Campaign condemned? One reason is that his own acquaintances were badly hit by it. Lord Granard, a Catholic Unionist, wrote in January 1887 asking him to press Salisbury to offer him the vacant governorship of Mauritius. 'In the present state of Ireland and of my finances, it is of the most vital importance to get something which would enable me to live out of Ireland for a few years' (Granard–Norfolk, 17/1/87, C767 Arundel archives; see also ibid., 28/1/87.)

51. Norfolk–Salisbury, 31/10/86, *SP*.

52. Petre–Salisbury, 13/10/85, *SP*.

53. Balfour–Salisbury. 14/3/88, Add. Ms. 49689 f. 15.

54. Denbigh–Salisbury, 4/3/87, *SP* (My italics).

    If the law officers can see their way to make out a good case against Archbp. Croke, *whether a conviction be secured or not*, the very publicity would force the Pope to intervene.... they are so sensitive to any ecclesiastical scandal in high places that action would be taken immediately. The Pope could no longer plead ignorance ...

55. 'I have heard quite recently a report that ... the Pope may make Dr. Walsh a Cardinal. If the position taken up by that prelate were clearly put before the world, I cannot believe this danger would be greatly reduced.... As regards this ... I shall of course do what I can.' (Norfolk–Salisbury, 19/10/91, *SP*.)

56. See Walsh, op. cit., pp. 320 sqq.

57. Norfolk admitted that much of the backroom work had been done by

Captain (later Sir) John Ross of Bladensburg, a strong Catholic Unionist. When asking for a knighthood for Ross, Norfolk wrote as follows:

> During the long and troublesome negotiations we conducted [in Rome], while I was the figurehead, Ross was the brain and the worker. Again, I think the fact that Dr. Walsh has not been made a Cardinal is probably greatly due to the continuous information with which Ross kept the Vatican supplied. (Norfolk–Salisbury, 22/6/92, *SP.*)

58. Norfolk–Salisbury, 28/7/87, *SP.*
59. Norfolk–Salisbury, 8/10/93, *SP.*
60. As even Archbishop Walsh seemed to concede. See P. J. Walsh, *William J. Walsh, Archbishop of Dublin* (Dublin, 1928), p. 321, 'On religious grounds' many Liberal candidates in English boroughs were 'entirely objectionable; he told Pope Leo XIII in February 1888.
61. Norfolk–Salisbury, 2/6/89, *SP.* There is an important point to be made here. As we have noticed (see p. 211, n. 18), Norfolk was capable of bluster on the question of Catholic schools. Witness, by contrast, equally striking slavishness whenever he was near to or in office: 'It is probable we shall shortly be having meetings of Catholics urging our views on the Schools question on the Government. I do not know whether it would be right for me to take part in such a meeting.... Will you please write me a line of information?' (Norfolk–Salisbury, 15/12/95); in December 1886, the tone was, if anything, even more paltry: '[Catholic] anxieties are not less keen and our hopes not less eager than when we last met. Are there any crumbs of comfort for us? I am speaking less of relations with Rome than of higher education.' (Norfolk–Salisbury, 7/12/86, *SP.*)
62. Norfolk–Salisbury, 27/6/97, *SP.*
63. Did Catholics make too much of voluntary schools anyway? Denominational education was often pointless unless part of a general Catholic culture. Witness this description of Derwent by its parish priest:

> The people here think little or nothing of their souls, and I should say they are the most God-forsaken set in Derbyshire.... Every child that has left our school has gone back to heresy with two exceptions, and it is painfully clear that it is only a matter of time with them.... If we had a few Catholic families in the neighbourhood we might make progress. (Rev. W. A. Hawkins-Norfolk, 25/2/84, C718, Arundel archives).

64. Salisbury was keen to help, at least in diplomatic appointments. As Lady Salisbury wrote in reference to a request on behalf of Lord Petre which would receive 'very favourable consideration': 'Setting politics aside, S. likes to have Catholics as they often get on better abroad.' (Lady Salisbury–Norfolk, 29/11/85, C. 765, Arundel archives.)
65. Norfolk–Salisbury, 8/9/92, *SP.*

66. See G. Lane-Fox–Norfolk, 17/8/92, C.767 (Arundel archives):

> I quite understand the feelings of Gog and Magog but ... much harm will be done to the Tory Party and to religion, and the Catholic Union etc. will all begin cackling after the mischief is done, just as they did after the Gladstonian Russell Relief bill was rejected, and the position of Catholics who are Roman and Tory will be more difficult than ever ... '

67. Norfolk–Salisbury, 28/6/95, *SP.*
68. Norfolk–Salisbury, 26/10/97, *SP.*
69. In this department Col. T. M. Sandys, long-time MP for the Bootle division of Lancashire, is not to be bettered.

> Only one mistake has been made in the appointment of the present Government and that is the appointment of the Post-Master General. You have no idea how unpopular this is up and down the country already. People can see no reason for having a Roman Catholic in the Cabinet – and the Duke of Norfolk is no man of business. He is known to be a tool in the hands of the Jesuits and ... the people object to have the Post Office and the Telegraphs in the hands of the Jesuit secret police – also thereby know [*sic*] all the secret policy of the Government – the movement of Troops & Fleets and police as well as individual members of the Community ... (Sandys–Salisbury, 16/7/95, *SP.*)

70. Salisbury–Balfour, 16/1/89, Add. Ms. 49689 f. 45.

> I send back Croke's letter [he wrote to Balfour] in order to suggest that you send it to your Roman adviser – Norfolk or Klein. (I should prefer Norfolk). I should do so with a letter civilly indicating that you fear the Pope is throwing us over. I suggest this only diplomatically – to place us in a better position in dealing with the R.C. educational demands.

71. Norfolk–Salisbury, 20/2/91. *SP.*
72. Ibid. Even the letter which began in anguish ended in accord: 'I have no fear [however] of any lasting feeling against the Government on the part of the Catholic body.'
73. Norfolk–Saunderson, 16/3/93, C.721 (Arundel archives).
74. *Tablet*, 25/3/93, p. 464.
75. Ibid., 1/4/93, p. 502.
76. Norfolk, it might be added, contributed £200 to Saunderson's election expenses in 1886. On that occasion the Colonel took a while to thank him because 'I have been all over the country on the political rampage'. (Saunderson–Norfolk, 23/6/86, C.766, Arundel archives.)
77. Norfolk–Salisbury, 10/10/95, *SP.*
78. Norfolk–Salisbury, 28/7/87, *SP.*
79. *The Times*, quoted by Gwendolen, Duchess of Norfolk, in *Sola Virtus Invicta* (London, 1917), p. 5, a privately printed collection of obituaries.

CONCLUSION

1. *Catholic Progress under Queen Victoria* (London, 1901), p. 3.
3. *Queen Victoria: Sixty Years of Catholic Progress* (London, 1897), p. 3.
3. Cardinal Moran, quoted ibid., p. 7.
4. *Catholic Progress in England* (Catholic Truth Society pamphlet) (London, 1897), p. 4.
5. T. Murphy, *The Catholic Church in England and Wales During the last two Centuries: Retrospect and Forecast* (London, 1892), p. 88.
6. Ibid., p. 101.
7. Ibid.
8. Ibid., p. 110.
9. Ibid., p. 101.
10. Ibid., p. 5.
11. Ibid.
12. Ibid., p. 10.
13. I. Sellers, *Nineteenth Century Nonconformity* (1977), p. 82. The following paragraphs are largely based on Sellers' lucid account.
14. Quoted ibid., p. 79.
15. Ibid., p. 78.
16. Bentinck–Croker, 29/9/74, in G. Alderman, *The Jewish Community in British Politics* (Oxford, 1983), p. 24. Alderman has been the main source of the following paragraphs.
17. Alderman, op. cit., p. 29.
18. Ibid., p. 34.
19. Ibid., p. 35.
20. Ibid., p. 37.
21. Ibid., p. 39.
22. See below p. 171, note 67.
23. Alderman, p. 43.
24. Bertram Straus, defeated at St. George's in 1900, quoted Alderman, p. 46.

Appendix: Constituency Catholicism

What was the strength of Catholicism in the constituencies? Victorian Catholics, prone to the statistics-worship of the age, thought it considerable. In 1851, there were 679,067 Catholics in England and Wales.[1] In 1886 the *Catholic Directory* estimated the number at 1,500,000 – an exaggeration, no doubt, as the directory then stuck to the figure until 1912, but evidence certainly of substantial growth.[2] By the turn of the century the number may indeed have been around a million and a half. In 1850 only three dioceses – Liverpool, Birmingham, Westminster – had between 100 and 200 priests; the other ten had less than 100. By 1900, all was change: two had less than 100 priests, five had between 100 and 200, three had between 200 and 300, and three had between 300 and 500.[3] Other figures – Easter communions, Sunday attendances, schools built, parishes formed – tell a similar story. Catholic 'progress' was a reality and it signalised a community ready to come into its political inheritance.

The figures represent, however, a *trompe l'oeil*. In any event, to establish Catholic numbers is not to establish Catholic votes. Indeed, because the greatest part of the increase is accounted for by an influx of the Irish working class, it is merely to establish the striking disproportion between the two. Numbers had to increase geometrically for votes to increase arithmetically. Consider the Catholics of Monmouthshire in the 1870s. Most were Irish and new to the district, most colliers and ironworkers, many eccentric or indifferent in their religious observance, and almost all of them voteless. Here was an existence reduced to elemental necessity: when they were not working they were 'almost without exception either asleep or drunk all the rest of their lives'.[4] Politics apparently did not matter. Engels queasily reported similar wretchedness in Lancashire:

> The Irishman loves his pig as the Arab his horse ... he eats and sleeps with it, his children play with it, ride upon it, roll in the dirt with it, as anyone may see a thousand times repeated in all the

great towns in England. The filth and comfortlessness that prevail
in the houses themselves it is impossible to describe.[5]

Examples need not be multiplied, but two points should be
noticed. First, many Catholics did not vote because they were not so
entitled. Likewise, others were entitled but had not registered – a
perennial theme of Catholic political literature. Among the lower
orders, there were two categories, both ineligible: the transient and
the vagrant, the first consisting of lodgers, seasonal harvesters and
the like, never in a constituency long enough to matter, the second
mainly those who received parish relief and therefore could not vote.
Perhaps no more than 150,000 Irish-born or second-generation Irish
Roman Catholics were enfranchised in 1885.[6]

Two considerations modify this picture. Look at Monmouthshire
again: Catholics there were either highly scattered or highly concentrated, and this was typical of all of Wales. In some places
Catholics were extremely thin on the ground. The six counties of
Northamptonshire, Bedfordshire, Buckinghamshire, Cambridge-
shire, Huntingdonshire, Norfolk and Suffolk had, in 1886, only forty-
nine priests between them.[7] Norwich in 1874 had 'two poor chapels
and ... scant evidences of Catholic life'.[8] In parts of deepest dissenting
Wales, amidst the Elims, the Bethels, the Ebenezers, 'here and there
amidst the heterogeneous elements of the place, an Irish family was
to be found, with very little of what they brought from their own
country save a love of whiskey and a notoriety for being foremost in
a row'.[9] Such isolation stands in contrast with Liverpool, which had
an enormous Catholic population. Northampton needed forty-nine
priests in 1886; Liverpool needed 323.[10]

The point is clear. In some places the Catholic 'vote' was derisive,
in others decisive. In addition, Catholic density engendered a high
degree of community self-consciousness. Many towns had an Irish
'quarter' and some paid dear for it. Ashton-under-Lyne, for instance,
witnessed a famous 'No Popery' riot in 1868, when the local church
came under attack from a mob inflamed by the well-known anti-
Catholic lecturer of the day, William Murphy. The Catholics gave as
good as they got. Not only was the parish priest adept in the use of
firearms, his flock constituted a formidable if unsubtle fighting force:

Their weapons were awful to behold – pokers, scythes, one or two
sword blades, heavily-loaded bludgeons, bayonets, pitchforks and
revolvers – and the owners of these murderous weapons were in

that state of excitement which made them heedless of danger. Certainly the Irish blood was ...[11]

Such episodes were exceptional. The Irish probably spent more time fighting each other than fighting their English neighbours. Even so, they were a force to be reckoned with, particularly if their priest cared to involve himself in politics. And if there were parochial organisations there were national ones, too. The Irish National League, founded in 1882 by T. P. O'Connor, was little more than a vote-marshalling machine, and for a while an apparently efficient one. In 1884 it had 4,600 members, in 1890 40,985.[12] In its heyday, that is before Parnell's fall from grace, it could send Parnellite MPs to constituencies all over England to preach the Home Rule gospel to the already converted Irish. This was important work, but its overall effect is not easily gauged: in strengthening the political faith of the Irish, the League also strengthened the resolve of their opponents. It is no accident that the only English seat ever won for Irish Home Rule was T. P. O'Connor's own, Liverpool Scotland.

These general considerations of the Catholic 'vote' can only yield general conclusions. It is more revealing to look at individual constituencies. Highly useful in this regard is a memorandum drawn up by Herbert Gladstone when he was Liberal Chief Whip. In it he lists seats won by the Liberals in 1886 and 1892 which were 'dominated' by the Irish vote, along with seats won by the Unionists which could be captured by the Liberals by an appeal to the Irish vote. The memorandum is incomplete in two senses: on the one hand, Gladstone seems to have left space for additional constituencies which he then thought the better of; on the other hand, he seems (reasonably enough) to have been unsure about some of the constituencies he included. Even so, it is the best account there is of the significance of the Catholic vote. Although it refers to the last quarter of the nineteenth century, it also has importance for the period covered by the opening chapters of this book. One would expect the Catholic vote to be most significant after the Reform and Redistribution Acts of 1884 and 1885, when many Irish people received the vote for the first time. If, however, this turns out not to be the case, we can certainly conclude that before that time the Catholic vote was even less decisive.

There are a few factual errors – the Tories won both Devonport seats in 1886, though they lost them again in 1892, the Liberals lost Bradford East in 1886, and the Tories gained one of the Newcastle upon Tyne seats in 1892 – but several curiosities. It is hard to see how the Irish vote 'dominated' in ELLAND (Yorkshire, West Riding), a largely Wesleyan seat with a very limited Catholic population. The same might be said of HOLMFIRTH (Yorkshire, W.R.), 'a Wesleyan stronghold'[13] without, indeed, a resident priest of its own, where the miners tended to decide the issue,[14] as they did also at WANSBECK (Northumberland).

Table 1   Liberal Seats 'dominated' by Irish vote (Add. Ms. 46107 ff. 28 sqq.)

Won in 1886	Won in 1892
Bradford West	Bristol North
Bradford Central	Bradford West
Bradford East	Bradford Central
Cardiff	Buckingham Northern
?Crewe	Burnley
?Camborne	Cardiff
Cockermouth	Crewe
Ilkeston	Northwich
Devonport	Camborne
Dewsbury	Egremont
?Chester-le-Street	Cockermouth
?	Chesterfield
?Durham Mid	Ilkeston
?Durham N.W.	Devonport
Gateshead	Dewsbury
?Gloucester	Durham
Halifax	Chester-le-Street
Hanley	Durham Mid
Lancaster	Durham N.W.
Gorton	Gateshead
?Heywood	Stroud
Radcliffe	Gloucester
Leigh	Halifax
Leeds East	Hanley
Leeds West	Hartlepool
Liverpool Exchange	Hull East
Manchester North	?North Lonsdale
Manchester South West	Lancaster

Middlesborough
Newcastle-on-Tyne (2)
Tyneside
?Wansbeck
?Nottingham West
?South Shields
Stockton on Tees
Stoke on Trent
Sunderland
Swansea Town
?Wednesbury
?Cleveland
?
?Holmfirth
Normanton
?Rotherham
Pudsey
?Barnsley

Accrington
Darwen
?Rossendale
Eccles
Heywood
Middleton
Radcliffe
Ince
Leigh
Leeds East
Leeds West
Liverpool Exchange
Manchester North
Manchester South
Manchester S.W.
Middlesborough
Monmouth Boroughs
Newcastle-on-Tyne (2)

Won in 1886

?Elland
?Spen Valley
?Shipley

Won in 1892

Newcastle-under-Lyme
Tyneside
Wansbeck
Oldham
Portsmouth
Salford North
Southampton
?South Shields
Stafford
Stockport
Stoke-on-Trent
Sunderland
Swansea District
Swansea Town
West Ham North
Whitehaven
Cleveland
Buckrose
Holmfirth

Normanton
Rotherham
Pudsey
Barnsley
Elland
Spen Valley
Shipley

Metropolitan Seats

Won in 1886	*Won in 1892*
Battersea	Bermondsey
Poplar	Camberwell
Whitechapel	?
	Battersea
	Limehouse
	St. George's in the East
	Whitechapel

Seats held by Unionists in 1886 and 1892 which may be won by an appeal to the Irish vote. (Add. Ms. 46107 f. 34)

Ashton-under-Lyne	Nottingham South
Birkenhead	St. Helen's
Bristol South	Salford South
Cheshire, Hyde	Salford West
Lancashire Widnes	Stalybridge
Manchester North East	Warrington
Monmouth South	Wigan

CLEVELAND is another oddity, where 'the Irish vote seems to have been small' and where Liberal fortunes, certainly in 1892, closely reflected the fortunes of the mining industry.

Appearances, however, can deceive. Little in SPEN VALLEY's profile would suggest much Catholic dominance: it was strong non-conformist territory, and its one Catholic chapel (in Heckmondwike) was only opened in the late 1880s. Yet elections to school boards reveal what elections to Parliament may obscure. They were fought with 'extraordinary vigour' between Bible-readers and Undenominationalists, the latter known for their slate-voting and strength. That fact notwithstanding, in June 1892 the parish priest topped the poll handsomely, with 1172 votes to his nearest rival's 802.[15] Not all his supporters need have been parishioners, but presumably all his parishioners were supporters. In matters of Catholic concern – and there was none greater than schooling – the vote was solid; in other matters, its solidity was less certain.

The curiosity of Spen Valley is to find a subterranean Irish 'dominance' where none might have been expected: the curiosity of DEVONPORT is to find Irish issues dominant but no Irish voters. The Catholic population of Devon and Cornwall was slight, but Home Rule bulked large in its politics. Traditional West Country Liberalism was not enough to carry Devonport for Gladstone in 1886, with its strategic and maritime reasons for fearing a hostile Ireland adjacent to it.[16] On the contrary, both there and in neighbouring PLYMOUTH, the Liberal vote collapsed: 'wholesale abstentions' in the first, ostentatious refusal to welcome the visiting Parnell in the second. It was therefore appropriate that Devonport's first Home Rule election should end in confusion. Outside the Royal Hotel 'the grotesque spectacle was witnessed of the successful members and defeated candidates endeavouring to address their friends at the same time from different windows'.[17] It took a triumphal West Country tour by Gladstone in 1891 to restore Liberal fortunes in the constituency in 1892.

Devonport was exceptional; the BRADFORD constituencies on the other hand are highly typical, both of Liberal strengths and weaknesses in the late 1880s and 1890s. Bradford had a large Catholic population (8 per cent in 1851), and a growing one.[18] In a town better known for stout nonconformity, the forces of Rome could muster surprising strength. The *Yorkshireman* noted on New Year's Eve 1881 'a significant if not alarming fact': that the largest congregation on the evening of 18 December 1881 was that of St Mary's Roman Catholic Church, the second largest being at St. Jude's Manningham, the local Ritualist parish.[19] Without the Irish vote in BRADFORD CENTRAL in 1886 the Liberals would have been in trouble. G. J. Shaw-Lefevre won it for them in a by-election (April 1886) after the death of W. E. Forster, and it was the Catholic vote which was decisive. 'So far as I could ascertain,' he told Herbert Gladstone, 'the Irish electors who voted for me about balanced the Tories who had voted for Forster and who went back to their own party, and the number of Liberals who abstained from voting did not exceed 500.'[20] The victory thus contained elements of future difficulty: only if the Irish vote remained firm could the threat of abstaining or cross-voting

Liberal Unionists be met. In 1892 the seat was retained, but in 1895 it was lost, along with the city's other two seats, to the Unionists. By that stage, Bradford politics had become increasingly dominated by Labour issues,[21] not Ireland, and the Liberals were as a result doubly vulnerable: with the collapse of the Irish alliance, they could no longer be sure of solid support from Catholics, who might in any case be attracted to Conservative education policy; nor could they confidently staunch the haemorrhage of votes (some of them Catholic, no doubt) to Labour candidates in BRADFORD EAST and, to a greater extent, WEST.

Herbert Gladstone was less certain of Irish dominance in other Yorkshire seats, and with reason. PUDSEY, which he did not query, was ambivalent: it lay between Bradford and Leeds, looking ecclesiastically to the former,[22] politically to the latter.[23] In either case, its Catholic population was not large. BARNSLEY, likewise, amidst a Babel of Wesleyan Methodists, Primitive Methodists, and Wesleyan Reformers, had a solitary Catholic church and a solitary priest.[24] It was dismal territory for Unionists, who could occasionally dent but never overturn a Liberal majority which was assured whichever way Catholics voted. The same might be said for DEWSBURY (North Riding), with one qualification: here Catholics did constitute a substantial section of the constituency. It had four priests, and enough parishioners between them to warrant seven Masses on a Sunday.[25] Perhaps that fact helps explain the relatively poor showing of socialist candidates in the constituency in 1895 and 1906.

As one of its five MPs, Gladstone was better qualified than most to speak of Leeds. His own constituency, LEEDS WEST, was largely English working-class in character; it was LEEDS EAST wherein lay the vast bulk of the city's Irish population. Without their support, the seat could not be won; with it, however, other seats might be lost: as when for instance, Lord Salisbury reminded the working classes of the city of the likely consequence of Home Rule – 'a large emigration of the pauperized Irish population into this country ... [bringing] more British workmen to starvation point'.[26] (It is a measure of his tactical acumen that, in the same speech Salisbury could court *English* Catholic votes *and* applaud the religious tolerance of Scottish Protestants.)[27] If Leeds Liberals were thus embarrassed by their Irish alliance, there was little they could do about it. On the other hand, some of the Irish – those involved in the growing Labour movement – were not themselves much enamoured of the Liberals. The result was curious: the Irish of Leeds reserved their bitterest antagonism either for the Tories or for each other.[28] Thus when a Labour Irish candidate was proposed for the LEEDS SOUTH by-election of 1892, it was the Irish themselves who quashed the candidacy, fearing it would split the Liberal vote and give the seat to the Tories. Their action evoked a memorable simile. H. H. Champion, former army officer and now Labour activist, was appalled. 'As I have never had an opportunity,' he told *Times* readers, 'of seeing political meetings of Hottentots, I cannot say how far it would be a libel on those inhabitants of Africa to compare them to ... Leeds Irishmen.'[29] The logic of such behaviour was not lost on Gladstone: it pointed clearly in the direction of Lib-Labism, the best means of harnessing forces which might otherwise be mutually destructive. Multiple honour was satisfied in 1906 when LEEDS EAST was taken by James O'Grady – sponsored by Labour, supported by the Liberals, and a friend to Irish Nationalists.[30] It would not always be so harmonious.

Gladstone was right to notice the influence of the Catholic vote in MIDDLESBOROUGH. A diocese had been created there in 1878 to cover the North and East Ridings of Yorkshire, and the new bishop, Richard Lacy, was of Irish birth. But the Catholics of the town did not speak with one voice. The usual English/Irish division manifested itself, the one tending towards Toryism, the other Liberalism. In addition, as the *Middlesbrough Daily Gazette* noticed in the 1880 election, a few 'renegade Irishmen' were to be found canvassing for the Tories,[31] never an easy task in those parts. The Tories indeed explicitly courted Catholic support. The secretary of the local Conservative Association, himself a Catholic, published a *Catholic Manifesto* urging that 'freedom can only be found in the Tory party'.[32] Most of his co-religionists chose slavery. In 1885 the Tories did disastrously (36.7 per cent) – in spite of Manning, Parnell, and, locally, Bishop Lacy – and in 1886 they withdrew altogether. In 1892 the Irish vote was split, not this time between Tory and Liberal, but between Liberal and Labour, both acceptable because both Home Rulers. Labour won narrowly, a worrying portent for the Liberals should their Irish alliance ever disintegrate. As with Leeds, Lib-Labism, in fact if not in name, offered a solution: the Labour candidate of 1892 was adopted by the Liberals in 1895 and won easily. The Tories again made a play for Catholic votes, battening on a local rumour that the bishop favoured their cause. If he did, he was not saying so. The Catholic clergy, reported the *North Eastern Daily Gazette* 'have resolved to leave the Catholic voters perfectly free to take what action they please'[33] – indication, no doubt, that the lessons of clerical dictation had been learned from the election of 1885. This pluralism was prophetic. The old order was changing. Middlesbrough Catholicism was not the political force it had been. In 1900 the Irish again supported the Liberal who had been endorsed by T. P. O'Connor. They backed a loser. The constituency celebrated a new century by turning Tory for the first time.

The rest of Yorkshire may now be briefly sketched. Gladstone had good reason for his doubts about Irish 'dominance' at ROTHERHAM: the place was a Unionist graveyard (26.4 per cent in 1885, 28.7 per cent in 1886, 30.2 per cent in 1892) and would have returned a Liberal whichever way its relatively small number of Catholics voted. SHIPLEY is less easily placed in the scheme of things – a seat which returned a Liberal in 1885 and 1886, an advanced radical Lib-Lab in 1892 and a Liberal Unionist in 1895. The Liberal theme was at least constant, whatever the variations. It did have a Catholic component, possibly boosted by the eligibility of Bradford freeholders in the constituency. A safe Liberal seat in 1885 (majority 2147) had become a highly marginal Unionist one ten years later (majority seventy-eight). In such circumstances *all* votes, not simply Catholic ones, mattered.

HALIFAX likewise (a two-seater) was safely Liberal in the mid-1880s, marginally Unionist in the mid-1890s. There was a very precise Catholic reason for this: John Lister. He was a convert both to Catholicism and to Fabianism, and his candidacy in 1895 split the vote and gave the seat to the Unionists.[34] How many of his 3818 supporters were co-religionists, how many of them voted for him because of that fact, cannot be known. But the town did have an important Catholic element, and unlike other Yorkshire towns where the Catholic Association was palpably Tory, Halifax's was Liberal. To that extent, Lister encapsulated Liberal difficulties in the 1890s – as the Irish alliance faded both nationally and in the constituencies, they had created organisations with nowhere to go except to the Tories or Labour. If Halifax's Unionists won their second seat in 1895 and 1900 because of ILP votes which the Liberals had been instrumental in registering in the first place, the Liberals had only themselves to blame.

Finally HULL EAST, lost by the Liberals in 1886, won in 1892. Local Liberals thought the 1886 defeat adventitious. 'The seat can easily be recovered,' an activist told Herbert Gladstone, '[for] though the Liberals have only one third of the representation, we polled a majority in Hull of 434 votes.'[35] This is perhaps another example of the eccentric reasoning of an eccentric town (the Liberals' uselessly large majority in the WEST ward could hardly be redistributed east), a town where 'the working class appears more Conservative than the middle class'.[36] The Catholic element – a considerable one – shared in the peculiarity. Most of them, between 1000 and 1500, lived in the CENTRAL ward and a combination of the Irish National League (Parnell's henchmen) and the Hull Catholic Registration Association (Manning's) helped give the seat to the Tories in 1885.[37] It might be expected with such a large Irish Catholic element the Tories would have been in trouble in the following years. Not so: their percentage of the vote went up from 50.9 to 56.3. Did Hull Central's Catholics care more for their schools than Ireland? The answer, one surmises, is that Hull Central's Protestants cared little for either.

Two other places in Yorkshire, though not on Gladstone's list, deserve notice. Gladstone himself acknowledged that WAKEFIELD had 'a considerable Irish vote ... and it was given for the Tory party' in 1885.[38] The political significance of this – apart from providing the Liberals with a comforting explanation of defeat – is questionable. Even if the Irish transferred to a man to the Liberals in 1886, it made no difference: on both occasions the Unionists received precisely the same proportion of the poll – 53.7 per cent. It is reasonable to suggest therefore that Wakefield Anglicanism (a bigger factor than in other parts of Yorkshire) negatived the potency of the Catholic vote. SHEFFIELD tells a similar story of apparent strength but actual weakness. The second half of the nineteenth century saw years of 'religious boom',[39] and although Nonconformity was the city's governing passion, Catholicism made more than steady advance also. In 1851 there was one place of Catholic worship, in 1881 there were six.[40] Politically, however, Sheffield Catholicism was a curious animal. In spite of several efforts over the years to organise a united front, eccentricity kept breaking through. Thus in 1868 the Tory, E. P. Price, was endorsed by the Protestant Defence League: several Catholics voted for him.[41] In 1874 there was another division, this time along standard lines. Irish Catholics were urged to vote Liberal for Ireland, English Catholics to vote Conservative for schools. Honour was satisfied. The constituency was a two-seater and candidates of both parties were returned. In 1880 it was the turn of the Irish camp to be split. English Catholics voted Tory as usual, but although the *Sheffield Telegraph* pronounced the Irish to be behind the Liberals 'to a man', [42] the evidence is against it. Some even troubled the letters pages with calls to vote Conservative, the party 'more trustworthy for Catholic interests than the so-called Liberal'. By 1885 the two-seater had become a five-seater, the majority of Catholic votes (between 600 and 800) in the CENTRAL division, with some others in BRIGHTSIDE and ATTERCLIFFE. At this point a Norfolk interest should be noticed. The 15th Duke was a considerable figure in the civic life of Sheffield: he was, for example, Mayor, then Lord Mayor between 1896 and 1897, and later first Chancellor of the city's new university.[43] Doubtless his name strengthened the Toryism of the town's English Catholics, but the Norfolk writ was by no means absolute. Lord Edmund Talbot, the Duke's brother, fought BRIGHT-SIDE for the Tories in 1885. His Irish co-religionists felt no sentimental urge to give him their votes. Ten years later, BRIGHTSIDE revisited yielded a similar result when the Duke's nephew, James Fitzalan Hope, was the Tory candidate. As for the CENTRAL ward, unwaveringly Unionist in every general election from 1885 to December 1910, the Catholic vote flattered to deceive. It was important, but never quite important enough. In the two elections that mattered, 1885 and 1886, it went in the first instance to the Tories, who were disposed to play down its value to them,[44] and in the second to the Liberals, who were not however compensated by it for the even greater number of Liberal Unionists who deserted them. Thereafter it declined in significance. It may however be allowed to stand for a more general theme. As with Sheffield Catholicism, so with Yorkshire Catholicism as a whole. It took itself seriously and was occasionally in turn taken seriously by the parties. But in its refusal to act unitedly, its resistance to dictation, and its capacity for antagonising Protestants into support for the other side, its undoubted strength represented a political optical illusion.

LONDON

In London, that 'modern Babylon' to which so many Irishmen exiled themselves in search of work, Catholics had a political importance less emphatic than might have been expected. Men of 'stout hearts and keen brains' they may have been, 'fighting successfully the battle of life',[45] but in Herbert Gladstone's estimation they could deliver only three metropolitan seats to the Liberals in 1886, seven in 1892: all of them, not co-incidentally, Category C seats (i.e. predominantly working-class) in which more often than not Liberal hopes would have been high anyway. (The exceptions to that rule were Bermondsey and St George's in the East.) The social impact of the Irish in London was of course formidable. Indeed it may have been for precisely that reason that their political impact was less so. 'They are spreading all over the metropolis,' recorded John Denvir in 1892, 'and, as a rule getting into far more satisfactory locations than formerly.'[46] This geographic dispersal and social acculturation may have diminished, not strengthened, their electoral power. And if the Irish impact on London was considerable, no less so was London's impact on the Irish.[47] It radicalised many of them: witness the extent of Irish involvement in New Unionism and the dock strike of 1889. It paganised many more: witness the standard clerical complaint of loss of faith, through indifference, materialism, lack of priests, or exposure to the manifold temptations of a non-Catholic culture. Metropolitan Catholicism was a significant force, but Gladstone was right not to overvalue it.

Electorally, the important pockets of Catholicism were in the East End. There were a sizeable number of Catholics in HOLBORN, but this was so much a Tory stronghold that any influence they may have had was not decisive. It is only by travelling several miles east and several rungs down that any real influence can be found. In BATTERSEA, for instance, they made a difference, though it lay only in strengthening John Burns's majority, not creating it. Burns and Battersea were admirably matched. A seat unconventional enough to refuse to fly the Union Jack for six years or pay the 1902 Coronation expenses[48] was well represented by an MP unconventional enough to number among his heroes the odd trio of Victor Hugo, Karl Marx and Cardinal Manning.[49] There were many Catholics in WHITECHAPEL, and even more Jews. Both were well catered for by Samuel Montagu, Jewish philanthropist and Irish Home Ruler. POPLAR, too, had a large Catholic community, requiring three Irish priests and five Masses on a Sunday in 1886,[50] the year, in fact, the Tories came closest to taking what was the safest of Liberal seats.

More heavily peopled with Irish than all these constituencies was ST GEORGE'S IN THE EAST, which was also the smallest of the London constituencies and therefore the one most liable to Irish influence. Yet it was almost as strongly Tory in 1886 as it had been in 1885 and although it went to the Liberals in 1892 it reverted to Toryism in the following election. The explanation is that the seat, being so small (an electorate of around 3,000), was notoriously hard fought and the Tories were simply better at 'treating' than their opponents.[51] The losing Liberal, J. W. Benn, sought to unseat Harry Marks in 1895, citing no fewer than 352 distinct instances of corrupt or illegal practices during or before the election, one of them the distribution of 500 soup kitchen tickets through Father Beckley, the parish priest.[52] The petition failed, the parliamentary committee evidently agreeing with one philanthropic rather than Machiavellian view of the election: 'Marks's soup is better than Benn's sympathy.' It should also be noticed that not all the Irish were Liberals anyway. Marks was careful to cultivate the Irish Unionist association in the constituency. The fact that they met on St Patrick's Day and that 'refreshments' were served may not be co-incidental.[53]

The remaining constituencies are briefly comprehended. BERMONDSEY had a goodly number of Catholics, most of them connected (as was much of the area) with the leather industry.[54] The Liberals won narrowly in 1885, lost rather less narrowly in 1886: the Catholics either stuck to their Parnell/Manning Toryism or, transferring, were unable to compensate for the greater reaction against the Liberals the following year. Whichever was the case (it was probably a bit of both) their vote was obviously not decisive. Likewise LIMEHOUSE, where the Liberal victory in 1892 was exceptional: the Tories comfortably took the seat in every other election between 1885 and 1900. Israel bulked larger than Ireland in the minds of the electorate, certainly towards the end of the century. The sizeable Jewish population of the area made restriction of alien immigration a more compelling issue than the establishment of a Parliament in distant Dublin. Finally, CAMBERWELL NORTH, where the Liberals were badly outnumbered in 1886 and again in 1895 but which otherwise did not return a Unionist candidate between 1885 and 1910. The social geography of the area has been impressively investigated,[55] but its politics remain opaque. It had more lower-middle-class Catholics than, for example, Whitechapel, but also some repellent Irish slums. On balance, its politics were more Nonconformist than Papal, and more class-based than either.[56]

LANCASHIRE

It is entirely fitting that Lancashire should have featured so prominently in Herbert Gladstone's calculations. It was the heartland of Catholicism in England, both indigenous and imported, and its politics reflected a denominationalism which other regions imitated but never surpassed. In 1881, 212,350 of its inhabitants had been born in Ireland,[57] not all of them Catholics, of course, though most were; to which may be added those born in England of Irish parents and also those substantial numbers of native English recusants who had always formed a notable part of the area. The result was a county with over half a million Catholics in the last two decades of the nineteenth century: densely clustered in places like Liverpool, Manchester and Preston, more thinly scattered in constituencies like Lonsdale, Blackpool and Barrow, but always a source of second thoughts for party managers and local agents. The usual corrective applies about the inequivalence of population and voting strengths. But a more significant point about Lancashire is this: Catholic electoral power often *was* great, and it was for just that reason that organised Protestantism was great also. Catholics did indeed influence elections in Lancashire, but not always in the way they intended. Where would Colonel Saunderson have been without the Pope to frighten his followers into the booths?

Gladstone was not alone in taking seriously the Catholic vote in BURNLEY, even though Nonconformity mattered more there.[58] In 1879 it numbered about 430.[59] In 1880 Lord Edmund Talbot, the Duke of Norfolk's brother, expected, but did not receive, the bulk of it. It split but went largely Liberal.[60] Norfolk himself on that occasion was warned to keep out of the constituency. 'Neither the clergy (Catholic) nor the Conservatives (Protestants) think it advisable as it might be interpreted as being too much bringing too much pressure on the Catholics.'[61] Later, H. M. Hyndman, founder and leader of the SDF, had reason to recognise the importance of Catholic support. He knew everything about the seat except how to win it. Having stood there four times he had only a well-developed repugnance to show for it:

Do you know Burnley? If not, don't. I do not say it is so wholly revolting a place as Dewsbury, or quite so depressing as Macclesfield, or so manifestly inhabited by inferior humans as parts of Manchester or Liverpool; but ... it look[s] quite bad enough ... [a] hideous Malebolge of carbon-laden fog and smoke ... [62]

Hyndman believed in 1895 that he had a claim on Catholic votes, but an early conversation with a supporter disabused him:

The Irish vote ... will never go for you, do what you may ... [They] are not only dead against Socialism, but they are absolutely bound to the Liberals and will never break away.[63]

The constituency was also corrupt, none more so in England, it was argued. 'Unless you can prevent bribery on a large scale the night before the election,' Hyndman was told, 'or secure the solid Irish vote' so as to outweigh the purchased vote, 'you will never be member for Burnley.' His own view was that 'on a fair poll without any queer dealings, the Tory would have won.'[64] One can conclude, therefore, four things: the Catholic vote in Burnley was large, solid, unbribable but not in the end decisive.

LEIGH resembled Burnley in its large number of Irish Catholic voters.[65] Where it differed was in its unvarying anti-Toryism, which penetrated the very soil: locals maintained that primroses would not grow there.[66] The Irish were partly responsible for this, the sizeable proportion of Welsh miners in the seat even more so. ACCRINGTON had fewer Catholics,[67] but, apart from 1886, a similar record of anti-Unionism. More interesting is its neighbouring constituency, DARWEN. Herbert Gladstone characterised it thus in 1899:

> R. C. vote there the determining factor c1700 strong. Const. requires a Radical R.C. candidate & agent suggest[s] Costelloe. But seat very expensive.[68]

Here, perhaps, was party management which was too clever by half. A candidate who was both radical and Catholic would not necessarily maximise both votes. On the contrary, the latter were inclined to Conservatism and no doubt would have been even more so if faced with B.F.C. Costelloe, the LCC Progressive. (Costelloe, in fact, is a good example of the candidate who, by trying to appeal to two interests, merely doubles the grounds for defeat. Witness his performance in St Pancras in 1899.)[69] Finally in this cotton-weaving district, there was ROSSENDALE. Gladstone was uncertain of the 'dominance' of the Irish vote there, and it was the scene of a hard-fought by-election in 1892 caused by Hartington's elevation to the peerage as Duke of Devonshire. It was his personal vote which had made the seat Liberal Unionist for one election, but after his departure to the Lords it became once again Gladstonian, which was so much its natural state that Herbert was right not to put too much weight on 'Irishness' as its determining feature.

The towns of Lancashire had their own distinctive identities, partly but by no means wholly determined by sectarian politics. OLDHAM, for instance, which had very few Catholics in the middle of the eighteenth century,[70] had enough in the middle of the nineteenth to antagonise the locals into vandalism of the church and the presbytery.[71] In a highly marginal seat, such tensions could make a difference, and in 1886 probably did: the Liberals were abandoned by between 800 and 1000 of their own followers and local organisers were at a loss as to how to get them back.[72] It is entirely improbable that any extra gain of Catholic votes might have compensated the Gladstone camp. LANCASTER had a higher proportion of Catholics – over 10 per cent[73] – and they seem to have obeyed instructions to vote Tory in 1885 and to have switched allegiance in 1886. ROCHDALE was always more Nonconformist than Catholic, though some contemporaries noticed the 'empty benches and pews' of 'abundant' indifference which affected both denominations.[74] The Catholic vote made little difference there.

Three Lancashire towns where the Catholic vote did make a substantial difference were Widnes, St. Helen's and Preston. WIDNES had about 1600 Catholics[75] and a large residential population: both told against the Liberals towards the end of the century. ST HELEN'S was summarised by Gladstone: 'Only RC allied with Non Cons cd. carry it.'[76] That was a very tall order for the Liberals, who came very close to winning the seat in 1885 and 1892 but had to wait until 1906 for success: first, because many of the Catholics were English recusants who were Tories anyway,[77] second because the Irish element among the Catholics of the town was enough to generate a fatally divisive Liberal Unionism which was in the end just enough to give the seat to the Conservatives:

> In St. Helen's dissent ruins the Liberal cause.... There is no captain, ... no recognized and trusted leader for the ranks to look up to and follow implicitly.... Success as a party is impossible under such conditions.[78]

The same cannot be said of PRESTON, where the Liberals were beaten fair and square between 1885 and 1900 and could not rely on Liberal Unionism as an excuse. Catholics had a highly instructive part to play in this, indeed the electoral history of the town may stand as an example of several general themes of this appendix. Both parties had for years courted the Catholic vote,[79] the Liberals usually with more assiduousness than success. But it was a risky business because, as H. W. Clemesha delicately put it, 'the presence of such a relatively large number of Roman Catholics has had the usual effect of producing that type of Anglican which is sometimes called Protestant and sometimes styled Low Church'.[80] Here no doubt is the key to the town's religious politics, the most convincing explanation of its loyalty to the Tories even in those elections the Liberals thought they could win. A cry of the 'Church in Danger' never went unheeded in Preston. Thus the dilemma of Catholics: when they were solidly Gladstonian, as in 1868, they encouraged a Protestant reaction even more solidly Disraelian;[81] and when they shifted to the Tories, as they did in 1885, they merely added to a majority which was untroubled anyway. The Liberals could not win with them (even though they tried hard in 1892, choosing a wealthy local recusant as a candidate)[82] and the Tories could win without them. It was an unusual fate for a community which formed over 20 per cent of the town's population.

Preston was barren for Liberals. Manchester, by contrast, was fruitful: four of its seats – MANCHESTER NORTH, MANCHESTER SOUTH WEST, SALFORD NORTH and GORTON – went Gladstonian in 1892 on the strength of the Irish vote. The difference between the two places was not, however, as great as that crop of victories might suggest. Like Preston, Catholic votes were certainly to be had, but the price of overeagerness in getting them was Protestant reaction. Mancunian Orangeism never attained the virulence of the Liverpudlian strain, but it lost little in the comparison. 'The fact of the matter is,' one contemporary noted, 'religious intolerance is a local tradition.'[83] Usually Tories were the beneficiaries. After 1868 – the election in which Gladstone had combined with 'infidels, Quakers, Independents, Fenians, Baptists, Reformers and ratteners' to overthrow Protestant institutions and bring England 'under the heel of priestly despotism'[84] – popular Conservatism in Manchester increasingly relied on anti-popery for its success. And yet 1868 was the only election in which the Liberals could be sure of Catholic votes. Thereafter they forfeited them on the question of religious schooling, and when some of them returned on the Home Rule issue the Protestant-Conservative alliance was too well entrenched for them to make much difference.[85]

Individual constituencies of course tell their own stories. Both MANCHESTER NORTH and MANCHESTER SOUTH-WEST went Liberal in 1886 on the strength of the Irish vote and stayed that way the following election.[86] GORTON is more interesting. The Liberals won in

1885 thanks to Irish support: the parish priest instructed his flock to ignore the Manning-Parnell injunction and they did so with enthusiasm. The Liberal was a prominent supporter of local religious charities, and the band of the Irish Nationalist League took to the streets when his victory was announced. T. P. O'Connor dissolved the branch as a result.[87]

STOCKPORT's Catholic population was mainly, but not exclusively Irish: one of its two parishes had been in existence as early as 1799,[88] long before the descent of the foreigner. The Irish worked in the town's cotton factories[89] and on the whole they had two reasons for voting Liberal: Ireland and Free Trade. On two occasions, however, these factors operated to the Conservatives' advantage: in 1885, when the Manning-Parnell injunction was in force; and ten years later, when the Indian cotton duties controversy cost the Liberals many votes in Lancashire. Otherwise Catholic support for Conservatives does not appear to be high. SALFORD NORTH's Liberalism in 1892 was exceptional, the only time between 1885 and 1906 that a Salford seat was lost by the Tories. Home Rule generally scuppered the Liberals in all three Salford seats[90] and their 1892 victory in one of them must be attributed to the national reaction against the Tories and a marginally higher Irish vote.

This is not the place to tell the story of the Catholic politics of Liverpool. An excellent account already exists[91] and it would be obtuse to try to condense its paradoxical story of sectarianism without belief. Only one Liverpool seat, EXCHANGE, was included by Herbert Gladstone in his list of Liberal seats dominated by the Irish vote in 1886 and 1892, though he had hopes (misplaced, it turned out) for BIRKENHEAD in 1895. Other constituencies were, of course, determined by the Irish vote, most notably LIVERPOOL SCOTLAND, where it constituted a majority (the only such British constituency) and where T. P. O'Connor held remarkable sway from 1885 to 1929. BOOTLE (technically a division of Lancashire, not Liverpool) was also heavily Irish,[92] sufficiently so to scare the electors into support for the egregious Colonel Sandys. KIRKDALE, on the other hand, though not as sparsely Catholic as some have suggested,[93] was nevertheless resistant to dictation, Liberal or Nationalist. Catholic voters did have minds of their own, but were not generally quick to exercise them.[94] Their choice in Liverpool was in any case an impoverished one: Tory Orangeism was out, Gladstonian Home Rule was natural but sterile, socialism potentially vote-splitting and, worse, soul-destroying.[95] Electorally this proved little match for a Protestantism which could unite, not divide, classes. 'The working classes hate most the Mass,' observed E. R. Russell, editor of the *Liverpool Daily Post*, 'the middle classes hate most the Confessional.'[96] Catholicism was catholic in the ammunition it gave its enemies.

The remaining Lancashire seats may be quickly dispatched. Both RADCLIFFE-cum-FARNWORTH and NORTH LONSDALE had Catholic populations under 10 per cent.[97] The first was a Liberal marginal. There were rather more Catholics in Farnworth than Radcliffe[98] and the Liberals tended to do slightly better there; but the two facts are most likely co-incidental.[99] The second was a Unionist marginal, where local factors, particularly the patronage of the Duke of Devonshire, played an important part; a more significant part than Catholicism ever did. MIDDLETON likewise had a Catholic population of under 10 per cent,[100] inclined to Toryism towards the end of the century because of the voluntary schools issue. Its neighbouring constituency, HEYWOOD, had a sizeable Catholic parish in Heywood itself and a smaller, more recent one at Ramsbottom.[101] Gladstone doubted the Irish 'dominance' there in 1886 but was more sure of it in 1892, when the Tory vote eased by 1 per cent. It is hard to tell either way.

INCE was an oddity: an enclave of Roman Catholics (they comprised over 20 per cent of the electorate) where politics oscillated between deference to recusant gentry and a desire for electoral radicalism. The latter eventually succeeded in the form of Stephen Walsh, who won the seat for Labour in 1906 and kept it until his death in 1929. His defeated opponent on that occasion was Colonel Henry Blundell-Hollinshead-Blundell, who, apart from a narrow defeat at the hands of a Lib/Lab candidate in 1892, had held the seat without great difficulty since November 1885. Two worlds met and parted in the 1906 election – Eton, Christ Church, Crimea and the Guards giving way to Kirkdale Elementary School, the pit at fourteen, and the Lancashire and Cheshire Miners' Federation. The constituency was unusual in that its pockets of Catholicism (Little Crosby, for instance) were peopled largely by English, not Irish Catholics – a boon to the Tories. Walsh was unusual in that he reversed the conventional pattern of religious odyssey: he was a cradle Catholic who converted to Anglicanism. The Irish of the seat were not unusual: they would have preferred a Home Rule candidate to a socialist.[102] Except in 1892, they never really got their way.

Lastly, three seats which may be grouped together: ECCLES, WARRINGTON and WIGAN, the first a highly marginal seat which the Liberals captured in 1892 (their only success between 1865 and 1906), the second and third on Gladstone's list of possibles for 1895, both nevertheless showing a swing to the Unionists in that election. Eccles was socially heterogeneous – cotton workers, engineers, miners, farm labourers – and the Irish vote, either in itself or as an influence on the rest of the electorate, seems to have been marginal.[103] WIGAN by contrast was a town with a much livelier Catholic tradition.[104] It had four parishes, eleven priests and its own Catholic grammar school:[105] this last fact doubtless making the Tory candidate's life easier. WARRINGTON's Catholics worked mainly in the town's cotton factories.[106] They formed a substantial community – 20 per cent of the population, nearly 10 per cent of the electorate.[107] Apart from 1900, 1885 was the year the Conservatives did best in the town, and it·is reasonable to surmise that this was partly attributable to the Manning-Parnell instruction. A strong tradition of voluntary education – the Catholics opened two schools, one in 1872, the other in 1896[108] – may have helped shore up the Conservative majority.

THE MIDLANDS

Why did the Midlands feature so little in Herbert Gladstone's calculations? The answer of course is that it was largely Unionist territory, but there were other reasons too, especially with regard to the nature of the Irish vote. It was an area in which Catholicism as a social identifier came away in the hands of those who tried to grasp it. Witness Birmingham. In 1813, the number of Catholics was 'inconsiderable compared with the whole population of the town'.[109] By 1855 it had grown to become 'an important centre of Roman Catholicism',[110] with seven churches or chapels serving the needs of its people. Yet by 1892 a 'great change' had taken place.[111] The Irish who came (and there were fewer and fewer after the famine) either did not stay or, if they did, merged into the city much more readily than elsewhere. Birmingham naturally had its Irish quarter – it fell mainly in BIRMINGHAM CENTRAL – but it was never as conspicuous a feature as in Liverpool or Manchester. The result was a loss of ardour, both national and religious, which distressed John Denvir, who had devoted so much time to its organisation. 'There is not,' he suggested, 'among our people in Birmingham, and the Midlands generally, that warmth of feeling [of] forty, or even twenty years ago.'[112] All over the region he noticed the signs of a creed and a community dying of inanition: 'undoubtedly a great decrease' of

Catholics in Wolverhampton 'and considerably greater' in Bilston and Darlaston; 'most of the Irish ... have gone from Worcester ... now'; 'there are few traces now' of the once 'considerable' number of Irish in Kidderminster; 'in Walsall ... only about half the Catholic baptisms that there were some thirty years ago'; in Northampton the Irish 'are not so numerous as before'.[113] They all aspired to America or, failing that, villadom.[114] Trooping obediently behind a Parnellite or Gladstonian flag was not a priority.

Denvir's lament for a vanishing species was nevertheless tempered by recognition that there were parts of the Midlands in which Catholicism still flourished. Gladstone recognised this too. His description of COVENTRY, for instance, is a fine example of his ability to capture the essence of a place in three telegrammatic sentences:

> There is an old Benedictine mission in div. + 4 to 5 hundred RC voters. Also about 1000 freeholders of Warwick and Leamington. Rads will vote for moderates but not mods for rads.[115]

The enumeration was exaggerated – 200 would have been nearer the mark, out of an electorate of nearly 10,000[116] – but the Irish element did have the advantage of consistency of purpose. When they voted, they voted very solidly indeed. In an 1881 by-election, for example, out of a possible 198 votes, 194 went to the Tory, as a protest against coercion in Ireland.[117] The Tory was duly elected and – a consequence perhaps not foreseen by the Catholics of Coventry – was introduced to the House of Commons by that arch-Protestant, C. N. Newdegate. The Tories held the seat in 1885, but in 1886 the Irish vote turned solidly against them.[118] It made no difference: the Liberal vote collapsed and the Tory was returned with a handsomely increased majority. Thereafter the Irish vote stayed with the Liberals, but although they won the seat in an 1887 by-election and later in 1892, Gladstone was not inclined to attribute it to Catholic support.

WEDNESBURY was similar: its Irish Catholic element made a difference in 1886, when it went with Gladstone, but otherwise it was marginally Tory for most of the 1885–1910 period. There is a hidden irony here. One of the boasts of its citizens was that Wednesbury was typical of England. Progress and Protestantism were synonymous:

> The inhabitants have been more or less affected by the changes that have taken place in the religion of the country – in the manners, customs and habits which have succeeded each other –

... from the despotic rule of the Druidical priesthood to the mild sway of Queen Victoria – from rude barbarism to modern civilisation – from the corrupt system of the Papacy and the usurpation of the Bishop of Rome, to the enjoyment of pure and undefiled religion, restored at the glorious period of the Reformation ... [119]

The author spoke truer than he realised. Shortly afterwards the town again shared a national experience, in the form of an influx of Irish Catholics, making up about a quarter of the population, bringing with them Romanism, recklessness and a rude alien tongue. 'Gaelic ... is now more often heard than the language in which Thor and Woden were praised and glorified.... In many of the houses not one of the women could speak English.' So wrote A. M. Sullivan in 1856.[120] Drinking, fighting, rioting became commonplace and the Irish 'would have gone wild and savage outright if it wasn't the mercy of God sent [them] a priest'.[121] So much for the Whig interpretation of Wednesbury history. It was this element which transformed a safe Tory seat into a marginal one, and which turned smug Anglicanism sour.

Riot was a occasional feature of Nottingham life too. Almost invariably, elections brought trouble: between 1865 and 1892 there was only one peaceful poll (1868), and the 1874 and 1885 disturbances amounted to serious threats to public order.[122] The Irish element in the city was substantial and initially far from welcome. In 1847 the council was alarmed by the 'number of sick and destitute Irish' making their way to the area and appointed a committee to stop them.[123] They need not have bothered. The Irish were in Nottingham to stay, deplorable hygiene and all.[124] Some of them became miners, which is why NOTTINGHAM WEST, among other factors, was so strongly Gladstonian in 1886.[125] In NOTTINGHAM EAST, however, more than half the Catholic population (1000 out of nearly 2000) was English, and their sympathies were Tory.[126] As a result, a reasonably safe Liberal seat became increasingly marginal until in 1895 it returned a Unionist and thereafter only returned a Liberal in the great landslide of 1906.

In STAFFORD in 1885 the Irish vote, about seventy strong,[127] followed its instructions and voted Tory. The Liberal won. In 1886 it followed its instincts and voted Liberal. The Tory won. This was not an impressive record of political potency. In truth, the seat was normally Liberal and therefore Home Rule was more of a hindrance than a help to the Gladstonian cause. HANLEY, another Staffordshire seat, was much the same, the only difference being that the Liberal vote was even greater and the Irish contribution to it ultimately even less decisive. STOKE-on-TRENT had a large Catholic population,[128] most of them, like their priests, Irish, many of them, like their neighbours, employed in the potteries.[129] Their support enabled the Liberals to emerge relatively unscathed from the flight of Liberal Unionists in 1886. They mattered less as a distinctive *bloc* in the 1890s when local matters (Liberal division and developing Labourism)[130] predominated over imperial questions. The neighbouring seat of NEWCASTLE under LYME had broadly similar characteristics. The Second Reform Act increased the electorate by 1,500 to 2,500, between 400 and 500 of whom were working-class Irish Catholics.[131] The Reform and Redistribution Acts of 1884 and 1885 completed the transformation. Class now mattered more than anything else in local politics.[132] The 1886 election was exceptional (about one-third of the Liberal vote turned Unionist): the following year normalcy was restored as the Liberals began to hear calls from the miners (whose support made all the difference in the constituency) for independent Labour representation.[133] By 1892 the Liberal W. S. Allen had 'virtually to transform himself into a Labour candidate to win'. The old order was not entirely dead, however. Allen loudly trumpeted his temperance politics to win local Nonconformist support. He won it too well. The abstainers were unassuagable when it was revealed that he had shares in a brewery company. End of career.

Cheshire was not much considered by Gladstone as a trawling ground for Irish Catholic votes. He had his doubts about CREWE in 1886, though a strong showing by the Liberal in 1892 (58.2 per cent) dispelled them. The Catholic population was concentrated in Crewe itself, with also a parish in Nantwich and a smaller mission station at Sandbach.[134] This imitated the population patterns of the constituency as a whole. The seat gives every appearance of sensitivity to local rather than national concerns, but it is reasonable to posit that the Liberal victory in 1892 owed its size to the Irish vote. Its near neighbour, NORTHWICH, only once returned a Tory between 1885 and 1910 – in 1886 – and the Liberal majority was rarely less than healthy. This suggests an Irish influence which was either negative or inconsequential.

Derbyshire was not much more fruitful, but in CHESTERFIELD and ILKESTON, two largely mining constituencies, Catholic elements may have helped the Liberal cause. In Chesterfield the prominent Liberal, J. Stores Smith, was a Catholic. His strong, at times controversial, support for denominational schooling[135] may have gained his party some of the votes of his co-religionists. Parliamentary elections, however, were affairs not of education or Ireland but increasingly of the mineworkers' desire to have an MP of their own, either under Liberal colours or, later, under Labour. It would be misleading therefore to put too much emphasis on Catholic matters as a determinant of Chesterfield politics. Likewise Ilkeston. As with Chesterfield, the Unionists did notably better in 1886 than 1885, unlike Chesterfield, they lost. They never stood much chance in the area and the existence of an exiguous Conservative Miners' Association (in 1900, its membership was seventy-eight) merely underlined that fact.[136] Catholics were plentiful in the seat, but Catholic issues were not.

THE NORTH

Gladstone was right to recognise Catholic electoral significance in a clutch of seats in the north of England. He would have been foolish not to: not only could Northumberland and Durham lay claims to an historic Catholicism even more venerable than Lancashire's, they could also boast a substantial number of the mid-century Irish diaspora, come to Tyneside in what locals called 'the rush' to avoid famine, disease and death. The 'rush', it was said, represented a chronological division as real as that between BC and AD and its effects were certainly profound.[137] Irish colonies sprang into being at Newcastle, Gateshead, Wallsend, Jarrow, Consett: 'clusters of wild flowers', one sentimentalist called them, grown from strange, wind-scattered seed;[138] in reality, communities of ship-builders, iron workers, jetty men, coalminers, chemical workers, wielders of pick and shovel. The social landscape was transformed, the political landscape also. By the 1850s, as one phrase vividly had it, 'Tyneside was honeycombed with fenians'.[139]

For the Irish in England, Fenianism sweetened exile and gave purpose to strange new factory existences; but it was politically hopeless. Constitutionalism offered a better path. As early as 1870 the strength of the Catholic vote in Newcastle was evident from school board elections. By 1874 the Irish in that city had in Joseph Cowen a Member of Parliament strikingly sympathetic to their cause.[140] By 1877 the Home Rule Confederation was well established on the Tyne, later to be followed by the Irish National League. Fenianism atrophied but took a long time to expire in the region. Its ultimate fate however was never in doubt. Not the least of the transformations of Northern political life was this: in the 1850s Newcastle Irishmen spent their nights planning and organising armed rebellion. Sixty years on they found themselves in the Tyneside Irish Brigade, formed by Colonel Joseph Cowen, son of the MP, to fight in the Great War for the defence of the Empire, King and Country. The odd casuistry of patriotism can have had few more impressive monuments.[141]

NEWCASTLE-UPON-TYNE itself fits slightly uneasily into Gladstone's inventory. With Cowen as candidate its Liberalism was always assured, but as Member his own Liberalism was of the awkwardly conscientious kind. Cowen was nothing less than the leading English Home Ruler. More than once he defied his party's policy of Irish coercion, and in 1885 he quarrelled with the local Liberal caucus, whose preferred candidate was John Morley. Cowen topped the poll, facing down some clerical opposition in the process.[142] His following among the Irish of Newcastle was formidable, and had not Parnell exempted them from the general instruction of 1885 they would probably have voted for him anyway. When he departed the scene in 1886, the city's politics began imperceptibly to alter.[143] The Irish vote, no less considerable, was rather less certain. The complexion of the constituency remained Liberal in the early 1890s, but as the century ended a Unionist revival may have owed something to Catholic votes. After all, education had mattered more to some priests than Ireland even in 1885, and with the disintegration of the Liberal-Irish alliance in the 1890s such crypto-Toryism would have appeared less like national betrayal than before. Besides, the social acculturation which was to reach its climax in the Tyneside Irish Brigade was presumably by now well under way. The seat was always more Liberal than Tory, but increasing marginalism was itself a reflection of how the Catholic vote had changed.

That SUNDERLAND had a sizeable Catholic population is reflected in the statistics: in 1886 it had four churches, seven priests, eight Sunday Masses.[144] This represented a substantial *bloc*, albeit one diminished by comparison with the strength of Nonconformity in the town. The vote was not as solid as it appeared. In 1885 Parnell countermanded his general injunction and instructed the Irish of the town to support Samuel Storey, the Liberal. Many of them did, but some defiantly voted Tory.[145] Storey topped the poll (8,295, 36.4 per cent) and did so again the following year when, on a lower turnout, his vote was down by over a thousand and his share of the poll down by 1.3 per cent. The Unionist vote increased by nearly 1 per cent. It may be concluded therefore that even if the Irish vote were solidly Liberal on both occasions – as it evidently was not – it nevertheless was a hindrance to the party in the latter election. The willingness of some Sunderland Catholics to follow clerical rather than Parnellite instruction in 1885 hints at a future Toryism which would be able to breathe more easily once Parnell, then Gladstone, had both departed the scene.

CHESTER LE STREET and HOUGHTON LE SPRING were virtually twin constituencies. In both of them the mining vote was crucial, and in neither was the Catholic element negligible. Houghton le Spring's Catholics were the more numerous and longer established as a community.[146] As for Chester le Street, the size and significance of its Catholic element has been doubted.[147] Perhaps: but it was one of the very few seats in 1885 in which the Irish were excused by Parnell their duty to vote Conservative and where the Conservative vote accordingly plummetted. The circumstances however were unusual. The caucus Liberal James Joicey was opposed by R. Lloyd Jones, Independent Liberal, 'a life-long advocate of Irish rights'[148] who stood as a labour representative. Joicey got 4,409 votes (44 per cent) to Lloyd-Jones's 3,606 (35.9 per cent); the Conservative trailed in at 2,018 (20.1 per cent). Joicey usually polled over 60 per cent, indeed was unopposed the following year. The 1885 result was more a spasm of pseudo-socialism than an Irish protest vote, but the latter element possibly went deeper in the constituency than has been acknowledged.

It may seem odd that JARROW, which had a Catholic vote of over 1000,[149] is not included in Gladstone's list, even though it had a very low percentage Unionist poll in 1886 and 1892. The answer is that the town's politics were so dominated by the local magnate Sir Charles Palmer – 'Good Old Charlie' to the workers of Jarrow, the most popular man in the North of England[150] – that Irish support for him merely copperbottomed a majority already secure. Even so, Catholic votes were never taken for granted, particularly in the face of a challenge to Liberal dominance from independent labour which had been developing as early as 1885. Strenuous efforts were made by the latter throughout the 1890s to wean the Irish working class of the town from their historic support for Liberalism. This might have worked better if Pete Curran, the LRC candidate in 1902, an Irishman by descent, had not also been a militant socialist, an atheist and possibly a common-law bigamist.[151] The abiding importance of the Irish vote is reflected in the fact that a Nationalist candidate polled 2,122 votes in a by-election in 1907; enough indeed to split the Liberal vote and give the seat to the contumacious Curran.

Durham, city and county, were at odds in their respective politics. In the city the catholic population was large though never electorally of much moment.[152] The cathedral saw to that. Even in 1885 when the Irish were instructed to vote for Thomas Thompson, a Liberal 'courageous and splendid'[153] in his support for their cause, the Conservative still won; the following year he won even more handsomely. DURHAM MID was a mining seat where Lib-Labism was the order of the day. Irish nationalism was a secondary sentimentality.[154] DURHAM NORTH WEST was the most Catholic of the three, the reason being the large Irish community at Consett attached to the ironworks. Evidently the Liberal, L. A. Atherley-Jones, won Irish votes even in 1885, his father having been Ernest Jones, Chartist and 'Friend of Ireland'. They were less inclined to support him in 1900 when his radicalism threatened their schools. He survived easily enough all the same.[155]

The Catholic electorate of GATESHEAD numbered about 2,000,[156] a formidable *bloc* when allied with the dominant mining interest in the constituency, less so if opposed to it. In a 1904 by-election, for example, they made common cause to support John Johnson of the Durham Miners Association, who was *inter alia* a vocal Home Ruler, and the result was a triumph which both sides claimed as their own. At the time it seemed as if the Irish had the better of the argument. They could, Joseph Devlin MP asserted on the eve of the poll, send a friend to the Commons and drive an enemy out of it.[157] It would have been less inspiring but nearer the truth to say that they could help send a friend there but could not keep him there on their own. Thus when Johnson, as sitting MP, stood again in January 1910, he had antagonised enough of his former supporters to encourage the Liberals to oppose him with a candidate of their own. He again got Irish Catholic support, but it did him little good in the end, the miners having deserted him to return to their former Liberal allegiance.[158] Gateshead thus typifies a general rule regarding seats with a large Catholic vote: when it did not engender a corresponding anti-Catholic vote, it was worth having; when it coincided with the dominant interest of the seat it was well worth having; when it did not so coincide, it was probably not worth worrying about.

Making allowance for local conditions, the rule applies to other Northern seats. TYNESIDE itself did not have a large Catholic vote but it tended towards Liberalism. SOUTH SHIELDS, a great centre of Primitive Methodism in the 1890s,[159] had a long post-Reformation Catholic history and an Irish vote which was estimated in 1885 as 10 per cent of the whole. Relations between Nonconformity and Catholicism in the constituency were surprisingly good – the first Catholic chapel had originally been used by the Baptists[160] – and politically they complemented each other in their Liberalism. The same could not be said of EGREMONT, the west division of Cumberland. Here the strength of Catholicism, especially in the Cleator Moor district, provoked violent Protestant response. In 1884 an Orange-led riot resulted in the death of a local Irish Catholic postman,[161] and the memory still lingered twenty years later. As late as 1916 the vicar recorded a need for 'wider charity all round'.[162] In such poisonous conditions the Liberals received Irish votes whenever they asked for them, but this also boosted the Unionist poll which otherwise might have regarded the territory as less than promising.[163] Neighbouring COCKERMOUTH also had sharp denominational division but it was capable of peculiar electoral ecumenism. Thus in 1885 the Liberal, Sir Wilfrid Lawson, was beaten by 'a Local Optionist round whom rallied Parnellites, Orangemen, Priests, Parsons, Publicans and some teetotallers'.[164] Here was comprehensive unpopularity. The Irish reversed their vote the following year and Lawson got back; but 1886 was the high point of Liberal-Irish co-operation. Thereafter the Catholic drift to Toryism on the schools question began to tell, though only in 1900 did the seat fall into Unionist hands. All told, there were about 500 Irish electors in the constituency.[165]

The large Catholic element in WHITEHAVEN is well attested, some from Wicklow, most from Ulster. The constituency also had an Orange faction associated mainly with the shipyards. When the yards fell on hard times so did the Protestants. Nationalists, with grim *schadenfreude*, claimed that this tended to deepen their attachment to Orangeism. Protestants, it was noticed, were 'so degraded as to be willing to live in slavery themselves, providing that they can still keep their feet on the necks of the "Papishes"'.[166] Of such material were angels in marble fashioned. But Catholics, too, voted

Conservative when it suited them, and in 1895 and 1900 they seem to have done so in number.[167] How they voted more often than not determined the result, Orangeism notwithstanding.

Finally STOCKTON-ON-TEES and the HARTLEPOOLS. Both of them had 'considerable'[168] Irish populations, but it would be misleading to claim too much for them. In Stockton, for instance, any transfer of votes from Tory to Liberal between 1885 and 1886 was precisely matched by transfers in the opposite direction of anti-Home Rulers. On both occasions the Liberal share of the poll (57.5 per cent) and the Conservative (42.5 per cent) were exactly the same. In Hartlepool, Nonconformity seems to have been a more potent factor, though the most powerful element of all was the Furness family, whose shipping line was a major source of local employment.

WALES

Four seats in Wales – Cardiff, Monmouth Boroughs, Swansea District and Swansea Town – figured in Gladstone's inventory. Not surprisingly all of them were in South Wales and, equally predictable, all were essentially urban in character. There was no Catholic influence worth speaking of in the north and east of the principality. The whole of Radnor, for instance, had only forty-seven Irish-born inhabitants in 1881, and Merioneth (with 136) and Montgomeryshire (with 199) were hardly much better.[169] A few expatriate Irish ended up in Bangor, Wrexham and Holywell, but not even wishful thinking could give them influence where plainly they had none. Even so, striking as is the contrast with South Wales, it should not be drawn with such starkness as to suggest that the latter was a place where Catholicism had strong political advantages. Outside Monmouthshire and Glamorgan, this was not so; and even within those two counties, Catholicism fell short of being the decisive element.

CARDIFF appears the most promising territory, if demography alone be deemed conclusive. At the beginning of the century, Catholics struggled to reach double figures. By 1850 there were 8,000 of them, by 1875 there 11,000, and by the turn of the century, 15,000.[170] Most of these were Irish, highly localised in their settlement, highly resistant to social integration, and more of a problem for sanitation engineers than local political managers.[171] Having avoided starvation, they could put up with mere squalor. Respectability only came much later. At the other end of the scale was the 3rd Marquess of Bute, Cardiff's leading landowner and best known Catholic convert. The Bute influence had always been strong in the town, but by the late nineteenth century it was perceptibly on the wane, for reasons less to do with the Marquess's Catholicism, more to do with simple democratic advance.[172] Besides, whatever power Bute had, it was certainly not due to the Irish of Stanley Street deferentially following his line. For the most part they voted on national grounds, following, for example, the Parnellite instruction of November 1885 to support the Conservative; who very nearly won. Ten years later the Conservative did win, and some Catholic votes may well have helped him do so, church schools and their maintenance being a dominant theme of Cardiff Catholic life.[173]

SWANSEA TOWN and DISTRICT were contiguous, but worlds apart in their politics. In the former the Unionist vote was usually around 45 per cent. In the latter it struggled to reach 20 per cent. This disparity may even have extended to their respective Catholic populations. Although in both instances they were overwhelmingly working-class – dockers in Swansea Town; iron, copper and tin workers in Swansea District – the Irish of Swansea Town were less solidly Liberal, possibly because of acquired disillusion at the workplace,[174] possibly because there were more Catholic schools in this con-stituency than in the neighbouring one. Perhaps there is irony here. 'Nowhere were Irish events watched with greater interest, nowhere were Irish aspirations were warmly endorsed'[175] than in South Wales. Some Irish may have shown their gratitude by voting Tory.

Something similar may have happened in MONMOUTH BOROUGHS, but the evidence is circumstantial. The Irish fondness for drink was a problem at Newport,[176] and the fact that the Liberal candidate in 1900 was a strong temperance campaigner may have cost him votes in that quarter. On the other hand, a growing congruence of Irish and Labour interests may also be witnessed in the constituency.[177] Liberal pains to cultivate Catholics in this seat were thus doubly ill-rewarded.

MISCELLANEOUS

A few miscellaneous seats remain. Some of them are puzzling. Why, for example, did Gladstone think that BUCKINGHAM NORTH was dominated by the Irish vote in 1892? The number of Catholics in the whole county was very slight. Perhaps Wolverton,[178] where most of them were to be found, was more loyal to Liberalism than he had expected. GLOUCESTER and STROUD do not quite fall into the same category because they had larger Catholic populations, but it is still hard to see either place, especially the latter, enthusiastically endorsing Home Rule. The same might be said of CAMBORNE (CORNWALL NORTH-WEST) where politics reflected very largely the concerns of the local copper and tin industry. Nonetheless, Gladstone was right to recognise a Catholic influence there. Camborne had an Irish quarter large enough to provoke native resentment, small enough to persuade the natives they could attack it with impunity. Community relations collapsed in April 1882 when, after an assault case against two Irish labourers, a virtual pogrom ensued in which Irish homes were destroyed and the Catholic church was desecrated.[179] Two hundred special constables had to be sworn in. In such circumstances, the low Unionist percentage in the constituency in 1886 no doubt indicates a desire less to do the Irish a favour as to be rid of them.

BRISTOL had a healthy Catholic population, with its own pro-cathedral and three other parishes, four convents and assorted homes for the poor.[180] The bishop lived in salubrious Clifton, spa town and home of the pro-cathedral, where the Catholic population was notably patriotic[181] and helped boost, no doubt, the natural Unionist majority of BRISTOL WEST. BRISTOL NORTH Catholics, on the other hand, were mainly Irish – possibly the reason the constituency turned so strongly Unionist in 1886 – and their influence (even if only negative) on a marginal seat should not be denied.

Finally PORTSMOUTH and SOUTHAMPTON, both of them two-seaters which returned Liberal members in 1982. Gladstone was unsure of Irish 'dominance' in the first, but does not seem to have questioned it in the second. In one respect, this is curious: it might have been thought that it would have been the other way round. Southampton in 1881 had only 767 Irish-born inhabitants to Portsmouth's 3,037.[182] Portsmouth, indeed was large enough to merit a Catholic diocese of its own, which was created in May 1882 under the leadership of the appropriately named Bishop John Virtue. But there was a reason for Gladstone's uncertainty. Many of Portsmouth's Catholics were in the army or navy (three of the town's seven priests were chaplains to the armed forces)[183] and to this extent, if they had a vote, tended to Toryism. The 'dockyard vote' itself was unsentimental: whichever party (it tended not to be the one in power) seemed better disposed to naval interests had its support.[184] As for Southampton, naval matters and Nonconformity[185] determined its allegiance more than

Romanism or Home Rule. Its Catholic vote was not large, but in closely-fought elections (such as that in 1892) it may have made a difference. Like some other seats, its place in Herbert Gladstone's inventory owes more to wishful thinking than electoral reality.

That reality was best captured by Lady Gwendolin Cecil in her biography of her father, Lord Salisbury. Her calculations were altogether simpler than Herbert's: the Irish vote in England was quite overrated. Party managers of both sides, 'deprived of all solid bases for calculation' because of the electoral reforms of 1884–5, 'had become a prey to panic anxieties,' she argued, and 'this state of feeling acted with complicating effect upon the relations of the Parnellite group to the two English parties [which] were in any case abnormal.' Parnell naturally exploited this anxiety, and it was only with hindsight that his real importance could be recognised:

> His influence could not, in fact, affect results in more than three or four English and Scottish seats, but the excited state of party nerves endowed his intentions with an exaggerated importance.[186]

Herbert Gladstone seems precisely the kind of manager she had in mind.

NOTES

1. P. Hughes, 'The English Catholics in 1850' in G. A. Beck (ed.), *The English Catholics 1850–1950* (London, 1950), p. 45. This is a valuable analysis of the difficulties of Catholic demography.
2. Quoted J. D. Baxendale, 'The Development of the Liberal Party in England, With Special Reference to the North-West' (unpublished Oxford D.Phil. thesis, 1971), p. 128. Pages 128–30 contain a useful summary of the topic.
3. D. Gwynn, 'The Growth of the Catholic Community' in Beck, op. cit., pp. 438–9. The 1900 figures represent the number of priests in the original dioceses, not the boundaries as they were occasionally altered before the end of the century.
4. *Franciscan Missions Among the Colliers and Ironworkers of Monmouthshire* (London, 1876), p. 33.
5. Quoted T. Barker and J. R. Harris, *A Merseyside Town in the Industrial Revolution: St. Helen's 1750–1900* (London, 1954), p. 281.
6. Baxendale, op. cit., p. 129. See also C.H.D. Howard, 'The Parnell Manifesto of 21 November, 1885 and the Schools question' in *English Historical Review* (62), January 1947, p. 42.
7. These counties constituted the Diocese of Northampton. See *Catholic*

Directory (1886), p. 194. Unless otherwise indicated, the references which follow are to the *Catholic Directory* of 1886.

8. F. H. Hibgame, quoted in *A Great Gothic Fane: A Retrospect of Catholicity in Norwich* (London, 1913), p. 269.

9. *Franciscan Mission Among the Colliers and Ironworkers of Monmouthshire* (London, 1876) p. 44.

10. *Catholic Directory*, p. 177, W. Glover (ed.).

11. The *Ashton-under-Lyne News* quoted in W. Glover (ed.), *The History of Ashton under Lyne* (Ashton-under-Lyne, 1984), p. 335.

12. C. C. O'Brien, *Parnell and His Party* (London, 1957), p. 274.

13. D. G. Hey (ed.), *Peasants and Clothiers* (Holmfirth, 1976), p. 66.

14. H. Pelling, *Social Geography of British Elections 1885–1910* (New York, 1967), p. 234. It will be clear that Dr. Pelling's work has been particularly valuable for some of the information contained in the following pages.

15. F. Peel, *Spen Valley Past and Present* (Leeds, n.d.), p. 363.

16. See Pelling, op. cit., p. 163.

17. H. F. Whitfield, *Plymouth and Devonport in Times of War and Peace* (Plymouth, 1900), p. 488.

18. See R. E. Chadwick, 'Church and People in Bradford and District 1880–1914: the Protestant Churches in an Urban Industrial Environment' (unpublished Oxford D.Phil. thesis, 1986), p. 77.

19. Ibid.

20. G. J. Shaw-Lefevre to Herbert Gladstone, 28/4/86, Add. Ms. 46052 f. 86. See also A. W. Roberts, 'Leeds Liberalism and Late-Victorian Politics' in *Northern History*, V (1970), p. 146, note 55.

21. For example, Herbert Gladstone notebook, Add. Ms. 46483 f. 4 (27/4/99). 'Hutton ... Re Bradford politics thinks E. Bradford shd. be given to Bell A.S.R.S. as best step towards settling the Labour dif. in West B.'

22. It had a school chapel, founded in 1883, which was served from St Mary's Bradford. Otherwise it had no resident priest. *Catholic Directory*, p. 155.

23. A third of the electorate consisted of Leeds freeholders. Pelling, op. cit., p. 302.

24. *Barnsley Historical Almanack and Year Book 1863*, p. 38. Altogether in 1863 there were three Anglican places of worship, one Wesleyan Methodist, one Methodist New Connexion, one Primitive Methodist, one United Methodist Free Church, one Wesleyan Reform Church, one Congregationalist, one Baptist, one Society of Friends, one Roman Catholic.

25. *Catholic Directory*, p. 153.

26. *Times*, 19/6/86, p. 12.

27. Thus, ibid.: 'In this country we get on as far as I know perfectly well with the Catholics.... It is [not] a matter of religious bigotry on the part of the Protestants. You do not find the Protestants in Scotland, who are quite as keen as the Protestants in Ulster, quarrelling with their Catholic neighbours' [sic].

28. For the Irish involvement in early Leeds socialism, see T. Woodhouse,

'The Working Class' in D. Fraser (ed.), *A History of Modern Leeds* (1980), pp. 366 sqq.

29. Quoted E. D. Steele, 'Imperialism and Leeds Politics' in Fraser, ibid., p. 349.
30. E. D. Steele, 'The Irish Presence in the North of England' in *Northern History*, XXI (1976), p. 241.
31. *Middlesborough Daily Gazette*, 31/3/80, quoted J. F. Supple, 'The political attitudes and Activities of Yorkshire Catholics, 1850–1900' In *Northern History*, XXII (1986), p. 241. Dr Supple's excellent piece was a useful source for the following paragraphs.
32. Ibid.
33. *North Eastern Daily Gazette*, 13/7/95, quoted Supple, p. 247.
34. See Supple, op. cit., p. 233.
35. J. Crake (Accountant)–H. Gladstone, 8/7/86, Add. Ms. 46052, f. 168.
36. Pelling, op. cit., p. 295323
37. Supple, p. 243.
38. See Add. Ms. 46051 f. 155. See also J. W. Walker, *Wakefield: Its History and People* (Wakefield, 1939), p. 362.
39. According to E. R. Wickham, *Church and People in an Industrial City* (London, 1957).
40. Ibid., pp. 109, 148.
41. Supple, op. cit., p. 239.
42. Quoted ibid., p. 240.
43. See D. Cannadine, *Lords and Landlords: the Aristocracy and the Towns, 1774–1967* (Leicester, 1980), pp. 44, 55.
44. Supple, op. cit., p. 243.
45. J. Denvir, *The Irish in Britain* (London, 1892), p. 389.
46. Ibid., p. 390.
47. An excellent account of both processes is L. H. Lees, *Exiles of Erin: Irish Migrants in Victorian London* (Manchester, 1979).
48. See Barry Kosmin, 'Political Identity in Battersea' in S. Wallman et al., *Living in South London* (London, 1982).
49. W. Kent, *John Burns: Labour's Lost Leader* (London, 1953).
50. *Catholic Directory*, p. 109.
51. It is clear from E. Benn, *Happier Days* (London, 1949), p. 34, that the Liberals were almost as bad as the Tories. In 1902 one of their canvassers ended up in the Old Bailey charged with perjury in connexion with the witnessing of lodger franchises, many of them, no doubt (p. 35) Irish. Although he was acquitted, 'the charge against him was justified many times over'.
52. Parl. Papers, *lxvii* (1896), p. 462.
53. Ibid., p. 466.
54. Denvir, op. cit., p. 394.
55. H. J. Dyos, *Victorian Suburb: A Study of the Growth of Camberwell* (Leicester, 1961).
56. Pelling, op. cit., pp. 52, 55.
57. Denvir, op. cit., p. 383.
58. See *Burnley 1861–1961* (Burnley, 1961), p. 57.
59. Lord Norreys-Duke of Norfolk, 17/12/79, c 718 (Arundel archives).

60. Lord E. Talbot-Norfolk, 17/3/80, c 765 (Arundel archives).
61. Ibid.
62. H. M. Hyndman, *Further Reminiscences* (London, 1912), p. 61.
63. Ibid., 66.
64. Ibid., p. 68. Hyndman, incidentally, could be a sharp if self-revealing social observer. 'There are two things to be noted in English upper-class life during the past twenty years: the growth of the influence of Catholics in "society," and the increase of the domination of German Jews in finance' (p. 199). There was also extensive bribery in 1880. See Ld. Norreys-Norfolk, 24/4/80 c 765 (Arundel archives).
65. *Catholic Directory*, p. 172. Also *Liverpool Daily Post*, 1/12/85, cited Pelling, op. cit., p. 267.
66. J. Lunn, *Leigh: The Historical Past of a Lancashire Borough* (Manchester, 1958), p. 266.
67. *Catholic Directory*, p. 219.
68. Add. Ms. 46483 f. 12 (Notebook, 18/5/99).
69. Add. Ms. 46483 f. 16 (Herbert Gladstone notebook, 7/6/99): 'Costelloe–Places all respt. for defeat on Local Veto (on other hand John Burns attributes it all to C's Roman Catholicism!).'
70. There were twenty-one Roman Catholics in Oldham in 1767. (*Annals of Oldham*, II, p. 163.)
71. H. Bateson, *The Centenary History of Oldham* (Oldham, 1949), p. 153.
72. Cf. Alfred Emmott (later 1st Baron Emmott)–H. Gladstone, 13/4/86, Add. Ms. 46052 f. 192 urging a lecture series on Irish history in Oldham. 'At the same time I fear it will not be possible to get any considerable number of the D[issentient] L[iberals] to attend these lectures ... I am speaking of the DLs as if we knew them all. We do not. To a large extent they are an unknown quantity.'
73. See J. D. Baxendale, op. cit., pp. 350, 359.
74. W. Robertson, *Rochdale Past and Present* (Rochdale, 1875), p. 97.
75. Add. Ms. 46483 f. 13 (Herbert Gladstone notebook, 31/5/99).
76. Add. Ms. 46483 f. 11 (notebook, 15/5/99). The two Catholics Gladstone considered for the seat were Joseph (later Sir Joseph) Walton, QC, Recorder of Wigan, and Sir Charles Russell QC – an indication that the seat would not sustain a radical candidacy.
77. Cf. T. Barker and J. R. Harris, *A Merseyside Town in the Industrial Revolution: St Helen's 1750–1900* (London, 1954), p. 174.
78. *St Helen's News*, 10/7/86, quoted ibid., p. 476.
79. See H. A. Taylor, 'Politics in Famine Stricken Preston: An Examination of Liberal Party Management 1861–5' in *Transactions of the Historic Society of Lancashire and Cheshire*, 107 (1955).
80. H. Clemesha, *The History of Preston-in-Amounderness* (Manchester, 1912), p. 285.
81. Ibid., p. 269.
82. Charles Weld-Blundell, who does seem to have won over Catholic votes to the Liberals. Ibid., p. 274.
83. *Manchester of Today* (Manchester, 1888), p. 38.
84. Rev. Henry Mead, quoted R. L. Greenall, 'Popular Conservatism in Salford' in *Northern History*, IX (1974), p. 132.

85. Ibid., p. 135 sqq.
86. Pelling, op. cit., p. 244.
87. C. H. D. Howard, 'The Parnell Manifesto of 21 November 1885 and the Schools Question' in *E.H.R.*, 62 (1947), p. 49.
88. *Catholic Directory*, p. 235.
89. Denvir, op. cit., p. 409.
90. R. L. Greenall, op. cit., p. 138.
91. P. J. Waller, *Democracy and Sectarianism: A Social and Political History of Liverpool 1850–1939* (Liverpool, 1981).
92. But cf. Denvir, op. cit., p. 432. The Irish of Bootle 'have not the political influence their numbers would give if they were a more settled population'.
93. Compare Pelling, op. cit., p. 249. ('The Irish were in a comparatively small minority') with Herbert Gladstone (Add. Ms. 46483 f. 59, 6/2/1900). '*Kirkdale*. Irish v. strong here, otherwise possible.'
94. For example, Waller, op. cit., p. 60.
95. Ibid., p. 234.
96. Ibid., p. 184.
97. Cf. Baxendale, op. cit., pp. 350, 359.
98. *Catholic Directory*, pp. 222, 226.
99. Pelling, op. cit., p. 259.
100. Baxendale, op. cit., loc. cit.
101. *Catholic Directory*, pp. 222, 227.
102. See P. F. Clarke, *Lancashire and the New Liberalism* (Cambridge, 1971), p. 254.
103. Pelling, op. cit., p. 267.
104. This included street festivals which oddly combined Merrie England (in the form of morris dancing) and Southern Italy (holy pictures, pious objects). See *Pictures of Wigan 1870–1920* (Wigan, 1978).
105. *Catholic Directory*, p. 173.
106. Denvir, op. cit., p. 433.
107. J. P. Aspden (ed.), *Warrington: One Hundred Years a Borough* (Warrington, 1947), p. 114.
108. Ibid.
109. C. Gill, *History of Birmingham* (London, 1952), p. 143.
110. Ibid., p. 375.
111. Denvir, op. cit., p. 414.
112. Denvir, op. cit., p. 415.
113. Ibid., pp. 417, 425, 429.
114. Ibid., p. 425.
115. Add. Ms. 46483 f. 57 (Notebook, 14/7/99).
116. Denvir, op. cit., p. 428.
117. T. W. Whitley, *Parliamentary Representation of Coventry* (Coventry, 1892), p. 385.
118. Ibid., p. 392.
119. J. N. Bagnall, *The History of Wednesbury* (London, 1854), p. 72.
120. Quoted Denvir, op. cit., p. 418.
121. Ibid.

122. *Records of the Borough of Nottingham*, IX (1839–1900) (Notts, 1956), pp. 172, 233–4, 275, 323–6, 359.
123. Ibid., p. 54.
124. Ibid., p. 90. [Report on Sanitation and Mortality in Nottingham, 15/3/52.]
125. Pelling, op. cit., p. 208.
126. Ibid., p. 209.
127. Ibid., p. 192.
128. *Catholic Directory*, pp. 127, 128. Six priests ministered in the constituency, though not all were Irish.
129. Denvir, op. cit., p. 426.
130. See Pelling, op. cit., p. 272.
131. F. Bealey, J. Blondel, W. P. McCann, *Constituency Politics: A Study of Newcastle-Under-Lyme* (London, 1965), p. 67.
132. Ibid., p. 61.
133. Ibid., p. 62.
134. *Catholic Directory*, pp. 234–5.
135. J. E. Williams, *The Derbyshire Miners: A Study in Industrial and Social History* (London, 1962), pp. 468–9, 489.
136. Ibid., p. 491.
137. J. Keating, 'History of the Tyneside Irish Brigade' in F. Lavery (compiler), *Irish Heroes in the War* (London, 1917), p. 41.
138. Ibid., p. 45.
139. Ibid., p. 46.
140. Ibid., pp. 51, 55–6.
141. Witness ibid., p. 108. 'A revered Fenian priest on Tyneside had his parish stripped naked of its young men. "It was agony to me at first," said his reverence, "to think of my fine lads going to fight for England, but now I feel proud, somehow, that they are going. I gave them my blessing....!" ' The argument was the one sponsored by John Redmond: loyalty in the war would be rewarded by Home Rule for Ireland.
142. C. H. Howard, op. cit., p. 49.
143. Pelling, op. cit., p. 325.
144. *Catholic Directory*, p. 147.
145. C. H. D. Howard, op. cit., p. 48.
146. *Catholic Directory*, pp. 145, 146.
147. Howard, op. cit., p. 49, note 10.
148. T. P. O'Connor, *The Parnell Movement* (London, 1886), p. 512.
149. See A. W. Purdue, 'Jarrow Politics, 1885–1914: the Challenge to Liberal Hegemony' in *Northern History*, XVIII (1982), p. 191.
150. Ibid., p. 185.
151. Ibid., p. 194.
152. Denvir, op. cit., p. 443, *Catholic Directory*, p. 144.
153. T. P. O'Connor, *The Parnell Movement* (1886), P. 512.
154. For instance, see Denvir, op. cit., pp. 442–3.
155. Pelling, op. cit., p. 336.
156. J. Keating, 'History of the Tyneside Irish Brigade' in Lavery, op. cit., p. 70.
157. Ibid., p. 71.

158. Pelling, op. cit., p. 327.
159. *South Shields 1850–1950* (South Shields, 1951), Section 4, p. 3.
160. Ibid.
161. Denvir, op. cit., p. 445.
162. C. Caine, *Cleator and Cleator Moor* (Kendal, 1916), p. 297.
163. Pelling, op. cit., p. 340.
164. J. W. Robertson Scott, *The Day before Yesterday* (1951), p. 48.
165. G. W. E. Russell, *Sir Wilfrid Lawson: A Memoir* (1909), p. 187.
166. Denvir, op. cit., p. 445.
167. Pelling, op. cit., p. 330.
168. Denvir, op. cit., p. 443.
169. Ibid., p. 384.
170. W. Rees, *Cardiff* (Cardiff, 1969), p. 313.
171. See J. Hickey, *Urban Catholics* (London, 1967), pp. 62 sqq.
172. See D. Cannadine, op. cit., pp. 49, 50, 56.
173. For the schools, see *Catholic Directory*, p. 187.
174. See L. J. Williams, 'The New Unionism in South Wales' in *Welsh History Review*, I (1963), p. 416.
175. Ibid., p. 428. See also, K. O. Morgan, 'Gladstone and Wales' in Ibid., I, pp. 73 sqq.
176. Denvir, op. cit., p. 299.
177. Pelling, op. cit., p. 354.
178. *Catholic Directory*, p. 191.
179. *Tablet*, 22/4/82, p. 619. Also *Times*, 24/4/82, p. 12, 'The miners ... openly declare that they shall not be satisfied till they have driven every Irishman out of the neighbourhood.'
180. *Catholic Directory*, pp. 133–4.
181. See, for instance, *Tablet*, 11/3/82, p. 380.
182. Denvir, op. cit., p. 384.
183. *Catholic Directory*, p. 211.
184. Pelling, op. cit., pp. 128, 129.
185. Ibid., p. 130.
186. Lady G. Cecil, *Life of Robert Marquis of Salisbury*, vol. III, p. 144 (1931).

Bibliography

Unless otherwise stated the place of publication is London.

OFFICIAL PUBLICATIONS AND WORKS OF REFERENCE

Annual Register
Annual Reports of the National Union of Conservative and Constitutional Associations
Birt, H. N., *Obit Book of the English Benedictines 1600–1912*, (1913)
Boase, F. (ed.), *Modern English Biography* (2nd imp. 1965)
Burke's Landed Gentry, I–III (18th edition, 1965–72)
Burnand, F. C. (ed.), *The Catholic Who's Who and Year Book* (1908)
Catholic Directory (1870–1880)
Craig, F. W. S. (ed.), *British Parliamentary Election Results 1832–1885* (1977); *British Parliamentary Election Results 1885–1918* (1974)
Cross, F. L. and Livingstone, E. A. (eds), *The Oxford Dictionary of the Christian Church* (Oxford, 1974)
Dictionary of National Biography
Dod's Parliamentary Companion
Foster, J., *Men at the Bar* (1885)
Gillow, J., *Bibliographical Dictionary of the English Catholics*, I–V (1885–1902)
Jubilee Report of the Monthly Tract Society (1887)
Parliamentary Debates (Hansard)
Pickrill, D. A., *Ministers of the Crown* (1981)
Vincent, J. and Stenton, M. (eds), *McCalmont's Parliamentary Poll Book*
Who Was Who

NEWSPAPERS AND PERIODICALS

Ampleforth Journal
Catholic Children's Magazine
The Catholic Critic
The Catholic Family Almanac
The Catholic Freethinker's Flysheet (1880)
Catholic Household (1893)
Catholic Literary Circular (1893)
The Chemist and Druggist
Contemporary Review

Daily News
Daily Telegraph
Dublin Review
Downside Review
Fortnightly Review
The Medical and Professional Review
Merry England
The Month
The Nineteenth Century
Porcupine
Primrose League Gazette
Punch
The Rambler [*Home and Foreign Review* after 1862]
The Ransomer
Saturday Review
The Tablet
The Times
Weekly Register and Catholic Standard

MANUSCRIPT AND ORIGINAL SOURCES

The following collections have been consulted in the writing of this book.

Bodleian Library, Oxford

H. H. Asquith
A. Birrell
J. E. C. Bodley
Viscount Bryce
4th Earl of Clarendon
W. M. Crook
B. Disraeli, Earl of Beaconsfield
J. Dodson, Baron Monk Bretton
G. J. Goschen
Sir W. V. Harcourt
L. Harcourt, 1st Viscount Harcourt
A. Macdonnell, 1st Baron Macdonnell
Cardinal Manning
    (not the papers hoarded for some three decades by the Revd. Professor A. Chapeau, but a small personal collection recently acquired by the Bodleian)
A. Milner, 1st Viscount Milner
Sir M. Nathan
Minute Books of the Grand Council of the Primrose League (1883–95)
J. S. Sandars (Henry Matthews Papers)
2nd Earl of Selborne

British Library

A. J. Balfour
Lady Anne Blunt (Wentworth Bequest)
W. S. Blunt (Wentworth Bequest)
J. Bright
4th Earl of Carnarvon
R. Cross
Sir C. Dilke
B. Disraeli, Earl of Beaconsfield (Supplementary Papers Add. Ms. 58210)
W. E. Gladstone
Lord Herbert of Lea and Lady Herbert
1st Marquis of Ripon
Sir S. H. Northcote, 1st Earl of Iddesleigh

Rhodes House Library, Oxford

Sir J. Pope Hennessy
Frederick, Lord Lugard

Churchill College, Cambridge

Lord R. Churchill
Mrs. V. M. Crawford
Sir C. Dilke (Supplementary Papers)

Hatfield House

3rd Marquis of Salisbury

National Library of Ireland

J. Redmond

BOOKS, ARTICLES, THESES

Acheson, S. J. 'Catholic Journalism in Victorian Catholic Society 1830–70 With Special Reference to the Tablet', unpublished Oxford M.Litt. thesis, 1981

Adams, P. 'Catholic Converts in England 1830–1870', unpublished Oxford B.Litt. thesis, 1977

Alderman, G., *Pressure Groups and Government in Great Britain* (1984)

Alderman, G., *The Jewish Community in British Politics* (Oxford, 1983)

Allies, T. W., 'Why I shall vote for the Unionists', *The Nineteenth Century,* 32 (July 1892)

Althaus, F. (ed.), *The Roman Journals of Ferdinand Gregorovius 1852–74* (1907)

Altholz, J. *The Liberal Catholic Movement in England 1848–1864* (1962)

Altholz, J. and McElrath, D. (eds), *The Correspondence of Lord Acton and Richard Simpson*, 3 vols (London, 1975)

Amhert, Rev. W. J., 'The Catholic Union of Great Britain', *The Month*, Sept.–Oct. 1872

Aspden, J. P. (ed.), *Warrington: One Hundred Years a Borough* (Warrington, 1947)

Auchmuty, J. 'Acton's Election as an Irish Member of Parliament', *English Historical Review*, LXI (1946)

Auchmuty, J. 'Acton as a Member of the House of Commons', *Bulletin of the Faculty of Arts, Farouk I University*, V (1949)

Anderton, Rev. W. H., *Sunday Afternoons with the Saints* (undated)

Anderton, Rev. W. H., *Secret Societies: A Quiet Talk About Them* (1882)

Anderton, Rev. W. H., *The Jesuits: A Sermon* (1880)

Armytage, W. H. G., 'The 1870 Education Act', *British Journal of Education Studies*, XVIII (June 1970)

Arnstein, W. L., *The Bradlaugh Case* (Oxford, 1965)

Austin, A., *Rome or Death!* (Edinburgh, 1873)

Austin, A., *Autobiography* (1911)

Bagenal, P. H., *The Priest in Politics* (1893)

Bagenal, P. H., *The Tory Policy of the Marquis of Salisbury* (1885)

Bagnall, J. N., *The History of Wednesbury* (1854)

Bahlam, D. W. R., 'Politics and Church Patronage in the Victorian Age', *Victorian Studies*, XXII, 3 (1979)

Bailey, P., *Leisure and Class in Victorian England* (1978)

Balfour, Lady B., *Personal and Literary Letters of the Earl of Lytton* (1906)

Barker, M., *Gladstone and Radicalism: The Reconstruction of Liberal Policy in Britain 1885–1894* (1974)

Barker, T. and Harris, J. R. *A Merseyside Town in the Industrial Revolution: St. Helen's 1750–1900* (1954)

Barnes, A. S., *The Catholic Schools of England* (1926)

Barnsley Historical Almanack and Year Book 1863

Bateson, H., *The Centenary History of Oldham* (Oldham, 1949)

Baxendale, R. D., 'The Liberal Party 1886–1900, Especially in the North West', unpublished Oxford D.Phil. thesis, 1971

Bealey, F. et al., *Constituency Politics: A Study of Newcastle-Under-Lyme* (1965)

Bebbington, D. B., 'Gladstone and the Nonconformists: A Religious Affinity in Politics', *Studies in Church History*, 12 (1975)

Beck, G. A. (ed.), *The English Catholics 1850–1950* (1951)

Benn, E., *Happier Days* (1949)

Best, G. F. A., 'The Religious Difficulties of National Education in England 1800–1870', *Cambridge Historical Journal*, XII, 2 (1956)

Birt, H. N., *The History of Downside* (1902)

Blair, D. H., *The Marquess of Bute: A Memoir* (1921)

Blake, R., *Disraeli* (1966)

Blake, R., *The Conservative Party from Peel to Churchill* (1970)

Blakiston, H. N. (ed.), *The Roman Question* (1961)

Blunt, W. S., *My Diaries 1888–1914* (1918)

Blunt, W. S., *Ripon in India: A Private Diary* (1909)

Bodley, J. E. C., *Cardinal Manning* (1913)

Bodley, J. E. C., 'Roman Catholicism in America', *The Nineteenth Century*, 26 (Nov. 1889)

Bolton, C. A. , *Salford Diocese and its Catholic Past* (Manchester, 1950)

Bourne, Cardinal, 'Henry, Duke of Norfolk', *Dublin Review* (April 1917)

Bouet, E. A., 'The Battle: On Which Side?' (1897)

Bowyer, G., *The Cardinal Archbishop of Westminster and the New Hierarchy* (1850)

Bowyer, G., *A Private History of the Creation of the Roman Hierarchy in Britain* (1868)

Braye, Lord, *The Present State of the Church in England* (1884)

Brett, M. V. (ed.), *The Letters and Journals of Reginald Viscount Esher* (1934)

Briggs, A., *Victorian People* (1982)

Bruce, C., *The Broad Stone of Empire* (1910)

Bruce, H. A., *Letters of Henry Bruce, Lord Aberdare*, I (Oxford, 1902)

Buckle, G. E., *The Letters of Queen Victoria 3rd Series 1886–1901*, 3 vols. (1931)

Burnley 1861–1961 (Burnley, 1961)

Butler, P., *Gladstone: Church, State and Tractarianism* (Oxford, 1982)

Butler, R. A. B. (ed.), *The Conservatives: A History From Their Origins Until 1965* (1977)

Campion, E. (ed.), *Lord Acton and the First Vatican Council: A Journal* (Sydney, 1975)

Caine, C., *Cleator and Cleator Moor* (Kendal, 1916)

Cannadine, D., *Lords and Landlords: The Aristocracy and the Towns, 1774–1967* (Leicester, 1980)

Carr, R., *Spain 1808–1939* (Oxford, 1966)

'Diaries of Bishop Casartelli of Salford', *The Ushaw Magazine*, June 1974

Casartelli, Bishop L. C., *A Forgotten Chapter of the Second Spring* (1895)

The Catholic Church and the Ritualists (1882)

Catholic Progress in England (1896)

Catholic Progress in England (1897)

Catholic Progress Under Queen Victoria (1901)

Cecil, Lady G., *The Life of Robert, Marquis of Salisbury* (1921)

Chadwick, R. E., 'Church and People in Bradford and District 1880–1914: The Protestant Churches in an Urban Industrial Environment', unpublished Oxford D.Phil. thesis, 1986

Chadwick, W. O., *Acton and Gladstone* (1976)

Chadwick, W. O., *The Victorian Church*, 2 vols (1966–1970)

Chilston, E. A. 3rd Viscount Chilston, *Chief Whip: The Political Life and Times of Aretas Akers Douglas* (1961)

Church, M. G., (ed.), *The Life and Letters of Dean Church* (1895)

Churchill, W. S., *Lord Randolph Churchill* (1907)

Clarke, P. F., *Lancashire and the New Liberalism* (Cambridge, 1971)

Clarke, R. F., S.J., *Father John Morris* (1894)

Clarke, R. F., S.J., *A Short Sketch of Fr. Albany James Christie, S.J.* (1891)

Clayton, J.D., 'Mr. Gladstone's Leadership of the Parliamentary Liberal Party 1868–1874', unpublished Oxford D.Phil. thesis, 1961

Clemesha, H., *The History of Preston-in-Amounderness* (Manchester, 1912)

Collier, E. C. F. (ed.), *A Victorian Diarist: The Journals of Mary, Lady Monkswell* (1944)

Collette, C. H., *Illegal Ecclesiastical Territorial Titles* (1895)

Colson, P. (ed.), *Lord Goschen and His Friends* (n.d.)

Colson, P., *The Coming Crisis: Is Mr. Gladstone the Foe of Protestantism and the Friend of Popery?* (1892)

Conzemius, V., 'Acton, Döllinger and Gladstone: A Strange Variety of Anti-Infallibilists', in J. D. Bastable (ed.), *Newman and Gladstone: Centennial Essays* (Dublin, 1978)

Cooke, A. B., 'A Conservative Party Leader in Ulster: Sir Stafford Northcote's Diary of a Visit to the Province, October 1883', *Proceedings of the Royal Irish Academy*, Section C, LXXV (1975)

Cooke, A. B. and Vincent, J. R., *The Governing Passion: Cabinet Government and Party Politics in Britain 1865–86* (1974)

Cooke, A. B. and Vincent, J. R., (eds), *Lord Carlingford's Journal* (Oxford, 1971)

Cooper, C. P., *The Common Law and the Pope's Apostolic Letters of September 1850: Extracts of Letters Addressed to C. P. Cooper* (1851)

Crowell, N. B., *Alfred Austin: Victorian* (1955)

Cruise-O'Brien, D. C., *Parnell and His Party 1880–90* (Oxford, 1957)

Curtis, L. P., *Coercion and Conciliation in Ireland 1880–1892* (Princeton, 1963)

Cwiekowski, F. J., *The English Bishops and the First Vatican Council* (Louvain, 1971)

Dale, R. W., 'Cardinal Manning's Demand on the Rates', *The Nineteenth Century*, XIII (Jan. 1883)

Dale, R. W., 'The Cardinal and the Schools: A Rejoinder', *The Nineteenth Century*, XIII (March 1883)

Davies, J. 'Aristocratic Town-makers and the Coal Metropolis: the Marquesses of Bute and Cardiff, 1776 to 1947' in D. Cannadine (ed.) *Patricians, Power and Politics in Nineteenth Century Towns* (Leicester, 1982)

Day, J., *John C.F.S. Day: His Forebears and Himself* (1916)

Denholm, A. F., *Lord Ripon* (1982)

Denholm, A. F., 'The Conversion of Lord Ripon in 1874', *Recusant History*, 10 (1969)

Denvir, J., *The Irish in Britain* (1892)

Dessain, C. S. (ed.), *The Letters and Diaries of John H. Newman*, XX–XXXI (1970–77)

Devas, C. S., *Labour and Capital in England From the Catholic Point of View* (1876)

Disraeli, B., *Coningsby* (World's Classics Edition, 1982)

Disraeli, B., *Lothair* (Oxford English Novels Edition, 1975)

Doherty, P., *A Word to Roman Catholics in Favour of the Irish Church* (1868)

Doyle, P., 'Bishop Goss of Liverpool (1856–72) and the Importance of Being English' in K. D. Baker (ed.), *Studies in Church History*, XV (1978)

Drake, M., 'The Mid-Victorian Voter', *Journal of Interdisciplinary History*, I, 3 (1971)

Drus, E., *The Kimberley Journal* in *Camden Third Series*, XCI

Duff, Sir M. Grant, *Notes From a Diary 1886–1888*, I (1889)

Duffy, C. G., *My Life in Two Hemispheres* (Athlone: Irish University Press reprint 1969)

Dyos, H. J., *Victorian Suburb: A Study of the Growth of Camberwell* (Leicester, 1961)

Endacott, G. B., *A History of Hong Kong* (Oxford, 1973)

Ensor, R. C. K., *England 1870–1914* (Oxford, 1936)

Evans, J. and Whitehouse, J. H. (eds), *The Diaries of John Ruskin* (Oxford, 1959)

Faber, G., *Oxford Apostles* (1954)

Fairhurst, J. R., 'Some Aspects of the Relationship Between Education, Religion and Politics 1895–1906', unpublished Oxford D.Phil. thesis 1974

Feheney, J. M., 'The Poor Law Board August Order, 1859: A Case Study of Protestant-Catholic Conflict', *Recusant History*, 17, 1 (May 1984)

Feuchtwanger, E. J., *Disraeli, Democracy and the Conservative Party* (Oxford, 1968)

Fenech, D. L., 'Britain and the Vatican 1880–1914', unpublished Oxford D.Phil. thesis, 1977

Figgis, J. N. and Lawrence, R. V. (eds), *Selections from the Correspondence of the 1st Lord Acton* (1917)

Finch, E., *Wilfrid Scawen Blunt* (1938)

Fitch, J. G., 'Religion in Primary Schools', *The Nineteenth Century*, XXXVI (July 1894)

Fitzgerald, P. H., *Fifty Years of Catholic Life and Social Progress* (1901)

Fitzmaurice, Lord E., *The Life of Granville George Leveson Gower, 2nd Earl Granville* (1905)

Fitzroy, Sir A., *Memoirs* (1925)

Foster, R. F., *Lord Randolph Churchill: A Political Life* (1981)

Franciscan Missions Among the Colliers and Ironworkers of Monmouthshire (1876)

Fraser, E. (ed.), *A History of Modern Leeds* (1980)

Fullerton, Lady Georgiana, *Ladybird* (1852)

Fullerton, Lady Georgiana, *Grantley Manor* (1854)

Fullerton, Lady Georgiana, *The Gold Digger and Other Verses* (Edinburgh, 1872)

Gardiner, A. G., *The Life of Sir William Harcourt* (1923)

Garvin, J. L., *The Life of Joseph Chamberlain* (1932)

Gasquet, Cardinal F. A., *Lord Acton and His Circle* (1906)

Gasquet, J. R., *Mr. Purcell's Life of Cardinal Manning* (1896)

Gill, C. *History of Birmingham* (1952)

Gilley, S., Review of W. L. Arnstein, *Protestant versus Catholic in Mid Victorian England: Mr. Newdegate and His Campaigns*, History, 68, pp. 344–6 (June 1983)

Gilley, S., 'The Garibaldi Riots of 1862', *The Historical Journal*, XVI (1973)

Gilley, S., 'Protestant London, No Popery and the Irish Poor 1830–60', *Recusant History*, X, XI (1970, 1971)

Gladstone, Ireland, Rome: Or the Pro-Romish Acts of Mr. Gladstone (1886)

Gladstone, W. E., *The Vatican Decrees in Their Bearing on Civil Allegiance: A Political Expostulation* (1874)

Gladstone, W. E., *Vaticanism* (1875)

Glover, W. (ed.), *The History of Ashton under Lyne* (Ashton under Lyne, 1984)

Gopal, S., *The Viceroyalty of Lord Ripon 1880–1884* (Oxford, 1953)

Gopal, S., *British Policy in India 1858–1905* (Cambridge, 1965)

Gordon, P. (ed.), 'The Red Earl: The Papers of the Fifth Earl Spencer', I, published by the Northamptonshire Record Society (1981)

Gregory, Rev. R., 'Religion and the Rates', *The Nineteenth Century*, XIII (February 1883)

Gruber, J. W., *A Conscience in Conflict: The Life of St. George Jackson Mivart* (New York, 1960)

Gwynn, S.L. and Tuckwell, G.M., *The Life of Sir Charles Dilke* (1918)

Hamer, D. A., *Liberal Politics in the Age of Gladstone and Rosebery* (Oxford, 1972)

Hamilton, Lord G., *Parliamentary Reminiscences and Reflections 1868–1885* (1916)

Hammond, J. L., *Gladstone and the Irish Nation* (1938)

Hanham, H. J., *Elections and Party Management* (1959)

Hardie, F., *The Political Influence of Queen Victoria 1861–1901* (1938)

Hawkins, R., 'An Army on Police Work, 1881–2: Ross of Bladenburg's Memorandum', *The Irish Sword*, XI 43 (1973)

Hedley, J. C., O.S.B., *The Public Spirit of the Catholic Laity* (1899)

Hennock, E. P., *Fit and Proper Persons* (1973)

Hey, D. G. (ed.), *Peasants and Clothiers* (Holmfirth, 1976)

Hibgame, F. H., *A Great Gothic Fane: A Retrospect of Catholicity in Norwich* (1913)

Hickey, J., *Urban Catholics: Urban Catholicism in England and Wales from 1829 to the Present Day* (1967)

Himmelfarb, G., *Lord Acton: A Study of Conscience in Politics* (1952)

Hobhouse, C., *Inside Asquith's Cabinet* (1977)

Holmes, J. D., 'English Catholicism from Wiseman to Bourne', *The Clergy Review*, LXI (1976)

Holmes, J. D., 'Factors in the Development of Newman's Political Attitudes' in J. D. Bastable (ed.), *Newman and Gladstone: Centennial Essays* (Dublin, 1978)

Holmes, J. D., *More Roman Than Rome: English Catholicism in the Nineteenth Century* (1978)

Hoppen, K. T., *Elections, Politics and Society in Ireland 1832–1885* (Oxford, 1984)

Hoppen, K. T., 'Tories, Catholics and the General Election of 1859', *The Historical Journal*, XIII, 1 (1970)

Hough, R., *First Sea Lord: The Life of Lord Fisher of Kilverstone* (1969)

Howard, C. H. D., 'The Parnell Manifesto of 21 November 1885 and the Schools Question' *English Historical Review*, LXII (January 1947)

Hurst, M. J., 'The Catholic Church in Ireland in the Age of Rebellion: Review Article', *The Historical Journal*, IX (1966)

Hurst, M. J., 'Joseph Chamberlain and West Midland Politics', *Dugdale Society Papers*, 15 (1962)

Hurst, M. J., *Joseph Chamberlain and the Liberal Reunion* (1967)

Hutton, A. W., *Cardinal Manning* (1892)

Hyndman, H. M., *Further Reminiscences* (1912)

Jackson, J. A., *The Irish in Britain* (1963)

James, R. R., *Lord Randolph Churchill* (1969)

Jarrett, H. S., 'Lord Ripon's Indian Administration', *The Month* (January 1885)

Jay, R., *Joseph Chamberlain: A Political Study* (Oxford, 1981)

Jenkins, R., *Sir Charles Dilke* (1958)

Johnson, N. E. (ed.), *The Diary of Gathorne-Hardy, Later Lord Cranbrook* (Oxford, 1981)

Johnstone, J. A. J., *A Catholic and Constitutional Platform: A Tract for 1885* (1885)

Jones, A., *The Politics of Reform 1884* (Cambridge, 1972)

Jones, W. D., *Lord Derby and Victorian Conservatism* (Oxford, 1956)

Kebbel, T. E., *Lord Beaconsfield and Other Tory Memories* (London, 1907)

Kennedy, A. L., *Salisbury 1830–1903: Portrait of a Statesman* (1953)

Kent, W. *John Burns: Labour's Lost Leader* (1953)

Knaplund, P. (ed.), 'The Correspondence of Gladstone and General Gordon', *Transactions of the American Philosophical Society*, 51 (1961)

Kosmin, Barry, 'Political Identity in Battersea' in S. Wallman et al. (eds), *Living in South London* (1982)

Koss, S., *Nonconformity in Modern British Politics* (1975)

Lang, A., *The Life, Letters and Diaries of Sir Stafford Northcote* (Edinburgh, 1890)

Lees, L. H., *Exiles of Erin* (Manchester, 1979)

Lescher, H., 'Have Catholic Englishmen a Mission?', *Downside Review* (1885)

Leslie, S. (ed.), *The Correspondence of Herbert, Cardinal Vaughan and Lady Herbert of Lea* (1942)

Lilly, W. S. and Wallis, J. P., *A Manual of the Law Specifically Affecting Catholics* (1893)

de Lisle, E., *Pastoral Politics: a Reply to Dr. Bagshawe, Catholic Bishop of Nottingham* (1885)

Lindsay, C., *Evidence for the Papacy* (1869)

Lloyd, T., 'The Passionists in England', *The Clergy Review*, LXI (1976)

Longford, E., *A Pilgrimage of Passion: The Life of Wilfrid Scawen Blunt* (1979)

Low, A., 'British Public Opinion and the Uganda Question October–December 1892', *Uganda Journal*, XVIII (1954)

Lucas, M., *Two Englishwomen in Rome* (1938)

Lucas, R., *Colonel Saunderson, M.P.* (1908)

Lucy, H. W., *A Diary of Two Parliaments 1885–86* (1886)

Lucy, H. W., *A Diary of the Salisbury Parliament 1886–92* (1892)

Lunn, J. *Leigh: The Historical Past of a Lancashire Borough* (Manchester, 1958)

Lyons, F. S. L., *The Irish Parliamentary Party* (1950)

Lyons, F. S. L., *The Fall of Parnell* (1962)

Lyons, F. S. L., *Charles Stewart Parnell* (1977)

McCarthy, J., *Reminiscences* (1899)

McClelland, V. A., *Cardinal Manning: His Public Life and Influence* (Oxford, 1962)

McClelland, V. A., *English Roman Catholics and Higher Education 1830–1903* (Oxford, 1973)

McCormack, A., *Cardinal Vaughan* (1966)

McDonald, W., *Reminiscences of a Maynooth Professor*, (ed. D. Gwynn) (1925)

McElrath, D., *The Syllabus of Pius IX: Some Reactions in England* (Louvain, 1964)

McElrath, D., *Richard Simpson: A Study in 19th Century Liberal Catholicism* (Louvain, 1972)

McEntee, G. P., *The Social Catholic Movement in Great Britain* (New York, 1927)

Mackenzie, N. and J. (eds), *The Diary of Beatrice Webb*, I (1982)

McLeod, H., *Religion and Class in the Late Victorian City* (1974)

Machin, G. I. T., *Politics and the Churches in Great Britain 1832–1868* (Oxford, 1975)

Machin, G. I. T., *Politics and the Churches in Great Britain 1868–1921* (Oxford, 1987)

Manchester of Today (Manchester, 1888)

Manning, H. E., Cardinal, 'Is the Education Act of 1870 a Just Law?', *The Nineteenth Century*, XII (December 1882)

Manning, H. E., Cardinal, 'Religion and the Rates', *The Nineteenth Century*, XIII (February 1883)

Marder, A. J., *Fear God and Dread Nought: The Correspondence of Admiral of the Fleet Lord Fisher of Kilverstone* (1952–9)

Marindin, G. E. (ed.), *Letters of Frederick Rogers, Lord Blachford* (1896)

Marmion, J. P., 'The Beginnings of the Catholic Poor Schools in England' in *Recusant History*, 17, 1 (May 1984)

Marsh, P. T., *The Victorian Church in Decline* (1969)

Mathew, D., *Lord Acton and His Times* (1968)

Matthew, H. C. G., 'Gladstone, Vaticanism and the Question of the East' in K. D. Baker (ed.), *Studies in Church History*, XV (1978)

Matthew, H. C. G., *The Liberal Imperialists: The Ideas and Politics of a Post-Gladstonian Elite* (1973)

Matthew, H. C. G. (ed.), *The Gladstone Diaries*, VI, VII and VIII (1978–1982)

Maurois, A., *Disraeli* (Bristol, 1944)

Maxwell, H., *The Life and Letters of George Frederick William, Fourth Earl of Clarendon* (1913)

Memorial Mass for Lady Georgiana Fullerton (1885)

Middleton, N., 'The Education Act of 1870 as the Start of the Modern Concept of the Child' in *British Journal of Educational Studies*, XVIII (June 1970)

Milburn, D., *A History of Ushaw College* (Durham, 1964)

Mivart, F. J. St. George, 'Catholic Politics' in *Dublin Review* (October 1883)

Monypenny, W. F. and Buckle, G. E., *Life of Benjamin Disraeli, Earl of Beaconsfield*, I–VI (1910–1920)

Morey, A., 'Benet House, Cambridge: Some Early Correspondence, 1895–1900', *The Downside Review* (July 1985)

Morley, J., *Life of Gladstone* (1903)

Mr. Gladstone Exposed! By a Nonconformist (1891)

Murphy, J., *The Religious Problem in English Education: The Crucial Experiment* (Liverpool, 1959)

Murphy, J., *Church, State and Schools in Britain 1800–1970* (1971)

Murphy, T., *The Position of the Catholic Church in England and Wales During the Last Two Centuries* (1892)

Nevill, R. (ed.), *The Reminiscences of Lady Dorothy Nevill* (1906)

Newman, J. H., *A Letter Addressed to His Grace the Duke of Norfolk* (1875)

Nicholls, D., 'Gladstone and the Anglican Critics of Newman' in J. D. Bastable (ed.), *Gladstone and Newman: Centennial Essays* (Dublin, 1978)

Nicholls, D., 'Gladstone, Newman and the Politics of Pluralism' in J. D. Bastable (ed.), *Newman and Gladstone: Centennial Essays* (Dublin, 1978)

Norfolk, Gwendolin, Duchess of, *Sola Virtus Invicta: A Collection of Obituaries of the 15th Duke of Norfolk* (Privately published, 1917)

Norman, E. R., *The Catholic Church and Ireland in the Age of Rebellion 1859–1873* (1965)

Norman, E. R., *Anti Catholicism in Victorian England* (1968)

Norman, E. R., *The English Catholic Church in the Nineteenth Century* (1984)

O'Brien, R. B., *The Life of Charles Stewart Parnell* (1911)

O'Connor, T. P., *The Parnell Movement* (1886)

O'Day, A., *The English Face of Irish Nationalism* (Toronto, 1977)

O'Meara, K., *Thomas Grant, First Bishop of Southwark* (1886)

Pattison, M., *Memoirs* (1885)

Paul, H. (ed.), *Letters of Lord Acton to Mary Gladstone* (New York, 1904)

Paul, H. *A History of Modern England*, v (1906)

Peel, F., *Spen Valley Past and Present* (n.d.)

Pellew, J., *The Home Office 1848–1914* (1982)

Pelling, H., *Social Geography of British Elections 1885–1910* (1967)

Perry, E. C., *Why Should Englishmen Support Home Rule for Ireland* (Exeter, 1886)

Pictures of Wigan 1870–1920 (Wigan, 1978)

Pollen, J. H., *The Life and Letters of Father John Morris, S.J.* (1896)

Pope Hennessy, J., *The Liberal Party and the Catholics* (1886)

Pope Hennessy, J., 'Lord Beaconsfield's Irish Policy', *The Nineteenth Century*, 92 (October 1884)

Pope Hennessy, J., 'The African Bubble', *The Nineteenth Century*, 161 (July 1890)

Pope Hennessy, J., 'Is Central Africa Worth Having?', *The Nineteenth Century*, 163 (September 1890)

Pope Hennessy, J., 'The Priesthood in Irish Politics', *The Dublin Review*, XIX (1872)

Pope Hennessy, J., *Verandah: Some Episodes in the Crown Colonies 1867–1889* (1964)

Prest, J., *Lord John Russell* (1972)

Pudney, T., *Religious Persecution: The Romish Inquisition in England in the Nineteenth Century* (London, 1892)

Purcell, E. S., *The Life of Cardinal Manning* (1896)

Purcell, E. S., *Life of Ambrose Phillipps de Lisle* (1900)

Purdue, A. W., 'Jarrow Politics, 1885–1914: The Challenge to Liberal Hegemony', *Northern History*, XVIII (1982)

Queen Victoria: Sixty Years of Catholic Progress (1897)

Ramm, A. (ed.), *The Correspondence of Mr. Gladstone and Lord Granville*, I, II (Oxford, 1962)

Randolph, E., *One of Us* (1882)

Records of the Borough of Nottingham, IX (1839–1900)

'*Reverence and Loyalty: Words Spoken in the College Church of Stonyhurst on the Occasion of the Jubilee of Her Majesty Queen Victoria 21st June 1887*'

Reynolds, E. E., *The Roman Catholic Church in England and Wales* (Wheathampstead, 1973)

Richards, N. J., 'Religious Controversy and the School Boards 1870–1902', *British Journal of Educational Studies*, XVIII, 2 (June 1970)

Ripon, Marquess of, 'Some Thoughts on International Morality', *The Month* (January 1879)

Roberts, A. W., 'Leeds Liberalism and Late-Victorian Politics', *Northern History*, V (1970)

Robertson, W., *Rochdale Past and Present* (Rochdale, 1875)

Robinson, J. M., *The Dukes of Norfolk: A Quincentennial History* (1983)

Robertson Scott, J. W., *The Day Before Yesterday* (1951)

Roland, D., 'The Struggle for the Elementary Education Act and Its Implementation 1870–73, unpublished Oxford B.Litt. thesis 1957

"*Rome's Recruits: A List of Protestants Who Have Become Roman Catholics Since the Tractarian Movement*" (1881)

Rossi, J. P., 'Lord Ripon's Resumption of Political Activity', *Recusant History*, XI, 1 (1971)

Rossi, J. P., 'Catholic Opinion on the Eastern Question 1876–1878', *Church History*, 51 (1982)

Royle, E., *Religion and Unbelief: Radical Politics 1790–1900* (1971)

Russell, G. W. E., 'Mr. Disraeli's *Lothair*', *The Month* (June 1870)

Russell, G. W. E., *Sir Wilfrid Lawson: A Memoir* (1909)

Russell, G. W. E., 'Government by Party', *The Month* (March 1874)

Russell, G. W. E., *Mr. Gladstone's Religious Development* (1899)

Russell, G. W. E., *Collections and Recollections* (1903)

St John, E., *Manning's Work for Children: A Second Chapter in Catholic Emancipation* (1929)

Selby, D. E., 'Henry Edward Manning and the Education Bill of 1870', *British Journal of Educational Studies*, XVIII, 2 (June 1970)

Sellers, I., *Nineteenth Century Nonconformity* (1977)

Seton-Watson, R. W., *Disraeli, Gladstone and the Eastern Question* (1935)

Shannon, R. T., *Gladstone and the Bulgarian Agitation 1876* (2nd ed., Brighton, 1975)

Sneyd-Kinnersley, E. M., *HMI: Passages in the Life of an Inspector of Schools* (1908)

Some First Lines of Catholic Politics (1880)

South Shields 1850–1950 (South Shields, 1951)

Spinner, T. J., *George Joachim Goschen* (Cambridge, 1973)

Stansky, P., *Ambitions and Strategies: The Struggle for the Leadership of the Liberal Party in the 1890s* (Oxford, 1964)

Steele, E. D., 'The Irish Presence in the North of England', *Northern History*, XXI (1976)

Steer, F., *Arundel Castle Archives* (Chichester, 1968)

Strachey, L. and Fulford, R. (eds), *The Greville Memoirs 1814–1860* (1938)

Supple, J. F., 'The Political Attitudes and Activities of Yorkshire Catholics, 1850–1900', *Northern History*, XXII (1986)

Sutherland, G., 'Administrators in Education After 1870: Patronage, Professionalism and Expertise', Sutherland, G. (ed.), *Studies in the Growth of Nineteenth Century Government* (1972)

Sutherland, G., *Policy Making in Elementary Education 1870–1895* (Oxford, 1973)

Swift, R. and Gilley, S. (eds), *The Irish in the Victorian City*, I (1989)

Taffs, W., *Ambassador to Bismarck: Lord Odo Russell, 1st Baron Ampthill* (1938)

Taunton, E. F., *Industrial Insurance* (1882)

Taylor, H. A. 'Politics in Famine Stricken Preston: An Examination of Liberal Party Management 1861–5', *Transactions of the Historic Society of Lancashire and Cheshire*, 107 (1955)

Thompson, A. F., 'Gladstone's Whips and the General Election of 1868', *English Historical Review*, LXIII (1948)

Thornley, D., *Isaac Butt and Home Rule* (1964)

Thorold, A., *Life of Henry Labouchere* (1913)

de Vere, A., *Recollections* (1902)

Vidler, A. R., *A Century of Social Catholicism 1820–1920* (1964)

Vincent, J. R., *The Formation of the Liberal Party 1857–1868* (1966)

Vincent, J. R. (ed.), *Pollbooks: How Victorians Voted* (Cambridge, 1967)

Vincent, J. R. (ed.), *Disraeli, Derby and the Conservative Party: The Political Journals of Lord Stanley* (1978)

Walker, J. W., *Wakefield: Its History and People* (Wakefield, 1939)

Waller, P. J., *Democracy and Sectarianism: A Political and Social History of Liverpool 1868–1939* (Liverpool, 1981)

Waller, P. J., *Town, City and Nation: England 1850–1914* (Oxford, 1983)

Walling, R. A. J. (ed.), *The Diary of John Bright* (1930)

Ward, Mgr. B., *Cardinal Vaughan* (1903)

Ward, W., *Ten Personal Studies* (1908)

Ward, W., 'Some Aspects of the Influence of Cardinal Newman' in *The Nineteenth Century*, 28 (Oct. 1890)

Ward, W., 'The Rigidity of Rome', *The Nineteenth Century*, 38 (November 1895)

Ward, W., 'Disraeli', *Dublin Review* (January 1913)

Warmoll, F. J., *A Short History of St. George and the Crusade of St. George for the Conversion of England and Especially of Stowmarket and its District* (1896)

Watkin, E. I., *Roman Catholicism in England from the Reformation to 1950* (1957)

Watson, G., *The English Ideology* (1973)

Whitfield, H. F. *Plymouth and Devonport in Times of War and Peace* (Plymouth, 1900)

Whitley, T. W., *Parliamentary Representation of Coventry* (Coventry, 1892)

Whyte, J. H., *The Indpendent Irish Party 1850–9* (Oxford, 1958)

Whyte, J. H., 'The Influence of the Catholic Clergy on Elections in Nineteenth Century Ireland', *English Historical Review*, LXXV (1960)

Whyte, J. H., 'Landlord Influence at Elections in Ireland', *English Historical Review*, LXXX (1965)

Wickham, E. R., *Church and People in an Industrial City* (1957)

Condé-Williams, F., *From Journalist to Judge: An Autobiography* (Edinburgh, 1903)

Williams, J. E., *The Derbyshire Miners: A Study in Industrial and Social History* (1962)

Williams, L. J., 'The New Unionism in South Wales', *Welsh History Review*, I (1963)

Williams, W. W., *The Life of Sir Charles Warren* (1941)

Willis, W., *Recollections of Sir John Day* (1908)

Wolf, L., *The Life of the First Marquis of Ripon* (1921)

Yates, E., *Broken to Harness* (1864)

Young, K., *Arthur James Balfour* (1963)

Zebel, S. H., *Balfour: A Political Biography* (Cambridge, 1973)

Zetland, The Marquis of, *The Letters of Disraeli to Lady Bradford and Lady Chesterfield* (1929)

Index